CLOUD COMPUTING 2020

The Eleventh International Conference on Cloud Computing, GRIDs, and Virtualization

October 25 - 29, 2020

CLOUD COMPUTING 2020 Editors

Bob Duncan, University of Aberdeen, UK

Magnus Westerlund, Arcada University of Applied Sciences, Finland

Andreas Aßmuth, Ostbayerische Technische Hochschule (OTH) Amberg-Weiden Germany

Sebastian Fischer, Fraunhofer AISEC, Germany

Aspen Olmsted, Ph.D., Fisher College, USA

Printed from e-media with permission by:

Curran Associates, Inc.
57 Morehouse Lane
Red Hook, NY 12571

Some format issues inherent in the e-media version may also appear in this print version.

Printed with permission by Curran Associates, Inc. (2020)

International Academy, Research, and Industry Association (IARIA)
412 Derby Way
Wilmington, DE 19810

Phone: (408) 893-6407
Fax: (408) 527-6351

petre@iaria.org

Additional copies of this publication are available from:

Curran Associates, Inc.
57 Morehouse Lane
Red Hook, NY 12571 USA
Phone: 845-758-0400
Fax: 845-758-2633
Email: curran@proceedings.com
Web: www.proceedings.com

Table of Contents

CLOUD COMPUTING 2020

Forward

The Eleventh International Conference on Cloud Computing, GRIDs, and Virtualization (CLOUD COMPUTING 2020), held on October 25 - 29, 2020, continued a series of events targeted to prospect the applications supported by the new paradigm and validate the techniques and the mechanisms. A complementary target was to identify the open issues and the challenges to fix them, especially on security, privacy, and inter- and intra-clouds protocols.

Cloud computing is a normal evolution of distributed computing combined with Service-oriented architecture, leveraging most of the GRID features and Virtualization merits. The technology foundations for cloud computing led to a new approach of reusing what was achieved in GRID computing with support from virtualization.

The conference had the following tracks:

- Cloud computing
- Computing in virtualization-based environments
- Platforms, infrastructures and applications
- Challenging features

Similar to the previous edition, this event attracted excellent contributions and active participation from all over the world. We were very pleased to receive top quality contributions.

We take here the opportunity to warmly thank all the members of the CLOUD COMPUTING 2020 technical program committee, as well as the numerous reviewers. The creation of such a high quality conference program would not have been possible without their involvement. We also kindly thank all the authors that dedicated much of their time and effort to contribute to CLOUD COMPUTING 2020. We truly believe that, thanks to all these efforts, the final conference program consisted of top quality contributions.

Also, this event could not have been a reality without the support of many individuals, organizations and sponsors. We also gratefully thank the members of the CLOUD COMPUTING 2020 organizing committee for their help in handling the logistics and for their work that made this professional meeting a success.

We hope that CLOUD COMPUTING 2020 was a successful international forum for the exchange of ideas and results between academia and industry and to promote further progress in the area of cloud computing, GRIDs and virtualization.

CLOUD COMPUTING 2020 Steering Committee

Carlos Becker Westphall, Federal University of Santa Catarina, Brazil
Yong Woo Lee, University of Seoul, Korea
Bob Duncan, University of Aberdeen, UK

Aspen Olmsted, College of Charleston, USA
Alex Sim, Lawrence Berkeley National Laboratory, USA
Sören Frey, Daimler TSS GmbH, Germany
Andreas Aßmuth, Ostbayerische Technische Hochschule (OTH) Amberg-Weiden, Germany
Uwe Hohenstein, Siemens AG, Germany

CLOUD COMPUTING 2020 Publicity Chair

Javier Rocher, Universitat Politecnica de Valencia, Spain

CLOUD COMPUTING 2020 Industry/Research Advisory Committee

Raul Valin Ferreiro, Fujitsu Laboratories of Europe, Spain
Bill Karakostas, VLTN gcv, Antwerp, Belgium
Matthias Olzmann, noventum consulting GmbH - Münster, Germany
Hong Zhu, Oxford Brookes University, UK

CLOUD COMPUTING 2020

Committee

CLOUD COMPUTING 2020 Steering Committee

Carlos Becker Westphall, Federal University of Santa Catarina, Brazil
Yong Woo Lee, University of Seoul, Korea
Bob Duncan, University of Aberdeen, UK
Aspen Olmsted, College of Charleston, USA
Alex Sim, Lawrence Berkeley National Laboratory, USA
Sören Frey, Daimler TSS GmbH, Germany
Andreas Aßmuth, Ostbayerische Technische Hochschule (OTH) Amberg-Weiden, Germany
Uwe Hohenstein, Siemens AG, Germany

CLOUD COMPUTING 2020 Publicity Chair

Javier Rocher, Universitat Politecnica de Valencia, Spain

CLOUD COMPUTING 2020 Industry/Research Advisory Committee

Raul Valin Ferreiro, Fujitsu Laboratories of Europe, Spain
Bill Karakostas, VLTN gcv, Antwerp, Belgium
Matthias Olzmann, noventum consulting GmbH - Münster, Germany
Hong Zhu, Oxford Brookes University, UK

CLOUD COMPUTING 2020 Technical Program Committee

Sherif Abdelwahed, Virginia Commonwealth University, USA
Maruf Ahmed, The University of Technology, Sydney, Australia
Abdulelah Alwabel, Prince Sattam Bin Abdulaziz University, Kingdom of Saudi Arabia
Ali Anwar, IBM Research, USA
Filipe Araujo, University of Coimbra, Portugal
Andreas Aßmuth, Ostbayerische Technische Hochschule (OTH) Amberg-Weiden, Germany
Luis-Eduardo Bautista-Villalpando, Autonomous University of Aguascalientes, Mexico
Carlos Becker Westphall, Federal University of Santa Catarina, Brazil
Andreas Berl, Technische Hochschule Deggendorf, Germany
Simona Bernardi, University of Zaragoza, Spain
Peter Bloodsworth, University of Oxford, UK
Jalil Boukhobza, University of Western Brittany, France
Roberta Calegari, Alma Mater Studiorum-Università di Bologna,Italy
Paolo Campegiani, Bit4id, Italy
Juan Vicente Capella Hernández, Universitat Politècnica de València, Spain
Ruay-Shiung Chang, National Taipei University of Business, Taipei, Taiwan

Yue Cheng, George Mason University, USA
Enrique Chirivella Perez, University West of Scotland, UK
Claudio Cicconetti, National Research Council, Italy
Noel De Palma, University Grenoble Alpes, France
Mª del Carmen Carrión Espinosa, University of Castilla-La Mancha, Spain
Chen Ding, Ryerson University, Canada
Ioanna Dionysiou, University of Nicosia, Cyprus
Bob Duncan, University of Aberdeen, UK
Nabil El Ioini, Free University of Bolzano, Italy
Rania Fahim El-Gazzar, Universty of South-Eastern Norway, Norway
Ibrahim El-Shekeil, Metropolitan State University, USA
Javier Fabra, Universidad de Zaragoza, Spain
Fairouz Fakhfakh, University of Sfax, Tunisia
Umar Farooq, University of California, Riverside, USA
Jan Fesl, Institute of Applied Informatics - University of South Bohemia, Czech Republic
Sebastian Fischer, Fraunhofer AISEC, Berlin, Germany
Stefano Forti, University of Pisa, Italy
Sören Frey, Daimler TSS GmbH, Germany
Somchart Fugkeaw, Thai Digital ID Co. Ltd., Thailand
Juan Fumero, UniversityofManchester, UK
Katja Gilly, Miguel Hernandez University, Spain
Jing Gong, KTH, Sweden
Nils Gruschka, University of Oslo, Norway
Jordi Guitart, Universitat Politècnica de Catalunya - Barcelona Supercomputing Center, Spain
Seif Haridi, KTH/SICS, Sweden
Herodotos Herodotou, Cyprus University of Technology, Cyprus
Uwe Hohenstein, Siemens AG Munich, Germany
Soamar Homsi, Air Force Research Laboratory (AFRL), USA
Luigi Lo Iacono, TH Köln - University of Applied Sciences, Germany
Anca Daniela Ionita, University Politehnica of Bucharest, Romania
Saba Jamalian, Relativity, Chicago, USA
Fuad Jamour, University of California, Riverside, USA
Weiwei Jia, New Jersey Institute of Technology, USA
Carlos Juiz, University of the Balearic Islands, Spain
Bill Karakostas, VLTN gcv, Antwerp, Belgium
Sokratis Katsikas, Norwegian University of Science and Technology, Norway
Zaheer Khan, University of the West of England, Bristol, UK
Ioannis Konstantinou, CSLAB - NTUA, Greece
Van Thanh Le, Free University of Bozen-Bolzano, Italy
Yong Woo Lee, University of Seoul, Korea
Panos Linos, Butler University, USA
Xiaodong Liu, Edinburgh Napier University, UK
Jay Lofstead, Sandia National Laboratories, USA
Hui Lu, Binghamton University (State University of New York), USA
Glenn Luecke, Iowa State University, USA
Hosein Mohammadi Makrani, University of California, Davis, USA
Salman Manzoor, Technical University Darmstadt, Germany
Stefano Mariani, University of Modena and Reggio Emilia, Italy

Olivier Markowitch, Universite Libre de Bruxelles, Belgium
Attila Csaba Marosi, Institute for Computer Science and Control - Hungarian Academy of Sciences, Hungary
Jean-Marc Menaud, IMT Atlantique, France
Philippe Merle, Inria, France
Francesc D. Muñoz-Escoí, Universitat Politècnica de València, Spain
Ioannis Mytilinis, National Technical University of Athens, Greece
Hidemoto Nakada, National Institute of Advanced Industrial Science and Technology (AIST), Japan
Richard Neill, RN Technologies LLC, USA
Marco Netto, IBM Research, Brazil
Jens Nicolay, Vrije Universiteit Brussel, Belgium
Ridwan Rashid Noel, Texas Lutheran University, USA
Aspen Olmsted, College of Charleston, USA
Matthias Olzmann, noventum consulting GmbH - Münster, Germany
Aida Omerovic, SINTEF, Norway
Brajendra Panda, University of Arkansas, USA
Alexander Papaspyrou, adesso AG, Germany
Paulo Pires, Fluminense Federal University (UFF), Brazil
Agostino Poggi, Università degli Studi di Parma, Italy
Walter Priesnitz Filho, Federal University of Santa Maria, Rio Grande do Sul, Brazil
Abena Primo, Huston-Tillotson University, USA
Mohammed A Qadeer, Aligarh Muslim University, India
Daniel A. Reed, University of Utah, USA
Christoph Reich, Hochschule Furtwangen University, Germany
Eduard Gibert Renart, Rutgers Unversity, USA
Ruben Ricart Sanchez, University West of Scotland, UK
Sashko Ristov, University of Innsbruck, Austria
Takfarinas Saber, University College Dublin, Ireland
Hemanta Sapkota, University of Nevada - Reno, USA
Lutz Schubert, University of Ulm, Germany
Wael Sellami, Higher Institute of Computer Sciences of Mahdia - ReDCAD laboratory, Tunisia
Jianchen Shan, Hofstra University, USA
Muhammad Abu Bakar Siddique, University of California, Riverside, USA
Altino Manuel Silva Sampaio, Escola Superior de Tecnologia e Gestão | Instituto Politécnico do Porto, Portugal
Alex Sim, Lawrence Berkeley National Laboratory, USA
Soeren Sonntag, Intel, Germany
Vasily Tarasov, IBM Research, USA
Bedir Tekinerdogan, Wageningen University, The Netherlands
Prashanth Thinakaran, Pennsylvania StateUniversity / Adobe Research, USA
Orazio Tomarchio, University of Catania, Italy
Raul Valin Ferreiro, Fujitsu Laboratories of Europe, Spain
AntonioVirdis, University of Pisa, Italy
Massimo Villari, Università di Messina, Italy
Teng Wang, Oracle, USA
Hironori Washizaki, Waseda University, Japan
Mandy Weißbach, Martin Luther University of Halle-Wittenberg, Germany
Christos Zaroliagis, CTI & University of Patras, Greece

Ahmed Zekri, Beirut Arab University, Lebanon
Hong Zhu, Oxford Brookes University, UK
Jan Henrik Ziegeldorf, RWTH Aachen University, Germany
Wolf Zimmermann, Martin Luther University Halle-Wittenberg, Germany
Markus Zoppelt, Nuremberg Institute of Technology (TH Nürnberg) / Friedrich-Alexander-Universität Erlangen Nürnberg (FAU), Germany

Secure Business Intelligence Markup Language (secBIML) for the Cloud

Aspen Olmsted
Fisher College
Department of Computer Science, Boston, MA 02116
e-mail: aolmsted@fisher.edu

Abstract— **Enterprise organizations have relied on correct data in business intelligence visualization and analytics for years. Before the adoption of the cloud, most data visualizations were executed and displayed inside enterprise applications. As application architectures have moved to the cloud, many cloud services now provide business intelligence functionality. The services are delivered in a way that is more accessible for end-users using web browsers, mobile devices, data feeds, and email attachments. Unfortunately, along with all the benefits of the cloud business intelligence services comes complexity. The complexity can lead to slow response times, errors, and integrity issues. An information technology department or service provider must get ahead of the problems by automating the execution of reports to know when availability or integrity issues exist and dealing with those issues before they turn into end-user trouble tickets. In this paper, we develop an Extensible Markup Language programming language that allows execution against many cloud documents and business intelligence services. The language enables issues to be proactively discovered before end-users experience the problems.**

Keywords-Business Intelligence; Cloud Computing; Heterogeneous Data

I. INTRODUCTION

Forrester Research defines business intelligence as "a set of methodologies, processes, architectures, and technologies that transform raw data into meaningful and useful information used to enable more effective strategic, tactical, and operational insights and decision-making [1]. For today's businesses, this mainly takes shape through data visualization (tabular and charts), business documents, data mining, customer interaction automation, and email marketing.

Data visualizations have been developed by enterprises for decades to allow users to analyze their data in tabular or chart format. The visualizations change based on runtime prompts that filter the data displayed in the visualization. Data from separate Online Transaction Processing (OTP) systems are often aggregated into data warehouses to allow visualizations that span data from multiple source systems. Unfortunately, little tooling was provided to ensure the visualizations guaranteed the required availability and integrity. This paper describes our work in developing a programming language to help an organization with these issues. We call our programming language, Secure Business Intelligence Markup Language (secBIML). Our programming language secBIML allows an organization to script the correctness requirements and receive proactive notification of security issues.

Data mining allows an enterprise to discover new knowledge from their OTP data using data science algorithms. Unfortunately, the integrity of the source data is often ignored, leading to new knowledge derived from bad information. Utilizing secBIML, an organization can script the correctness requirements into comparison tables and receive proactive notification of integrity issues in the source data.

Many cloud application providers sell customer relationship management (CRM) and email marketing solutions and advertise their ability to automate interactions with customers based on changes in the data. Unfortunately, little attention is provided to how the data is aggregated and the availability and integrity of the information that is used as the source of the automation or email marketing. Our programming language secBIML can alert an organization of issues so they can proactively solve the problems with the correctness of the data used in the process.

The organization of the paper is as follows. Section II describes the related work and the limitations of current methods. In Section III, we describe the elements in the secBIML programming language. Section IV provides the motivating example behind our work. Section V describes how we developed our runtime engine. Section VI drills into the data we gather in our experimentation with data visualizations. Section VII investigates the tests we used in our experimentation with business document integrity. Section VIII describes the test implementation used in our experimentation with business email integrity. We conclude in Section IX and discuss future work.

II. RELATED WORK

The large corporate cloud providers such as Microsoft, Google, Amazon, and IBM hold many patents in the domain of recognizing application availability. The patents are designed for business to consumer websites where there is less control than we have in our enterprise BI environment. The lower level of control stems from the client machines in business to consumer architectures are unknown to the provider. One example of such a patent is from Letca et al.[7]. In the patent, Microsoft inserts a stub between the calling client and the web application. The stub gathers performance data as the user is using the web application. Unfortunately, with such a solution, a flaw in the stub can reduce the availability of the service. In our work, we utilize the network during off-hours for the enterprise to gather application data. The information gathered informs the information technology staff of priorities to proactively solve problems before they are filed as end-user trouble tickets.

Codd [1] describes integrity constraints in his original work on relational databases. Codd's original work assumed the data sources are two-dimensional tables that are normalized to eliminate redundancy. Codd's ideas made it into most online transaction processing (OTP) databases but never made it to the BI or document level. The data layer behind most BI architectures often increases availability by allowing dirty data through the use of database hints. In our work, we are looking for integrity errors by defining constraints in the document testing language itself and not in the data layer behind the documents.

TABLE I. secBIML TAGS.

Tag	*Type*	*Parent*
Credential	*Statement*	
Report	*Statement*	*Credential*
Execution	*Statement*	*Report*
Parameter	*Statement*	*Execution*
Alert	*Statement*	*Comparison or Execution*
RestAction	*Statement*	*Alert*
DBAction	*Statement*	*Alert*
LogAction	*Statement*	*Alert*
Reference	*Expression*	*Comparison*
Comparison	*Expression*	*Comparison*
Literal	*Expression*	*Comparison*
ActionValue	*Expression*	*RESTAction, DBAction or LogAction*

Many security software vendors offer a web application security scanner. These scanners try to break a web application to find common vulnerabilities such as cross-site scripting and SQL injection. Khoury et al. [8] evaluate the state of art black-box scanners that support detecting stored SQL injection vulnerabilities. Our work utilizes white box testing to find vulnerabilities in access control on both the docuememt or data element level.

III. LANGUAGE ELEMENTS

The programming language secBIML is defined in Extensible Markup Language (XML) with elements expressing the statements and expressions. Attributes or child elements express the parameters to the statements and expressions. Elements are identified in a SecBIML program as a start-tag, which gives the element name and attributes, followed by the content, followed by the end tag. Start-tags are delimited by `<, ' and `>'; end tags are delimited by `</' and `>'. TABLE I shows a breakdown of the tags available in the secBIML language.

```
<report name="eventbyhour"
server=https://logireports.fi.edu?rdName=Reports.Admissio
ns.Event_ByHour credential="bilogin"/>

<execution name="eventbyhourjuly"
report="eventbyhour"/>

<parameter execution="eventbyhourjuly"
name="BeginDate" value="07/01/2019"/>

<parameter execution="eventbyhourjuly"
name="EndDate" value="07/31/2019"/>
```

Figure 1. Example Report, Execution and Parameter Declaration Elements

A. *Statement Tags*

secBIML syntax is made up of declarative statements that define one of eight statement entities: credential, report, execution, parameter, alert, RESTaction, DBaction, and LOGaction. Figure 1 shows an example set of declarations to define a single implementation of a report with two runtime parameters. The parameters are set for a date range of the entire month of July 2019. The following is the set of language elements currently supported by secBIML:

- Credentials – The credential tag declare
- Reports – The report tag states the details on the server and the name of a specific report that is tested.
- Executions – The execution tag declares a specific test case for a report.
- Parameters – The parameter tag declares the runtime values used in the test of a specific execution.
- Alerts – The alert tag defines the data that is tested specify actions to take on failures. Actions can add tuples to a datastore, send emails, or call web-services. Parent tags for Alerts can either be comparison entities or execution entities.
- RESTactions – The RESTaction tag defines actions that call to web-services. The web-services call has the key-value pairs in the delivery.
- DBActions – The DB actions tag defines tuples written to a database table. The key in the key-value pair returned from the ActionValue entity matches with a table column, and the value is inserted in the tuple.
- Logactions – The "Logaction" tag is used to define values written to a log file.

B. *Expression Tags*

Expressions in the secBIML are entities where the syntax returns one of five different data types: list, boolean, numbers, text, or key-value pairs. Expressions are used to find a specific value in the report output, aggregate a set of values in the report output, express literal values, or define what data is sent to actions. Operators can combine expressions to be used in complex relational comparisons. There are four expression elements that return values in the secBIML language. The four elements are reference, literal, comparison, and ActionValue. We document the four elements below:

- References – The reference tag allows for the retrieval of a value from a report. The values are specified in the output by the hypertext markup language (HTML) id or a position in an HTML table. The type attribute allows values to be accumulated, counted, or averaged. The selector attribute is used to aggregate the values in a row or column within an HTML table. Selectors are patterns that match against elements in a tree and are the primary method used to select nodes in an XML document. secBIML supports CSS Level 3 selectors [9].

- Literals - The literal tag allows the expression of a constant value. Literal tags are used when comparing a value in a report to a static value defined at the time the test is created.
- Comparisons – The comparison tag allows values to be compared. A comparison tag returns a Boolean value based on the results of the comparison. The comparison tag requires an operator attribute to specify the comparison operation type. There are six supported comparison operator abbreviations: equal (EQ), not equal (NE), greater than (GT), less than (LT), great than or equal to (GE), less than or equal to (LE). The value in the parenthesis is the abbreviated version of the comparison operator. Figure 2 shows the declaration of a reference to a cell within the last row of a table in the report output. A comparison of a literal value of 23,201 is made to the value on the report, and if the data is different, a REST web service call is made to save the data. By default, actions include the data used in the comparison, the name, the compared values, and a timestamp marking the comparison evaluation time.
- ActionValues – The ActionValue tag allows the delivery and storage of key-value pairs in response to the alert. The type attribute defaults to a comparison name but can be a comparison, reference, literal, or execution result. There are two available values from the execution results; the HTTP status and the duration of the execution.

C. *Attributes & Child Elements*

In both the statement and expression tags, white space and attributes are allowed between the element name and the closing delimiter. An attribute specification consists of an attribute name, an equal sign, and a value. A child element is a tag fully enclosed between the open tag of another statement or expression and the matching closing tag. White space is allowed around the equal sign. Attributes and child elements in the secBIML syntax specify the parameters in the statements or the expressions. It is possible to express any parameter either through an attribute or through a child element. The expression of a child element allows for more complicated parameters including collections of values. Figure 2 shows how the RestAction and ActionValue entities can be rolled up into attributes. Attribute parameters are similar to read but do not allow for more than one value of the same attribute type.

```
<reference name="attendancetotal"
execution="eventbyhourjuly" type="sum"
selector="#attendance"/>

<comparison name="totalattendance"
reference="attendancetotal" literal="23201"/>

<alert comparison="totalattendance"
action="writeerror"/>

<action name="writeerror" restaction="
http://https.logireports.fi.edu/saveerror"/
actionvalue="totalattendance">
```

Figure 2. Example Alert and Supporting Elements

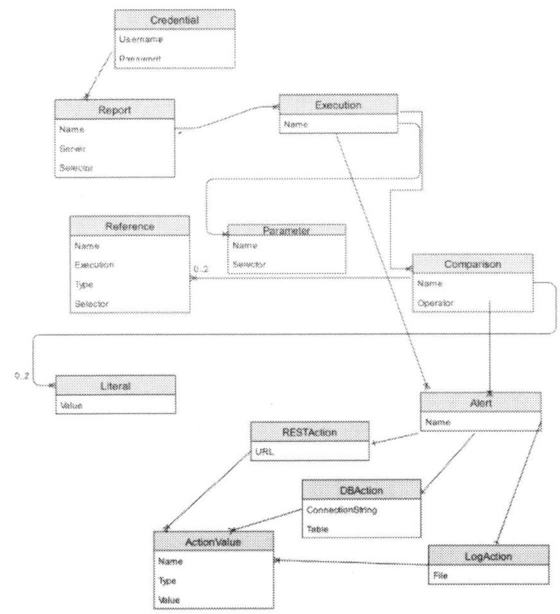

Figure 3. secBISQL ER Diagram

IV. secBISQL& Motivating Example

To facilitate the usage of the programming language by non-programmers, we developed a version of the language that has the tags stored in a SQL database. The SQL version is called secBISQL. The semantics of the two versions secBIML and secBISQL are identical. The difference is in how the programming language is stored in the source format. Figure 3 shows an entity-relationship diagram (ER) for secBISQL.

secBISQL was developed for The Franklin Institute (TFI) in Philadelphia, PA [10] to allow them to identiy availability and integrity errors in their business intelligence operations. In their business intelligence operations, TFI had one hundred and twenty custom reports that ran in the cloud using a business intelligence tool name Logi Analytics [11]. The custom reports were developed over many years by several different developers. Unfortunately, the end-users were experiencing errors and timeouts throughout the day.

In our first iteration, we used secBISQL to measure the security of data visualizations. We followed this iteration up by experimenting with other generated business documents and communications. The documents we experimented with can be categorized into three primary categories; word processing, presentation, and spreadsheet documents. Each document we looked at had aggregation of values or references to data from business intelligence reports. We also looked at automated emails sent to patrons after activities with the patrons, along with mass emails that were sent for marketing future events to patrons.

For the word processing, presentation, and spreadsheet documents, we utilized Microsoft™ Office 365 [8]. Office 365 is a cloud-based software as a service (SAAS) solution for word processing. To programmatically reference the word processing document, the URL of the office 365 document is added in the entity object as a "report" entity. Comparisons can be defined to compare individual values in the document to other values or aggregated values in the same document or a data visualization. For example, an invoice document laid out in Microsoft™ Word can be verified to ensure that the columns for quantity and amount are equal to the total column. A spreadsheet document has the functionality to aggregate values but a word processing document is often used for the end printed business document because of layout concerns. Integrity checks can be established in secBIML to ensure the word processing data is correct. Values in a business document could also be compared to a source business visualization. Often data is pulled from a data visualization and placed in a flyer or presentation, but that data may change in the source system. secBIML can ensure that data remains correct. This same technique can be used with documents stored in competitive cloud SAAS word processing solution providers such as Google™ GSuite [9].

After tackling the business documents, we looked at emails generated from back-end business transactional data. We were able to retrieve emails from an email service provider (ESP) through the Representational state transfer (REST) application programmer interface (API)s. REST is a software architectural style that defines a set of constraints for Web services creation. Web services that conform to the REST architectural style, called RESTful Web services, provide interoperability between computer systems on the Internet. The "report" entity was used to specify a REST front end URL, and the parameters were used to call out to the web-service for the specific REST data. The data was then compared to a report that listed the source data consumed in the generation of the email marketing or business automation.

V. Runtime Engine

The language compiler and execution engine were built using the C Sharp programming language on the .NET Core runtime engine [12]. .NET Core is an open-source, managed execution framework that allows execution on the Microsoft Windows, Linux, and macOS operating systems. The framework is a cross-platform successor to the .NET Framework. The framework allows the implementation of secBIML on any modern operating system.

secBIML links to a .NET library named Puppeteer Sharp [13]. Puppeteer Sharp is a .NET port of the Node.JS Puppeteer API [14]. Puppeteer is a Node programming language library that provides a high-level API to control the Chrome browser. Puppeteer allows a program to run the browser headless so that the browser interface is not exposed to the console. This layer of browser execution is critical in the execution of the business intelligence reports to ensure proper execution of JavaScript rendered HTML reports.

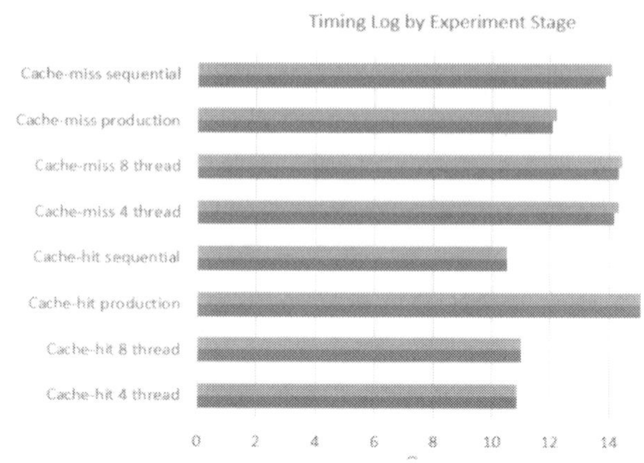

Figure 4. Average Timing

VI. Empirical Data – Data Visualization

In this section, we look at the empirical data we gathered to support our hypothesis that the usage of the secBIML language could increase the security of business intelligence reports and visualizations. To measure the availability of the business intelligence reports, we scheduled one hundred and twenty reports to run overnight in six modes. The six modes were sequential with a cache and without a cache, four

TABLE II SECBIML PRE-TESTING DATA

Data Point	Timing	Executions
Cache-miss sequential	17652	120
Cache-hit sequential	1464	120
Cache-miss 4 thread	20556	120
Cache-hit 4 thread	1824	120
Cache-miss 8 thread	22380	120
Cache-hit 8 thread	2016	120
Cache-hit production	145873	910
Cache-miss production	4864	320

TABLE IV SECBIML BUSINESS DOCUMENT TESTS

Document Type	Count	Internal	External	Initial Integrity	Continuous Integrity
Word Documents	102	24	82	82%	94%
PowerPoint Documents	55	2	53	86%	92%
Excel Documents	1	0	1	100%	100%

concurrent threads with a cache and without a cache, and eight current threads with a cache and without a cache. The tests were run over thirty days, and the average execution is shown in TABLE III. Also, include in the table is the average production data for the same period. The production data was gathered by parsing the web server logs for calls to the business intelligence report.

The reports that exhibit slow behavior were optimized based on the data gathered in the first phase and were optimized, and the experiment was run again for thirty days. TABLE III shows the average timing data collected in the post-optimization period. Figure 4 shows the comparison of the average per report timing for both pre-optimization and post-optimization timing experiments. The data clearly shows that the availability was increased in every mode of data gathering based on the knowledge gathered from the secBIML executions.

VII. Empirical Data – Business Documents

In this section, we look at the empirical data we gathered to support our hypothesis that the usage of the secBIML language could increase the security of business documents. We sampled fifty-seven business documents stored as Microsoft™ Office 365 documents. The data was either stored in Word, PowerPoint, or Excel applications. TABLE IV shows the documents used in our tests. The internal and external columns represent the number of tests that we established in each category. The internal tests compare values within the document, and the external tests compare values across documents. The initial integrity column displays the percentage of the correctness of the numbers returned from the first execution of the test. The continuous integrity displays the rate of accuracy over 12 weeks. After the initial test, corrections were applied to the documents, and continuous integrity tests ran nightly. The test demonstrates how often the data changed in the source data. We only found one excel document that had external budget data, and the data was correct and did not change over the 12-week test period. Discovery and setup of tests for business documents was a tedious process. In our future work, we plan to develop a Chrome web browser plugin to allow the automation of the test creation within the document. Nightly executions of the tests for business documents helped to improve the integrity, but trigger-based test execution would be a better solution. Both Microsoft Office 365 and Google GSuite offer API hooks that can be used to launch the test when a document is saved. The test could then run and immediately notify the user of the error. We would also plan to add web browser notifications immediately when an integrity error occurs.

VIII. Empirical Data –Emails

In this section, we look at the empirical data we gathered to support our hypothesis that the usage of the secBIML language could increase the security of email marketing and business automation. Many CRM and email marketing vendors claim functionality to allow artificial intelligence with email marketing and continuous communication with customers based on business automation. We believe this is a more difficult process than vendors imply. The difficulty comes from the fact that the data used to generate these emails and automation must be accurate and current. So, we wanted to test the correctness of data used in a production system. To measure the integrity of the data, we used an email services provider (ESP) Mailgun [13]. An ESP is a cloud service provider that manages the delivery of email messages. Some vendors provide analytic data on email delivery, such as the number of messages delivered, suppressed, and dropped. Data about the email clients, click-throughs, and unsubscribe data is also maintained. An added benefit of the provider we chose is that a free version is available through the GitHub Student Developer Pack [14].

A Standard Query Language (SQL) Server Common Language Runtime (CLR) extension was developed to send

TABLE III SECBIML POST-TESTING DATA

Data Point	Timing	Executions
Cache-miss sequential	14808	120
Cache-hit sequential	1452	120
Cache-miss 4 thread	18324	120
Cache-hit 4 thread	1812	120
Cache-miss 8 thread	20556	120
Cache-hit 8 thread	2016	120
Cache-hit production	139647	989
Cache-miss production	4393	289

TABLE V SECBIML EMAIL AND AUTOMATION TESTS

Type	Count	Errors
Visitation Email Automation	18,114	13
Email Merge Errors	756,123	1,243

the emails with proper tagging and retrieve the sent email data through the APIs. Database triggers were used to send automation responses based on the visitation of patrons. For example, an email was sent before a visitation that included details on arrival, directions to the venue, and the group's itinerary. Surveys were also sent to the patrons the day after visitation. Using the APIs from Mailgun, we were able to retrieve the data about the sent emails and check the integrity of the merged fields, appropriateness of the content in the email, and problems with delivery. TABLE V shows the errors found over a month of tests. The errors fell into two categories; data errors with the automated emails and data merge errors where data was truncated or displayed improperly in the final layout. The automation errors originated from data entry errors from operators entering transaction data and poor design in the transactional systems to allow the data inconsistencies to exist. The merge errors originated from live data that did not look like the data used in the testing of the email templates. In both cases, the percentage of error is small, but if an organization works hard to acquire a customer, these types of errors can negate that hard work.

IX. CONCLUSIONS AND FUTURE WORK

Based on our research, we demonstrate that the availability and integrity of business visualizations, documents, and communications increase using the secBIML programming language. This work demonstrates the successful implementation of the tests written in secBIML for an actual organization utilizeing their production environment. Our future work will develop tooling to make it easier to create business document tests while doing layout in the document. The tooling will make it more likely that an end-user will specify the correctness of a document. We will also create trigger-based executions of our testing programs. The triggers will enable on the fly verification instead of a point in time testing.

REFERENCES

[1] B. Evelson, "Topic Overview: Business Intelligence," Forrester, 2018.

[2] I. Letca et al., "Measuring Actual End User Performance And Availability Of Web Applications". Patent US 8,938,721 B2, 2015.

[3] C. E. F., "A relational model of data for large shared data banks," *Communications of the ACM*, vol. 13, no. 6, pp. 377-387 , 1970.

[4] N. Khoury, P. Zavarsky, D. Lindskog and R. Ruhl, "An Analysis of Black-Box Web Application Security Scanners against Stored SQL Injection," in *2011 IEEE Third International Conference on Privacy, Security, Risk and Trust and 2011 IEEE Third International Conference on Social Computing*, Boston, MA, 2011, pp 1095-1101.

[5] World Wide Web Consortium (W3C), "Selectors Level 3," 18 November 2018. [Online]. Available: https://www.w3.org/TR/selectors-3/. [Accessed 16 October 2019].

[6] The Franklin Institute, "The Franklin Institute," 2019. [Online]. Available: http://www.fi.edu. [Accessed 16 October 2019].

[7] Logi Analytics, "Business Intelligence is Dead," 2019, [Online]. Available: https://www.logianalytics.com. [Accessed 16 October 2019].

[8] Microsoft Corporation, "What is Office 365," [Online]. Available: https://www.office.com/. [Accessed 12 November 2019].

[9] Google, Inc., "About Google Docs," [Online]. Available: https://www.google.com/docs/about/. [Accessed 12 November 2019].

[10] Microsoft, ".NET Core Guide," [Online]. Available: https://docs.microsoft.com/en-us/dotnet/core/. [Accessed 23 October 2019].

[11] D. Kondratiuk, "Puppeteer Sharp," [Online]. Available: https://www.puppeteersharp.com/. [Accessed 23 October 2019].

[12] Google, "Puppeteer," [Online]. Available: https://developers.google.com/web/tools/puppeteer. [Accessed 23 October 2019].

[13] Mailgun Technologies, Inc, "The Email Service for Developers," [Online]. Available: https://www.mailgun.com/. [Accessed 3 December 2019].

[14] GitHub, "GitHub Education," [Online]. Available: https://education.github.com/pack. [Accessed 3 December 2019].

Web Application Firewalls and Ways of Seeing Imperfect Tools

Andrew Zitek
New York University
New York, USA
e-mail: alz236@nyu.edu

Aspen Olmsted
Fisher College
Boston, USA
e-mail: aolmsted@fisher.edu

Abstract— **Common wisdom on how to evaluate preventative goods is weak, and as a result cybersecurity suppliers provide tools without hard evidence or guarantees. While it may be naive to expect any one tool to act as a silver bullet, information asymmetry is a problem that can and should be addressed. We argue that well-informed consumers are essential to responding to the security, privacy, and usability challenges associated with developing web applications hosted in the cloud. Accordingly, we study Web Application Firewalls to draw attention to the status quo, and provide questions that allow the public to readily identify information asymmetry in the goods they consider.**

Keywords- application firewalls; secure coding;

I. Introduction

A number of market studies indicate the demand for Web Application Firewalls (WAFs) is increasing rapidly [1]-[4]. At the same time, the InfoSec community readily offers concrete examples of how to carry out attacks on systems protected by WAFs [5]-[8]. We are confused by these two observations. Do consumers understand the extent of the limitations of their tooling? Are better options not available? Are they obligated the purchase by compliance requirements? The modern cybersecurity consumer faces many challenges. We argue that a broad survey of the WAF landscape will serve as a means to identify the paradigms with which researchers should equip consumers, so they make prudent and informed decisions.

A quick internet search will show that much published research on WAFs focuses on measuring and improving specific aspects of attack detection via involved techniques like machine learning [9]-[12]. Although none of the authors say so directly, the papers offer the impression that researchers are well aware that WAFs are flawed and that energies are focused narrowly on making these flaws smaller. While we agree that novel techniques may in the end improve these tools, we find it implausible that WAFs will ever provide the same protection as bug-free code. We'll support this theory and explain why you should care in later sections. First though, we'll step back and ask the natural question, what problems are WAFs actually intended to solve?

A good challenge for readers would perhaps include exploring a few vendor sites and, using only the information there, explain the purpose of WAFs. We found this task somewhat onerous, but in good faith we'll offer the following non-comprehensive list of uses: (1) protect applications, (2) detect attacks, (3) provide reporting and (4) meet compliance [13]-[16]. Upon compiling this list of uses, we found something to admire in each—they represent genuine concerns that consumers need to address and for which they seek out solutions. On closer inspection, however, we wondered how one could quibble with such broad objectives? Were they so broad as to be rendered meaningless? We find that savvy consumers are left still wondering a number of questions. First, how do WAFs accomplish their intended purpose? Second, to what extent do WAFs actually solve the problems that vendors claim they solve? Third, are WAFs in particular better suited to address these problems than other tools or processes?

Some cybersecurity specialists have argued that Payment Card Industry (PCI) requirement 6.6 explains the proliferation of WAFs without necessarily answering these questions. Requirement 6.6 states that organizations must either (1) use an application firewall *or* (2) implement a process for code reviews [17]. Wicket offers the somewhat critical conclusion that, given the unappealing nature of the second option, most organizations read this as a WAF mandate [18]. His argument is that organizations don't install WAFs for their security value, but instead out of a desire to pass their mandatory PCI certification. While we agree that PCI probably does drive some demand for WAFs, we disagree that this alone could explain such high demand for WAFs. This is simply due to the fact that a vast number of organizations don't actually pursue PCI certification. We considered the possibility that organizations look to PCI as a defacto standard, essentially "if it's good enough for banks it's good enough for us." We would be more inclined to expand on that theory, however, provided more evidence. Our debate of PCI is, in fact, addressing a larger matter—that some in the cybersecurity community believe it is safe to forgo the proactive process of removing bugs from code as long as one installs some type of reactive tool like a WAF. This is at best misleading and at worst wrong.

Other popular channels of information, like Wikipedia, are more realistic in their description of WAFs, but in our opinion, are not without problems. Although Wikipedia does give some matter of fact information such as, "By inspecting HTTP traffic, WAFs can prevent attacks stemming from web application security flaws, such as SQL injection, cross-site scripting, file inclusion, and security misconfigurations," it also makes hard-to-support claims such as, "The Open Web Application Security Project (OWASP) produces a list of the top ten web application security flaws. All commercial WAF offerings cover these ten flaws at a minimum [19]." We argue that less savvy readers may be misled into feeling a false sense of security due to the fact that the meaning of the word *coverage* is unclear. We have to ask, is this just a poorly worded sentence, or is it evidence of bona fide embellishment?

In their recent work, Muegge and Craigen have offered the conclusion that cybersecurity specialists manipulate cognitive limitations to over dramatize and oversimplify risks [20]. Essentially, Muegge and Craigen maintain that, because there is a lack of reliable information around cybersecurity, processes should be anchored around what they call "evidence-based design principles." We agree that it's not easy to find reliable data, or data that's not oversimplified, in cybersecurity because our experience researching WAFs confirms it. Muegge and Craigen's theory on the absence of quality information is extremely useful because it sheds light on the problem of how difficult it is for consumers to make well-informed decisions without sufficient evidence.

At this point we would like to raise some objections inspired by our own internal skepticism. We feel that we may have been ignoring the fact that eliminating risk entirely is considered impossible. "Tools will never be perfect", we say, "we should reduce harm in any ways we can afford." Cybersecurity specialists in particular will note that the goal is less about perfection and more about reducing risk. Our point is not that we should cast aside tools simply because they're not perfect. Our point is that if suppliers are not offering a guarantee for their claims about the quality of services provided, consumers should be given information that lets the cold sting of these limitations sink in.

We are not the first to make the connection between cybersecurity tools and Akerlof's Market for Lemons [21]-[23]. Putting to use the example of used car sales, Akerlof famously put forth that quality will degrade in markets where it is not possible for consumers to validate the quality of goods being offered [24]. He maintains that these markets lead to weary consumers, willing to pay only lower prices for specific classes of goods no matter the quality [25]. Still more interesting, others have made the claim that information asymmetry has been solved in the market of used cars by guarantees like pre-certified used car programs and reputable third-party quality information sources like Carfax [26]. Arguments like this make us optimistic about the future, and we would like to see efforts toward analogous solutions for the problems of information asymmetry in markets for cybersecurity goods.

During the course of the COVID-19 pandemic, firms capable of working in the cloud have benefited, and those yet to shift to the cloud are accelerating plans to do so [27]. As the cloud continues to prove itself essential, the selection processes consumers use for tools to secure applications run in the cloud grows proportionally. We encourage researchers to acknowledge these trends and focus on addressing security, privacy, and usability challenges with solutions that lead to well informed consumers.

The organization of the paper is as follows: Section II reviews work related to assessing WAFs, and we provide a motivating example along with explanations of our empirical evidence. Section III provides discussion of our solution—a mental paradigm for savvy consumers. We conclude and describe future work in Section IV.

II. Measuring the Extent To Which WAFs Solve Problems

Many assume that the capability of WAFs to analyze and filter requests at the application level is new technology. In fact, application-level access control systems that embody the firewall design have existed since at least 1998 [28]. In these systems, depicted as a flow diagram in Figure 1, just like in traditional network firewalls a special intermediate server establishes a barrier between a trusted internal domain and an untrusted external domain. These self-contained, generally configurable firewalls provide a chokepoint from which a policy of security rules may be enforced with the intent of denying suspicious traffic while allowing other credible seeming traffic. Toward this goal, a negative or positive security model can be used as a basis for access decisions. We focus only on the negative security model, as we have found this to be more popular by far, likely due to the fact that it requires little manual configuration by administrators when compared with the positive security model. We construct a basic threat model for this generic system using the STRIDE methodology in Table I.

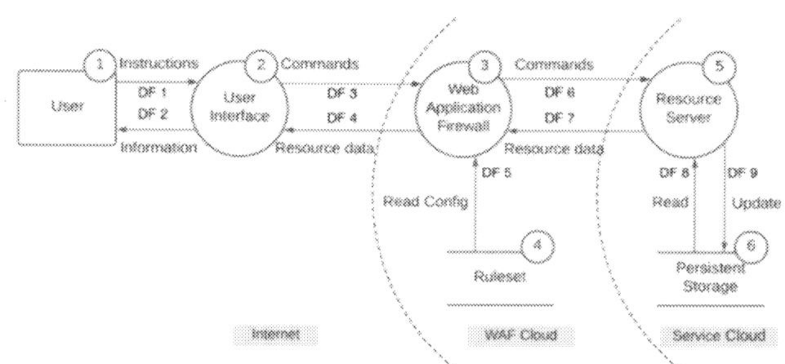

Figure 1. Data Flow Diagram

TABLE I. STRIDE Threat Analysis of Figure I

Data Flow Diagram Element	S	T	R	I	D	E
1) User	✓		✓			
2) User Interface	✓	✓	✓			
3) Web Application Firewall	✓	✓	✓	✓	✓	
4) Ruleset					✓	
5) Resource Server	✓	✓	✓	✓	✓	✓
6) Persistent Storage	✓	✓	✓	✓	✓	✓
7) DFs 3-4, 6-9		✓		✓	✓	

There are numerous closed- and open-source initiatives attempting to provide tools for measuring the performance of WAFs, most with an emphasis on regression testing [29]-[31]. Azaria and Shulman, affiliated with Imperva, presented a methodology for assessing the performance of WAFs with a focus on two qualities: legitimate traffic that is blocked, and malicious traffic that is not blocked [31]. In their benchmark analysis, it was demonstrated that in the set of sample requests shown in Table II, there existed no instance of legitimate traffic that was blocked and there existed many instances of malicious traffic that was not blocked. This presentation is instructive because it sheds light on the fact that the complexities of binary classification systems are central to the issues that WAF developers face. Using this information, we can speculate that False Negatives are preferred over False Positives, probably because they do not cause service interruptions for clients using the WAF.

TABLE II. BENCHMARK OF CLASSIFICATION OF ATTACKS BY WAF

Attack Type	*Total Attacks*	*Misclassified*	*%*
False Negative	67	67	100
False Positive	148	0	0

a. False Negative Attacks are malicious requests that should be blocked
b. False Positive Attacks are legitimate requests that should not be blocked

We may expand on this speculation with a theoretical example. Consider the situation given in Figure 2 when 2 percent of all traffic received by a web server is malicious. We then integrate a WAF that returns a positive classification result 95 percent of the time for requests that are actually malicious. If a request is not malicious, the WAF returns a negative classification result 99 percent of the time.

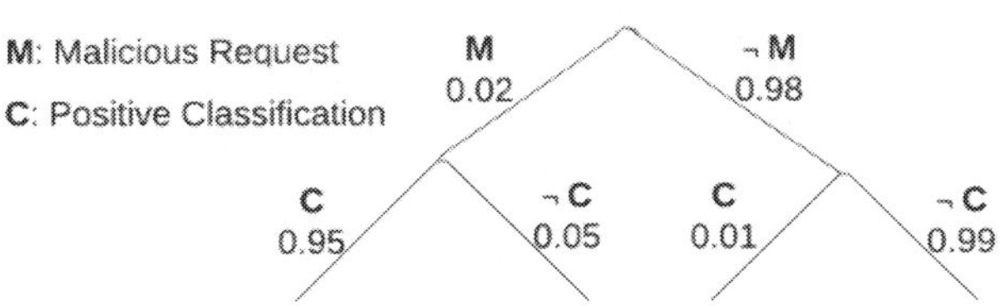

Figure 2. Tree Diagram of Request Classification

If the WAF returns a positive classification for a request, the probability the request is actually malicious is given by (2),

$$P(C) = (0.02)(0.95) + (0.98)(0.01) = 0.029 \quad (1)$$

$$P(M|C) = P(M \cap C) / P(C) = (0.02)(0.95) / 0.029 = 0.655 \quad (2)$$

If the WAF returns a negative classification for a request, the probability the request is actually not malicious is given by (4),

$$P(\neg C) = (0.02)(0.05) + (0.98)(0.99) = 0.971 \quad (3)$$

$$P(\neg M|\neg C) = P(\neg M \cap \neg C) / P(\neg C) = (0.98)(0.99) / 0.971 = 0.999 \quad (4)$$

We remark that the sensitivity we assigned to our WAF in this example is high and would drastically reduce the *total number* of malicious requests received by the webserver. For a webserver responding to 1 million requests daily this would result in a 95 percent decrease from 20K to 1K malicious requests. While this improvement, if reflective of real-world scenarios, seems encouraging, we are left with the thought that a webservice absent of its own well-designed security mechanisms processing 1K malicious requests on a daily basis seems far from secure. Basically, it seems that no matter how advanced the sensitivity of our WAF, the reality appears that our webservice will always have the responsibility to respond appropriately to a nonzero number of malicious requests. This, in a nutshell would imply that the benefits of WAFs are strictly supplementary and not substitutionary.

Bonneau, Herley, Oorschot, and Stajano describe the use of passwords for authentication purposes as an, at first, seemingly analogous situation where organizations settle for more lax security policies involving binary classification systems, due to usability challenges [32]. They offer the fairly sympathetic argument that organizations do not expect to achieve ironclad invulnerability, so they instead seek only to reduce harm at acceptable cost. We agree that this is the status quo and we believe, in the case of authentication strategies, that this compromise seems justified because it is likely to impact only individual users rather than an organization as a whole. We find this reminder helpful because it sheds light on the fact that consumers are in fact very accustomed to making compromises in their security strategies.

If we had an imaginary dial for the sensitivity of a system of authentication signals, we could imagine, at the highest setting, many users would have a hard time logging in, but fewer accounts would be hijacked. As we lowered this imaginary setting, we could foresee these numbers shifting until, at the lowest setting, few users would have problems authenticating, but most accounts could be easily hijacked. Despite having sensitivity configurations, WAFs simply do not provide an analogous type of tradeoff because application-specific implementation bugs can lead to all-or-nothing types of attacks, for example database dumps instead of attacks that only impact specific users. We find that making this distinction is essential. There is no blanket one-size-fits-all policy suggesting what compromises to security strategies are favorable.

In the remainder of this section we will refute the idea that WAFs provide coverage of vulnerabilities created by application-specific implementation bugs. We have elected to test injection attacks, because they represent the number one web application security risk per the OWASP Top Ten 2017 list [33]. Additionally, we document things of interest that arise in the process of integrating the WAF with our basic webservice.

A. Technology Stack

We use the following tools to conduct this experiment.

- IBM Public Virtual Server C1
- Ubuntu 18.04-64
- Node.js 12.14.1
- MySQL 5.7.28
- Cloudflare Web Application Firewall

LISTING I. VULNERABLE CODE SNIPPET

```
const userInput = req.query.itemID;
const statement = `
  SELECT
    ItemID,
```

```
5    ItemName,
6    ItemDescription
7   FROM Items
8   WHERE ItemID = ${userInput};
9 `;
10
11 connection.query(
12   statement,
13   function callback(err, rows) { ... }
14 );
```

In Listing 1, representing a snippet of the vulnerable code, on line 8 an unsanitized user input is interpolated into the string representing the SQL statement. This bug represents the source of the vulnerability we will use to test the WAF.

B. Attacks

We start with three basic SQL-injection (SQLi) attacks [34] and enhance each version by applying a technique called obfuscation [5].

i. Basic Tautology – the goal of tautology is to inject SQL tokens that cause the conditional statement of a query to evaluate true, like

   GET /items?itemID=1 or 1=1

ii. Basic Union Query – the goal of a union query is to manipulate the where clause of a query so that multiple sub-queries can be made in addition to the one the programmer intended, like

   GET /items?itemID=1 UNION SELECT UserID, UserName, UserPassword FROM Users

iii. Basic Piggyback Query – the goal of a piggyback query is to exploit a misconfiguration where it is sometimes possible to append a query to another query, like

   GET /items?itemID=1; DROP TABLE Users

iv. Obfuscated Tautology – the goal of this obfuscation is to use quotation marks to trick the WAF into thinking the attack is legitimate traffic, like

   GET /items?itemID=1 OR 1#"OR"'OR''='"="'OR''='

v. Obfuscated Union Query – the goal of this obfuscation is to use different encodings to trick the WAF into thinking the attack is legitimate traffic, like

   GET /items?itemID=1 union%23foo*%2F*bar%0D%0Aselect%23foo%0D%0A UserID,UserName, UserPassword+FROM+Users

vi. Obfuscated Piggyback Query – we can use similar techniques for piggyback queries, like

   GET /items?itemID=1; +DROP%20TABLE%20Users

In further consideration of the STRIDE classification model, the tautology and union query attacks represent information disclosure threats, while the piggyback query represents a tampering threat. In the DREAD threat rating methodology, SQLi attacks are given the highest possible score of ten out of ten [35]. These styles of attacks are prolific, decades-old and have impacted significant players like the World Health Organization and the Wall Street Journal [36].

C. Integration

We find some snafus encountered during the integration process noteworthy. At first, the process of activating the WAF appeared to involve updating our DNS provider and clicking a button next to our CNAME entry to turn an icon from grey to color. We were unsure what to think when, at first, all of our attacks succeeded. We reviewed the configuration settings in the provided dashboard several times and, after a few days, contacted customer support. Customer support explained that the service tier we were using would protect against only DDoS attacks, not OWASP sourced attacks like the ones we were testing.

Later, we upgraded our service tier and ran our tests a second time. Again, all of our attacks succeeded. We returned to our configuration settings and discovered that upon upgrading plans, new options had become available and, by default, were not active. After toggling these to active, we, at last, observed our first blocked attack. Still, we later uncovered more configurations for the sensitivity of the WAF. All tests in the next section were performed with the sensitivity set to the highest possible setting. These snafus may represent human-usability issues and demonstrate how a pivotal ingredient to usable cybersecurity is informative feedback, especially visibility of the system state [37]. Basically, integrating a WAF adds a nontrivial level of operational complexity to a system, and this is a drawback because it can sometimes make it difficult to measure the security integrity of a system.

D. Results

The results of the experiment, provided in Table III, concluded that the WAF is unable to guarantee protection from the risk of injection attacks caused by application-specific bugs. A trivial level of obfuscation makes it possible for an adversary to succeed at all three flavors of the attacks tested. This result makes us doubt the significance of the calculations made in Section II. At first, the possibility that under certain conditions we could reduce the total number of malicious requests received by a webservice seemed promising, but in retrospect, when there still exists in reality a nonzero number of *known* attacks that the WAF does not correctly classify, it is not straightforward to describe what benefit this would provide, if any.

TABLE III. CLASSIFICATION OF ATTACKS ON VULNERABLE WEBSERVICE BY WAF

Attack Class	*True-negative*	*False-negative*	*Misclassified*
B. Tautology	yes	no	no
B. Union	yes	no	no
B. Piggyback	no	yes	yes
O. Tautology	no	yes	yes
O. Union	no	yes	yes
O. Piggyback	no	yes	yes

a. For each of the six attack classes we send one request in order to observe the result. Because each of the six instances represent a malicious request, each should result in a True-negative outcome. We label all requests with different outcomes as Misclassified.

We contacted Cloudflare customer support and provided the obfuscated versions of each example attack along with links to a live server for demonstration purposes. A customer support representative communicated that the keywords we provided were, "not a combination we have connected to an active software vulnerability we are ware [sic] of currently." The representative suggested that we create a custom ruleset to block these exact requests from our system using the web interface. The same representative later added that, "for our global rulesets we need to balance coverage and avoiding false positive(s) from over agrresive [sic] rules in our network." We find that this commentary further supports the hypothesis made in this paper regarding inherent weaknesses of systems involving binary-classification. In the end, a different customer support representative in the same conversation wrote, "our WAF Engineering team will add the first two examples to our WAF engine so this will be picked up by Cloudflare WAF rules. I am afraid we are not yet on a position to provide you with a [sic] ETA but it will be taken care of soon." Another representative later reiterated that they were unable to share further details regarding how or when these changes would take effect.

E. Guaranteeing Protection

We will briefly demonstrate the effort involved in patching the application bug using secure coding. We know where the bug resides in our source code because we designed it intentionally. We are aware of course, that the writers of applications do not always know about the bugs in their code.

The patch will involve changing two lines of code, lines 8 and 13, to leverage a technique called parameterized queries, or prepared statements. Parameterized queries guarantee protection from SQLi attacks by ensuring that the SQL engine parses and compiles the query separately from the variables. The variables are escaped and inserted into the query later, so that no matter their content, they will be interpreted as ordinary strings [38].

LISTING 2. PATCHED CODE SNIPPET

```
1 const userInput = req.query.itemID;
2 const statement = `
3   SELECT
4     ItemID,
5     ItemName,
6     ItemDescription
7   FROM Items
8   WHERE ItemID = ?;
9 `;
10
11 connection.query(
12   statement,
13   [userInput],
14   function callback(err, rows) { ... }
15 );
```

In Listing 2, representing a snippet of the patched code, a placeholder is put in line 8 indicating that the second argument to the query function on line 13 will contain the variable that should be escaped and inserted into the query after it has been parsed and compiled.

After our modifications, the attacks are unsuccessful at tampering with the integrity of the database and disclosing information additional to what the author intended. This solution is low effort and highly effective but depends on knowledge.

III. A MENTAL PARADIGM FOR THE SAVVY CONSUMER

To paraphrase John Berger on art, it isn't so much the WAFs we want to consider, but the ways we see them [39]. Essentially, our point is not to convince consumers to reject tools like WAFs because they are imperfect. Our point is to convince consumers that they must resist the potential peace of mind and assurance that comes with preventative goods like WAFs. These delusions may become reasons to not carry out other prudent behaviors.

Although much of this paper may make this idea seem obvious, we argue that, in fact, it's difficult for consumers to recognize the extent to which the position they hold in the market for cybersecurity tools lacks quality information. As we have discussed, while organizations are desperate for meaningful solutions, suppliers offer tools without guarantees and it is difficult to research credible information on the quality of tools offered. In situations like these, we wish to provide a paradigm allowing consumers to readily identify information asymmetry in the goods they consider. Due to the nature of cybersecurity tools we will focus specifically on preventative goods that aim to forestall negative outcomes.

We are aware that in economics, goods are often given labels when they exhibit particular qualities that make them special. In the case of luxury, or Veblen goods for instance, demand can appear to increase as price increases contradicting the law of demand [40]. In this close study of tools like WAFs, it is possible to make the argument that many cybersecurity products embody their own unique set of characteristics, and we have yet to discover an economic term for this type of good. These unique properties are:

1. You pay for it hoping to stop something undesirable
2. If you observe nothing, you might assume it worked
3. If you observe anything, you will know it did not

Standing alone, we think these observations may not seem striking, so, in an attempt to promote sticky mental associations between the domain of our problem and the solution, we surveyed a few students and colleagues, asking them to name a familiar product that has these characteristics. The list below represents the responses. The entries do not necessarily reflect our own opinions.

- Flu Vaccinations
- Vaccinations (Other)
- Vitamin C Supplements
- Supplements (Other)
- Surgical Masks
- Mosquito Repellent
- Pest Extermination Service
- Antivirus Software
- Anti-Aging Treatments (Beauty Industry)
- Contraceptives
- Light Therapy Lamps
- "Paying off the mob"
- "A rock that keeps tigers away"

To make it clear, this paper has no interest in making arguments for nor against any of these goods. The observation that many of these goods are controversial however, is interesting because it sheds light on the fact that goods with the particular qualities highlighted above may present special challenges for consumers. Basically, we argue that thinking about a few preventative goods that consumers are already familiar with may enable us to more quickly grasp the challenges present in markets for cybersecurity tooling. Complexity of subject matter, lack of data, supplier reputation, industry regulations and social pressure appear to be key factors that these markets share in common.

In the end, we cannot provide a blanket prescription regarding whether or not organizations should use preventative tools like WAFs to protect their cloud hosted web applications. What we can do is ask the consumer an analogous question like, do you think you should take a vitamin C supplement to prevent illness? To what extent does the supplement prevent you from getting sick? How will you know? Specifically, how will you measure whether the claims the supplement supplier makes are true using valid data? If you cannot obtain the data needed to make this analysis, will the supplier provide you a guarantee? Ultimately, if you have a few extra dollars, and taking a supplement would give you peace of mind, the negative impacts of doing so, on the surface, seem low, but that's no excuse to not wash your hands in the first place.

IV. Conclusion

In this paper, we address the problem of how to assess preventative goods. We argue that consumers are left to trust suppliers who provide imperfect technology for cybersecurity without guarantees. In this paper, we evaluate problems with WAFs and how they can be compared and contrasted. We utilize the STRIDE threat model in an applied experiment on a WAF analyzing a SQLi attack. Our conclusion is that small changes in configuration can lead to very different results with the tooling and implementation knowledge is currently the most important ingredient in the equation. Our future work will calculate a measure of dependency on outside knowledge that is required for individual cybersecurity tools.

References

[1] CISOMAG. Web application firewall market worth $5.48 Billion by 2022. [Online]. Available from: https://www.cisomag.com/web-application-firewall-market-worth-5-48-billion-2022/ 2020.02.27

[2] MarketWatch. Web Application Firewall Market Research Reports 2019. [Online]. Available from: https://www.marketwatch.com/press-release/web-application-firewall-market-research-reports-2019-global-industry-size-in-depth-qualitative-insights-explosive-growth-opportunity-regional-analysis-by-market-reports-world-2019-06-14 2020.03.16

[3] C. Rodriguez. Web Application Firewall (WAF) Global Market Analysis New Technologies and Threats Collide to Create Expanded Opportunities. [Online]. Available from: https://www.akamai.com/us/en/multimedia/documents/content/frost-sullivan-web-application-firewall-global-market-analysis-research-excerpt-report.pdf 2020.03.16

[4] KBV Research. Web Application Firewall Market Size. [Online]. Available from: https://www.kbvresearch.com/web-application-firewall-market/ 2020.03.18

[5] R. Salgado. SQL Injection Optimization and Obfuscation Techniques. [Online]. Available from: https://media.blackhat.com/us-13/US-13-Salgado-SQLi-Optimization-and-Obfuscation-Techniques-WP.pdf 2020.03.20

[6] Z. Allen. WAFs FTW: A Modern DevOps Approach to Security Testing your WAF. [Online]. Availale from: https://www.youtube.com/watch?v=05Uy0R7UdFw 2020.08.20

[7] V. Ivanov. Web Application Firewalls: Analysis of Detection Logic. [Online]. Available from: https://www.youtube.com/watch?v=dMFJLicdaC0 2020.08.20

[8] I. Schmitt and S. Schinzel. WAFFLe: Fingerprinting Filter Rules of Web Application Firewalls. [Online]. Available from: https://www.usenix.org/conference/woot12/workshop-program/presentation/schmitt 2020.08.20

[9] A. Moosa, "Artificial Neural Network based Web Application Firewall for SQL Injection" World Academy of Science, Engineering and Technology International Journal of Computer and Information, 2010, pp. 12-21, ISSN: 2010-3778

[10] K. Demertzis and L. Iliadis, "Cognitive Web Application Firewall to Critical Infrastructures Protection from Phishing Attacks" Journal of Computations & Modelling, 2019, pp. 1-26, ISSN: 1792-8850

[11] D. Appelt, C.D. Nguyen and L. Briand, "Behind an application firewall, are we safe from SQL injection attacks?" IEEE 8th International Conference on Software Testing, Verification and Validation, May 2015, 10.1109/ICST.2015.7102581

[12] A. Makiou, Y. Begriche and A. Serhrouchni, "Improving Web Application Firewalls to Detect Advanced SQL Injection Attacks" International Conference on Information Assurance and Security (IAS), Mar. 2014, pp. 35-40, 10.1109/ISIAS.2014.7064617

[13] F5 Security Products. Advanced Web Application Firewall (WAF). [Online]. Available from: https://www.f5.com/products/security/advanced-waf 2020.03.2020

[14] Cloudflare. Web Application Firewall. [Online]. Available from: https://www.cloudflare.com/waf/ 2020.03.18

[15] Imperva. Web Application Firewall (WAF). [Online]. Available from: https://www.imperva.com/products/web-application-firewall-waf/ 2020.03.18

[16] Trustwave Managed Security. Managed Web Application Firewall. [Online]. Available from: https://www.trustwave.com/en-us/services/managed-security/managed-web-application-firewall/ 2020.03.18

[17] Security Standards Council. Payment Card Industry Data Security Standard (PCI DSS) Requirement 6.6 Code Reviews and Application Firewalls. [Online]. Available from: https://www.pcisecuritystandards.org/pdfs/infosupp_6_6_applicationfirewalls_codereviews.pdf 2020.08.20

[18] J. Wickett. Three Ways Legacy WAFs Fail, Signal Sciences Blog. [Online]. Available from: https://www.signalsciences.com/blog/three-ways-wafs-fail/ 2020.03.05

[19] Internet Archive WayBack Machine. [Online]. Available from: https://web.archive.org/web/20161104030043/https://en.wikipedia.org/wiki/Web_application_firewall 2020.08.20

[20] S. Muegge and D. Craigen, "A Design Science Approach to Constructing Critical Infrastructure and Communicating Cybersecurity Risks" Technology Innovation Management Review, Jun. 2015, vol. 5, pp. 6-16, ISSN 19270321

[21] M. Lesk, "Cybersecurity and economics" IEEE Security & Privacy, Nov. 2011, vol. 9, pp.76-79, 10.1109/MSP.2011.160

[22] T. Moore, "The economics of cybersecurity: Principles and policy options" International Journal of Critical Infrastructure Protection, Dec. 2010, vol. 3, pp. 103-117, 10.1016/j.ijcip.2010.10.002

[23] C. Dacus and P. Yannakogeorgos, "Designing Cybersecurity into Defense Systems: An Information Economics Approach" IEEE Security & Privacy, May. 2016, vol. 14, pp. 44-51, 10.1109/MSP.2016.49

[24] G. Akerlof. "The Market for 'Lemons': Quality Uncertainty and the Market Mechanism" The Quarterly Journal of Economics, Aug. 1970, vol. 84, pp. 488-500, ISSN 1531-4650

[25] Wikipedia. The Market for Lemons. [Online]. Available from: https://en.wikipedia.org/wiki/The_Market_for_Lemons#Criticism 2020.02.29

[26] D. Maimon. An Evidence Based Cybersecurity Approach to Risk Management: Risk Management and "Market for Lemons". [Online]. Available from: https://scholarworks.gsu.edu/cgi/viewcontent.cgi?article=1000&context=ebcs_presentations 2020.08.20

[27] J. Rubenstone. Cloud Infrastructure Keeps Firms Afloat During Coronavirus Pandemic. [Online]. Available from: https://www.enr.com/articles/48975-cloud-infrastructure-keeps-firms-afloat-during-coronavirus-pandemic 2020.08.20

[28] R. Hunt, "Internet/Intranet firewall security—policy, architecture and transaction services" Computer Communications (Elsevier), Sep. 1998, vol. 21, pp. 1107-1123, ISSN 0140-3664

[29] Microsoft. WAFBench. [Online]. Available from: https://github.com/microsoft/WAFBench 2020.08.20

[30] Fastly. FTW. [Online]. Available from: https://github.com/fastly/ftw 2020.08.20

[31] Y. Azaria and A. Shulman. WTF - WAF Testing Framework. [Online]. Available from: https://www.youtube.com/watch?v=ixb-L5JWJgI 2020.08.20

[32] J. Bonneau, C. Herley, P. Van Oorschot and F. Stajano, "Passwords and the evolution of imperfect authentication" Communications of the ACM, Jul. 2015, vol. 58, pp. 78-87, 10.1145/2699390

[33] OWASP Foundation. OWASP Top Ten. [Online]. Available from: https://owasp.org/www-project-top-ten/ 2020.03.26

[34] S. Shanmughhaneethi, S. Shyni and S. Swamynathan, "SBSQLID: Securing Web Applications with Service Based SQL Injection Detection" International Conference on Advances in Computing, Control, and Telecommunication Technologies, Dec. 2009, pp. 702-704, 10.1109/ACT.2009.178

[35] P. Carter, "Threat Analysis and Compliance," Securing SQL Server: DBAs Defending the Database, 2018, Apress, pp. 12–16

[36] J. Cox. The History of SQL Injection, the Hack That Will Never Go Away. [Online]. Available from: https://www.vice.com/en_us/article/aekzez/the-history-of-sql-injection-the-hack-that-will-never-go-away 2020.02.22

[37] J. Nurse, S. Creese, M. Goldsmith and K. Lamberts, "Guidelines for usable cybersecurity: Past and present" Third International Workshop on Cyberspace Safety and Security (CSS), Sep. 2011, pp. 21-26, 10.1109/CSS.2011.6058566

[38] A. Sadeghian, M. Zamani and S. Ibrahim, "SQL Injection is Still Alive:A Study on SQL Injection Signature Evasion Techniques" International Conference on Informatics and Creative Multimedia (ICICM), Sep. 2013, pp. 265-268, 10.1109/ICICM.2013.52

[39] J. Berger. Ways of Seeing Episode 1. [Online]. Available from: https://www.youtube.com/watch?v=0pDE4VX_9Kk 2020.08.20

[40] Wikipedia. Veblen Good. [Online]. Available from: https://en.wikipedia.org/wiki/Veblen_good 2020.08.20

Using Bayesian Networks to Reduce SLO Violations in a Dynamic Cloud-based Environment

Agam G. Dua

Tandon School of Engineering
New York University
Brooklyn, New York
Email: agam@nyu.edu

Aspen Olmsted

Fisher College
Boston, Massachusetts
Email: aolmsted@fisher.edu

***Abstract*—As more organizations move critical infrastructure to the cloud and leverage features like auto-scaling to grow according to the customer demand, we see a new set of challenges specific to this class of dynamic, distributed systems. In this paper, we propose a model leveraging Bayesian networks to help in the diagnostics of these systems during failures to considerably shorten the time to localize the cause of Service Level Objectives violations. The model subsequently reduces the violation duration by reducing the Mean Time To Resolution.**

Keywords–Bayesian network, Machine Learning, Cloud Computing, Auto scaling, Service Level Objective, Availability.

I. INTRODUCTION

The move of modern software to the cloud has been increasing over the past decade, and organizations are migrating more distributed systems to execute in the cloud environment. One of the reasons for this migration is the advanced custom auto-scaling abilities [1] provided by the cloud vendors. While deploying distributed systems has become a lot easier, improvements like these make it radically different from the older model of deploying systems on a mostly static infrastructure and introduces its own set of challenges.

However, businesses must continue to be actively mindful of the availability that their users expect. Most organizations design deployments around a set of metrics known as Service Level Objectives (SLOs). We define SLOs in terms of performance, reliability, and availability of the application and quantify the SLOs in metrics such as downtime, error rates, end-to-end request latencies, etc. An example latency metric would be to expect an average of 200ms response time over 5 minutes for a server side HTTP application. Exceeding this threshold would be considered an SLO violation. The expectations for a well-engineered application is high availability, i.e., infrequent SLO violations. This infrequency, and many metrics that are recorded for each system make it especially complicated to detect, localize and fix the system during a violation. This complication can result in the Mean Time To Resolution (MTTR) being unacceptable to the stakeholders of the system.

This paper focuses on the automated localization of the problem in a distributed system with each service leveraging shared infrastructure, such as network equipment, resource capacity, and even a shared database. We assume that an issue has been detected in at least one part of the distributed system. We do not specifically attempt to surface the root cause of the problem. However, we expect that by localizing the problem automatically, the MTTR decreases significantly. The decrease comes by allowing further human intervention to determine the root cause faster. In the proposed strategy, we leverage Bayesian networks and as a custom reactive probing framework that observes the state of a subset of previously hidden nodes in the Bayesian network.

The paper's organization is as follows: Section II describes the related work and the implementations of current methods. In Section III, we provide a motivating example where this application is useful. Section IV details the underlying framework and the methodology, along with the results, while Section V concludes and describes future work.

II. RELATED RESEARCH

There is an existing body of literature that tackles the problem of automated diagnosis of SLO violations in distributed systems, which broadly categorizes the diagnosis into two parts. The first part is localizing the issue to a specific subset of the system. Zhang, et al. [2] focus on response time problems caused by abnormally slow services, and use Bayesian networks to diagnose the issues. This approach's primary focus is using the response time of individual observed services and total end-to-end response time to infer time taken by unobserved (uninstrumented) services. A limitation of this model is that the localization's granularity is only up to a specific service, which itself could be a complex system and hard to debug. The research assumes that parts of the system which are not instrumented to report SLO violations of their own. Our research will aim at yielding a more granular diagnosis by introspecting services and their dependencies.

Cohen et al. [3], attempt to correlate system metrics in a distributed system with the SLO violations. They explicitly do not use application metrics, focusing instead on system-level metrics from the server such as CPU time in user mode, disk read frequency, etc. where each metric they use is specific to the system of a particular application, enabling a more granular localization of the problem. However, they require training the classifier on past data which is hard to come by since SLO violations are infrequent in a well-engineered system. Our research leverages Bayesian networks, where the prior probabilities are calibrated by a domain expert who has access to past data. Furthermore, the study mentioned above does not consider the cloud platform, which can be responsible for a separate class of SLO violations related to newer features they provide.

The second part of the problem is root cause analysis, which can be computationally intensive and therefore is not viable for large volumes of data or compromises accuracy due to many metrics and a large number of data points for the metrics. Natu et al. [4] apply feature selection to prune the search space of irrelevant and redundant metrics. Our approach does not attempt to prune the search space but does try and glean as much information as possible from the available metrics while maintaining focus on solving the first part of the problem.

III. Motivating Example

When an error occurs in a dynamically scaled distributed system SLO violations are often caused by time spent collecting the information needed to understand the root cause. In the case of the services we are researching, we consider a response latency over 400ms to be an SLO violation as this has been demonstrated to cause user impact.

We measure this SLO on a subset of the distributed system that corresponds to synchronous operations that directly impact the "real-time" user experience. We do not consider scheduled or deferred jobs in this. For example, we observe the time to load a specific URL on the website, or a view in the mobile application, but we do not consider a violation of a queued email sending job.

The following graph shows the full duration of SLO violations by time period that have been recorded in official postmortems in the company:

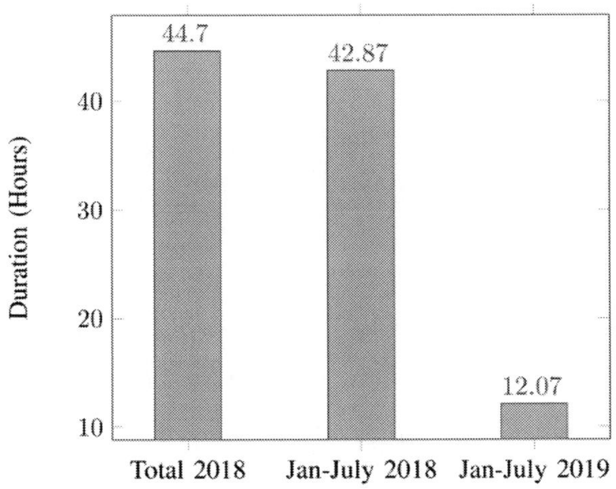

Figure 1. SLO Violations in Hours.

In particular, there was one incident where the cloud provider the company infrastructure is deployed on was facing issues in one subnet, which prevented scaling new servers to accommodate user load. It took 6 hours to mitigate user impact, 2.5 hours (~42%) of which was spent in localizing the issue to that particular subnet. In this incident, we were alerted that we had scaling issues, without further specificity.

IV. Methodology and Empirical Evidence

To form the model, one should reason about what the SLO violation in such a distributed systems setup in the cloud could be caused by:

- *Database issues*: If the database was under load, e.g. due to too many queries per second, or other availability concerns.
- *Application Errors*: If there were application errors due to a bug or application level dependency issues.
- *Resource starvation*: If the servers were being limited by CPU, memory, network, etc.
- *Bad deployment*: If there was an issue with the deployment process itself.

Similarly, resource starvation can be caused by buggy code or scaling issues. Here, the buggy code would likely be unrelated to the business logic of the application. An example of such a problem one might encounter is a memory leak by the application not correctly freeing the memory allocated for an operation. In a database-backed application, as we are examining, this can be discovered in a bug in the database access layer where too many connections are open, tying up the resources of both the application and the database server.

Scaling issues are best described as the service's inability to receive more capacity, despite the metrics indicating a need for this extra provisioning. An example here would be when a service exceeds the aggregate CPU utilization threshold over a cluster of hosts for a service and triggers the cloud configuration scaling but is denied extra capacity.

Furthermore, resource starvation can be caused by buggy code or scaling issues, and scaling issues can be caused by:

- *Cloud limits*: If the cloud resource limits set by an agreement with the company and the cloud vendors was hit.
- *Recent configuration change in the infrastructure*: If a potential new bug was introduced.
- *Infrastructure or external dependency issue*: If there was an issue with other services or infrastructure that we depend on for scaling up.

With this in mind, a causal, directed acyclic graph on which the Bayesian network would be built was created to reflect the infrastructure:

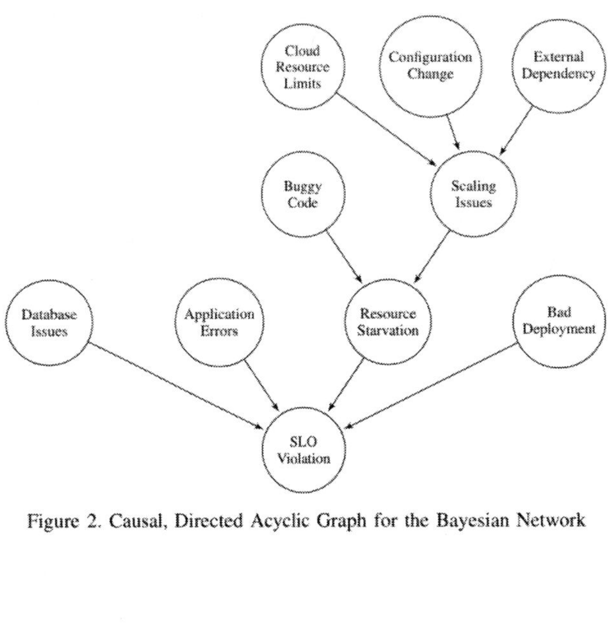

Figure 2. Causal, Directed Acyclic Graph for the Bayesian Network

The model's implementation used the pomegranate python library [5], and a series of implemented checks to make some of the nodes "observed". The checks linked into various monitoring systems and ruled out cloud limits, recent configuration changes, database issues, and application errors. This was determined by leveraging APIs (Application Programming Interfaces, in this case over the HTTPS protocol) of the monitoring systems and comparing with the conditions for the nodes in the Bayesian network, e.g., whether a deployment occurred in a period of time that correlates with the timeline of the incident.

The nodes for which information is not available are known as unobserved nodes and form the crux of the model. With the help of the pomegranate library, the output of the model results in the unobserved nodes of the Bayesian network being associated with their updated probabilities, given the information gathered from the monitoring systems, i.e., the observed nodes. These calculated probability values show with reasonable certainty that the issue was an external dependency or infrastructure issue and that deploy issues and errors are unlikely. This also indicates that there is a high chance the alerted scaling issues are causing an SLO violation. The specific probabilities generated with the above mentioned methodology associated with the nodes in the Bayesian network can be seen in Table I.

TABLE I. CALCULATED PROBABILITIES OF OUTCOMES

Node Name	*P(True)*	*P(False)*
Resource Starvation	0.9899687033177891	0.10031296682210913
SLO	0.9810724570630289	0.018927542936970975
External Dependencies	0.6070287539936117	0.39297124600638844
Bad Deployment	0.10035812797969593	0.8996418720203041
Application Errors	0.09677684818274046	0.9032231518172594

V. CONCLUSION AND FUTURE WORK

In this paper, we addressed the problem of minimizing SLO violations in an organization's infrastructure. We argued that using Bayesian networks and leveraging past data to assist with localizing of the problem can drastically reduce the Mean Time To Resolution of incidents. In this paper, we addressed this issue of minimizing SLO violations by designing a Bayesian network that incorporates causal relations and is initialized by a subject matter expert leveraging past data and experience with the system. We demonstrated in a specific type of incident that the model could correctly determine the cause and provide alternative paths in decreasing order of likelihood of occurrence.

In the future, we will prove the model can be generalized across a variety of incidents, and not just the specific motivating example in this paper. Furthermore, the model should be able to update itself with new data over time, so the relevance of the prior probabilities defined by a subject matter expert will decrease. Eventually, a pluggable architecture can be provided where the prior probabilities can be generated by automation leveraging historical data in the various monitoring systems.

REFERENCES

[1] "Big Day for Amazon EC2: Production, SLA, Windows, and 4 New Capabilities," 2008, URL: https://aws.amazon.com/blogs/aws/big-day-for-ec2/ [accessed: 2020-03-03].

[2] R. Zhang, S. Moyle, S. Mckeever, and A. Bivens, "Performance problem localization in self-healing, service-oriented systems using bayesian networks abstract," in *Proceedings of the ACM Symposium on Applied Computing*, 01 2007, pp. 104–109.

[3] I. Cohen, J. S. Chase, M. Goldszmidt, T. Kelly, and J. Symons, "Correlating instrumentation data to system states: A building block for automated diagnosis and control," in *Proceedings of the 6th conference on Symposium on Operating Systems Design —& Implementation - Volume 6*, 01 2004, pp. 231–244.

[4] M. Natu, S. Patil, V. Paithankar sadaphal, and H. Vin, "Automated debugging of slo violations in enterprise systems," in *2010 2nd International Conference on COMmunication Systems and NETworks, COMSNETS 2010*, 02 2010, pp. 1 – 10.

[5] J. Schreiber, "pomegranate," 2016, URL: https://github.com/jmschrei/pomegranate/ [accessed: 2020-03-03].

IoT Device IdentificAtion and RecoGnition (*IoTAG*)

Lukas Hinterberger* and Bernhard Weber†
Dept. Electrical Engineering and Information Technology
Ostbayerische Technische Hochschule
Regensburg, Germany
email:
lukas.hinterberger@st.oth-regensburg.de*
bernhard1.weber@st.oth-regensburg.de†

Sebastian Fischer
Secure Systems Engineering
Fraunhofer AISEC
Berlin, Germany
email:
sebastian.fischer@aisec.fraunhofer.de

Katrin Neubauer‡ and Rudolf Hackenberg§
Dept. Computer Science and Mathematics
Ostbayerische Technische Hochschule
Regensburg, Germany
email:
katrin1.neubauer@oth-regensburg.de‡
rudolf.hackenberg@oth-regensburg.de§

***Abstract*—To ensure the secure operation of IoT devices in the future, they must be continuously monitored. This starts with an inventory of the devices, checking for a current software version and extends to the encryption algorithms and active services used. Based on this information, a security analysis and rating of the whole network is possible. To solve this challenge in the growing network environments, we present a proposal for a standard. With the *IoT* Device IdentificAtion and RecoGnition (*IoTAG*), each IoT device reports its current status to a central location as required and provides information on security. This information includes a unique ID, the exact device name, the current software version, active services, cryptographic methods used, etc. The information is signed to make misuse more difficult and to ensure that the device can always be uniquely identified. In this paper, we introduce IoTAG in detail and describe the necessary requirements.**

Keywords*—*Internet of Things; device identification; open standard; IoTAG; security rating.

I. Introduction

It has been shown that the use of Internet of Things (IoT) technologies is always associated with risks. Both, in terms of data protection and the reliability and security of an IoT environment. It is not always possible to completely eliminate all sources of risk. However, the threat potential can be reduced by introducing new technologies to simplify system maintenance. The Federal Office for Information Security in Germany lists measures to protect IoT devices [1]. Based on this, requirements for a compatibility interface will be defined, which can be used to implement a central and manufacturer-independent security management of IoT systems. The data to be provided and the security requirements to be fulfilled by the interface will be based on the draft of the European standard for the security of IoT devices ETSI EN 303 645 v2.0.0 [2]. This standard defines basic requirements for the security of IoT devices.

In order to be able to monitor and evaluate each component individually, even in complex IoT environments, a way to identify each device is required. This means that each device must have a unique identifier, which may only be assigned at least once within a closed system. At best, the identifier is unique worldwide.

After each device has been recorded individually, it must also be possible to identify the product type. This enables the devices to be classified in safety categories. For example, the failure of an individual telephone must be considered less critical than the failure of an alarm system. It is only possible to test a device for existing weak points or for information published by the manufacturer if the product type is known. In the latter case, at least the manufacturer and a clear product designation is required.

In order to be able to check whether the firmware of a device is up-to-date, it is necessary for a device to provide its currently running firmware version. In addition, information about the update behaviour of the device must be provided. This includes information on whether the device can be updated, whether it has an automatic update mechanism and up to which point in time updates are provided by the manufacturer.

IoT devices are by definition in exchange with other network components. This can be done either locally isolated in a separate network or globally over the Internet. To protect sensitive data from unauthorized access, the use of verified algorithms and communication protocols is required. By providing an overview of the encryption and hashing algorithms used by a device, it is possible to check whether outdated or insecure procedures are used. The same applies to network protocols and network technologies in use. If a device provides all network protocols it supports, including the protocol version, it can be checked whether the device is vulnerable to attacks against its communication.

To meet these requirements, we present a proposal for a standard for the detection of IoT devices: *IoT* Device IdentificAtion and RecoGnition (*IoTAG*). It focuses on the security of the devices and will provide necessary information to estimate the security of all devices in the network.

This paper is based on our previous publication [3] and extends the idea of IoTAG with the necessary descriptions and more details. It is structured as follows: Section II shows some related work and Section III consists of the IoTAG definition, subdivided into the dataset, the serialization, the integrity and the communication. In Section IV, a brief conclusion is given.

II. Related Work

There are several suggestions to detect IoT devices automatically. However, most of them only consider functionality and not security. Two concepts which also consider security are the Thing Description and the Device Description Language.

A. *Thing Description*

The concept of Thing Description (TD), presented by the World Wide Web Consortium (W3C), is a uniform representation of metadata of a device, as well as the interfaces provided by the device. It can be either physical or purely virtual properties. These include device properties, such as currently stored settings or sensor data.

In addition, information is provided on available control actions or events that can be used to interact with the devices. Furthermore, an optional "Security" field provides information on the authorization procedures available for accessing device resources. According to the W3C specifications, the TD is exclusively a data exchange format for device metadata that can be provided by the device itself or by an independent resource [4].

For the use of this technology as a security interface, the device-independent provision of information proves to be problematic. As a result, it cannot be guaranteed that the information actually refers to the device and that the data records are up-to-date and correct. The Thing Description specification does not provide any procedures for the transmitted values to be signed by the device or another instance [4].

Also, the small amount of security related information described above excludes TD for use in an automated monitoring and testing scenario. Our requirements for the predefined dataset, data integrity, as well as the availability of predefined communication procedures can be regarded as not fulfilled.

B. *Device Description Language*

The IoT Device Description Language (IoT-DDL) is a machine- and human-readable XML-based description for IoT devices. The IoT-DDL is used by a device to provide information about its capabilities, resources, entities and services, as well as cloud-based functionalities. This includes information about the hardware installed in a device (e.g., Secure Elements), software functions (e.g., switching the device on or off) or external services (e.g., log server), as well as descriptive metadata, which can include the device manufacturer or the device name. But the scope of this information has not been firmly defined.

The IoT-DDL focuses on both device-to-device and device-to-cloud communication and is intended to simplify the creation of heterogeneous IoT scenarios. Message Queuing Telemetry Transport (MQTT) and the Constrained Application Protocol (CoAP) are supported for communication between devices. The security mechanisms supported by these protocols are not used to secure the communication. Instead, a specially developed AES-based procedure is used to encrypt the transmitted data [5].

Thus, in the case of the IoT-DDL, the requirement for a firmly defined dataset and its integrity are also violated.

III. IoTAG Definition

In contrast to existing interoperability procedures for facilitating the setup and control of IoT infrastructures, as presented in Section II, a new technical proposal for the automated identification and recognition of IoT devices (called IoTAG) will be defined.

The focus of the IoTAG definition lies on the standardized provision of security-critical device data, the integrity preservation of the datasets to be transmitted and the relevance of the information for an individual classification of each device with regard to the implementation of security specifications and recommendations. When designing the necessary guidelines for this purpose, the requirements defined at the beginning of this document for such a communication standard are taken into account.

The implementation of IoTAG on the devices is done by the manufacturers.

A. *Dataset*

The section "Dataset" consists of subsections which represent some of the attributes. These give an explanation why this information must be provided by an IoTAG compatible device and a description of the attribute's content.

1) Manufacturer: The provision of a manufacturer's designation is useful for several reasons. On the one hand, there is always the possibility that devices with identical or very similar designations are sold by different companies. On the other hand, this information can be used to contact the manufacturer and inform them about software errors or to be able to make use of support services.

The information about the manufacturer thus contains the name of the company that provides the firmware and its updates. This is a string value that contains the official company name according to the respective entry in the commercial register.

2) Name: The name or designation of a device serves to identify the product. This attribute contains the product name under which the device is sold by the manufacturer in the form of a string.

3) Serial number: The serial number of a product is a unique marking of a device assigned by the manufacturer and enables its identification within a product line. In the event of production faults, the affected devices can be identified by their serial numbers.

The representation of the serial number is manufacturer-specific. Basically, it is an arbitrary string of characters that is unique for each device in a product series and thus, in conjunction with the manufacturer and product name, allows a clear conclusion to be drawn about the object.

4) Type: The device type provides information about the type of product. It indicates the main functionality of the device and can be used to draw conclusions about the complexity of the device. This information is important for the security of an IoT system in that it allows conclusions to be drawn about the effects an attack on a device may have. For example, an attack on a surveillance camera is a greater problem from the perspective of data protection than an attack on a smoke detector, for example. A locking system or an alarm system, must also be classified as more security-critical than a TV.

Possible values for the product type specification are:

- alarm system
- camera
- smart lock
- smart speaker
- smart TV
- smoke detector

This list contains first suggestions and can be extended at any time by further product definitions.

5) ID: In order to be able to identify a device at any time, it must have a unique identifier. For this reason, a combination of existing information is created for device identification: the manufacturer, the product name and the serial number. Although this information can be calculated by software, it is also stored for manual linking of a dataset to a device.

The specifications included in the generation of the device ID are to be regarded as constants and must not be changed subsequently after the device has been taken into operation.

The device ID is a character string that contains a hash value in alphanumeric representation. It is generated by concatenating the information about manufacturer, product name and serial number, then generating the hash value of this string using the SHA-256 algorithm [6] and finally encoding the resulting binary data as base16 string [7]. The use of SHA2 and SHA3 family algorithms is recommended by the National Institute of Standards and Technology (NIST). For performance reasons, the SHA2 algorithms are preferred to the SHA3 algorithms [8] [9] [10].

6) Category: The product category fulfills a purpose comparable to that of the product type. An additional security-related assessment can be carried out by dividing devices into categories that describe their area of application or use scenario. If the two categories "lighting" and "assisted living" are considered as two different areas, the failure of a device can have different effects. If a motion sensor responsible for the lighting fails, the user must activate the light manually. However, if a motion sensor from the assisted living area, which is supposed to report whether the occupant of a house is entering and leaving the bathtub, fails, the help hoped for by using this system can be missed in an emergency like a fall in the bathtub. Thus, devices in the assisted living area are to be classified as more security-critical than pure comfort functions.

The device category attribute can have the following values, among others:

- assisted living
- entertainment
- household
- industry
- infrastructure
- lighting
- personal assistance
- security

These are also initial proposals. With the increasing spread of IoT devices, the fields of application are also expanding, so that further definitions are necessary.

7) Secure boot: Secure boot mechanisms can be used to ensure the integrity of a device's firmware at system startup. When a device is started securely, signature mechanisms are used to check whether the components involved, such as the boot loader and operating system, are unchanged originals. The information required for this verification is stored in a suitable hardware module, such as a Trusted Platform Module (TPM) [11] [12].

The secure boot attribute uses a boolean value. If no software integrity check is performed, the value is "false".

8) Firmware: In order to be able to check that the firmware of a device is up-to-date, it must publish the firmware version currently being executed. If a device requires a manual installation of the firmware, there must be a possibility to retrieve it from the manufacturer. To prevent software from being obtained from dubious sources, the IoTAG dataset also provides an internet address for downloading the firmware.

In contrast to the specifications described so far, the firmware is not an atomic value, but two strings to be considered separately: the firmware version (referred to as "version") as published by the device manufacturer, and a Uniform Resource Locator (URL) [13], which refers to the download resource for this firmware.

For consecutive versions, lexicographically ascending terms are recommended so that the order of release can be determined.

9) Client software: If software for third-party devices is required for the use of an IoT device, IoTAG will provide the latest version supported by the device. In addition, a link to a resource is also provided here from which this software can be obtained. This eliminates the need for the user to search for a source of supply, which in turn reduces the risk of obtaining software from untrusted sources.

The specifications of the client software are analogous to those of the device firmware (see 3.2.8). However, if no client software is required, empty strings are specified.

10) Updates: The update behaviour of a device provides information on whether a device updates itself automatically, i.e., whether it checks for the availability of new firmware versions and obtains and installs them, or whether it must be manually updated to the new version.

It should be noted, that even if a device is configured for automatic updating, the provision of new firmware by the device manufacturer is also necessary. In order to be able to take a device out of service when it is no longer supplied with new software, it is necessary to specify the point in time from which this is the case.

The update configuration information is also a multi-part record within the update item. A boolean value is used to indicate whether a device has an automatic update mechanism and also uses it. "Automatic updates" is chosen as the name for this value.

The end of support is a date formatted as a string according to ISO 8601 [14] and integrated into IoTAG under the name "end of life".

11) Cryptography: In order to be able to make predictions about the cryptographic capabilities of a device, it is necessary that the algorithms used by a device to secure its communication are known and a statement can be made as to whether these are implemented in hardware or software. It must also be specified whether secret keys are stored exclusively in secure hardware or also in memory areas accessible via software.

The private key required for the signature of IoTAG as described in subsection C is treated individually. A separate variable is introduced to show how this key is managed, as it is essential for the reliability of IoTAG.

Two identical structures are subordinated to the superordinate term cryptography. Each contains an attribute "IoTAG key", which is a boolean value. If the signature key is managed in a secure hardware environment and cannot be read by software, it takes the value "true" in the hardware structure and the value "false" in the software structure. The reverse is true if the key is accessible via software.

Another boolean value is the variable "key store". This indicates whether cryptographic keys to be kept secret are stored in this area. This specification can be true in both structures. An overview of the cryptographic algorithms used in a device is given by the variable "algorithms". This contains a collection of character strings. Each element of this collection contains a cryptographic algorithm according to its standardised designation (example: "ecdsa-sha2-nistp256", as defined in RFC 5656 [15]).

12) Connectivity: The connectivity of a device describes its physical possibilities to connect to communication partners. Different technologies are used for data exchange. These include the standards under IEEE 802.3 and IEEE 802.11 [16] developed by the Institute of Electrical and Electronics Engineers (IEEE) as well as industrial standards such as Bluetooth [17], ZigBee [18] or other.

For compatibility reasons, IoT devices can support older versions in addition to the current standard of a communication method. But if these have security problems, an attacker can use them to gain access to confidential information [19] [20].

For the transmission of the supported communication standards, a multi-part data structure is used. For example, it will have the attributes "IEEE802_11", "Bluetooth" and "ZigBee". Each of them forms a collection of strings. While in the case of Bluetooth and ZigBee the alphanumeric version numbers are included, for the IEEE family of standards, the suffixes of the individual standards are entered. If the suffix begins with a hyphen, it is removed. The first standard of the family is specified with an empty character string. Additionally, the collection can contain the values "WEP", "WPA", "WPA2" and "WPS". These inform whether the respective technology is used by a device.

13) Services: Network devices offer various services to interact with them. Analogous to securing the communication against external attacks as described in subsection D, the interception of the connection by devices within the network must also be prevented. This goal can be achieved, among other things, by dispensing with unencrypted transmission protocols. It should be noted, however, that the implementation of these protocols can also contain errors and therefore the version of the software used must be checked and published by IoTAG.

A separate data structure is defined to describe a network service. This contains the name of the service (Name), the network port (Port), the protocol used (Protocol) including any version designations, as well as the name and version of the software (Software) that offers the service in the format <designation>-<version>. Since the information whether the connection is UDP or TCP-based is also required to specify the network port, the port is specified in the format <Port>/<UDP|TCP>.

The actual IoTAG attribute is ultimately a collection that contains such a data structure for each service offered.

B. Serialization

To prevent incompatibilities due to incorrect interpretations, the serialization format Javascript Object Notation (JSON), according to the specification in ECMA-404 [21] and RFC 8259 [22] with UTF-8 encoding, is selected.

JSON is preferred over the Extensible Markup Language (XML) because it has a higher performance in terms of memory resource consumption and computing power [23].

Listing 1 shows a serialized IoTAG data set. The attribute names to be used can be taken from this example. For space reasons, the value of the "ID" attribute has been wrapped into two lines.


```
{
 "Manufacturer": "Beispiel GmbH",
 "Name": "Example-Device",
 "SerialNumber": "D1.0",
 "Type": "example device",
 "ID": "2071c7736acd16f6cea3727d3b7ecde5
```

```
        3f4c2e97b421f3550248e19d7309c636",
    "Category": "infrastructure",
    "SecureBoot": false,
    "Firmware": {
        "Version": "1.0",
        "URL": "https://192.168.102.94:10000/FirmwareInfo"
    },
    "ClientSoftware": {
        "Version": "",
        "URL": ""
    },
    "Updates": {
        "AutomaticUpdates": false,
        "EndOfLife": "2021-01-01T00:00:00"
    },
    "Cryptography": {
        "Software": {
            "IoTAGKey": true,
            "KeyStore": true,
            "Algorithms": [
                "RSASSA-PSS",
                "SHA-256",
                "TLS_AES_128_GCM_SHA256",
                "TLS_CHACHA20_POLY1305_SHA256",
                "aes256-ctr",
                "ecdsa-sha2-nistp521",
                "diffie-hellman-group-exchange-sha256",
                "hmac-sha2-256,hmac-sha2-512"
            ]
        },
        "Hardware": {
            "IoTAGKey": false,
            "KeyStore": false,
            "Algorithms": []
        }
    },
    "Connectivity": {
        "IEEE802_3": [
            "WPA2",
            "b",
            "g",
            "n"
        ],
        "Bluetooth": [
            "4.2"
        ],
        "ZigBee": []
    },
    "Services": [
        {
            "Name": "IoTAG",
            "Port": "27795/TCP",
            "Protocol": "HTTP/2",
            "Software": "IoTAG-Server"
        },
        {
            "Name": "SSH",
            "Port": "22/TCP",
            "Protocol": "SSH-2",
            "Software": "OpenSSH-8.1"
        }
    ]
}
```


Listing 1. IoTAG example

C. Integrity

1) Signature algorithm and authentication: The RSA procedure serves as the basis for the signature mechanism of IoTAG. A minimum length of 2048 bits is recommended for the keys required by this procedure [24]. Since the RSA algorithm would always generate the same encryption text for identical messages, methods have been developed that combine the plaintext with a random value, the padding, before each encryption process. The Public-Key Cryptography Standards (PKCS) define in PKCS#1 with RSASSA-PKCS1-v1_5 and RSASSA-PSS two signing procedures for RSA that take such padding into account. The latter is preferable for new developments, which is why it is used for IoTAG signatures using the standard options defined in PKCS#1 [25].

To verify the signature, the message recipient must know the sender's public key. However, this must also ensure that an attacker has not mistakenly published his key to the recipient and is therefore able to generate misleading messages whose signature is considered valid by the recipient. To counteract this, the signer's public key is published in conjunction with a certificate, which in turn is signed by a trusted third party [12]. In IoTAG certificates are used according to the specification in ITU-T X.509 [26] and RFC 2459 [27]. Such a certificate can be issued directly by the manufacturer of a device and stored on the device, or it can be created when the device is set up and then signed by a local or external certification authority.

2) Signed dataset: Basically, the target of the signature is always the IoTAG dataset in serialized form and thus a UTF-8 encoded character string (see subsection B). However, not this entire string is used for the signature, but instead a hash sum is calculated from it, which is then signed. As recommended by NIST, the SHA-256 algorithm is used to generate this sum [28].

Before the hash algorithm can be applied, the IoTAG string is converted into a byte array. Only from this array the hash sum is calculated, to which the signature algorithm is then applied. If the array contains a terminating null byte, this is ignored in the hash calculation.

D. Communication

The last open point to be defined is the IoTAG related communication behaviour. This includes not only the retrieval of IoTAG data from a device, but also the retrieval of software resources via an URL, provided inside the IoTAG dataset. The same technologies are used for both procedures, which is why a general description of the communication endpoint, the transmission protocol and the data format is given before the two procedures are explained in more detail.

1) General description: The Hypertext Transfer Protocol Version 2 with Transport Layer Security (TLS) [29] is selected as the transmission protocol (HTTPS) [30]. This means that an HTTPS-capable server application must be provided as the communication endpoint for querying information, which has a trustworthy certificate for encrypted communication. This application does not have to support the full scope of operations defined in RFC 2616 [31], it only has to be able to respond to a single GET request by providing the respective data record. The addressed resource is determined by the respective URL.

For formatting the data for transmission within HTTP packets, JSON is used.

2) Retrieving Software Resources: It is defined that the IoTAG data set provided by a device always contains a URL to obtain the latest available device firmware or, if necessary, the software for client systems. It is not possible to download the software directly via this URL. Instead, it is used to execute the HTTP request described in subsection A. The response to this request contains a JSON object, which in turn has the string attributes "URL" and "Version". This URL can now be used directly to download the firmware. The second specification informs about the version of the software.

3) Retrieving IoTAG: Every IoTAG compatible device must provide a communication interface to retrieve the IoTAG data set. In order to make this procedure uniform, a unique HTTP URL must be defined via which a corresponding resource can be accessed. This requires a uniform port number and a predefined path for the request to the HTTP server. 27795 is specified as the network port. The path consists of a single segment called "iotag". This results in the following URL scheme, whereby the "<host>" statement is to be interpreted according to the definition in RFC 3986 paragraph 3.2.2. [13]: https://<host>:27795/iotag

4) Transmitted data record: The specification of the signature process shows that in addition to the actual IoTAG data set, additional information is required to verify its correctness. This is a certificate containing the key needed to verify the signature as well as the signature itself. A separate JSON object is also defined for this, which contains this information in the form of the attributes "IoTAG", "Certificates" and "Signature".

Since the signature is present as a byte sequence during its calculation, it is encoded for transmission to base64 and can thus be integrated into the JSON object as a string.

A uniform form for the transfer of the certificate must be ensured. For the transmission of ITU-T X.509 certificates in non-binary form, the coding according to RFC 7468 [32] is suitable. Basically, the certificate is first converted into a binary structure, taking into account the coding rules specified in ITU-T X.690 [33], and then encoded to base64, which also allows it to be embedded as a string in the JSON object. If additional certificates are required for the verification of the certificate, all certificates are first encoded and the resulting character strings are then concatenated. The order of the certificates must be observed according to the specification in RFC 5246 chapter 7.4.2 [29].

The IoTAG dataset could be entered directly as an object, since it is JSON-serialized for transmission anyway. To check the signature, the IoTAG object must be extracted from the parent object. This can be done in two ways: the recipient can still treat the transmitted data as a string and try to extract the IoTAG object by manipulating it. However, this procedure is unusual and involves additional development effort, since the corresponding extraction routine must be implemented. Alternatively, the received JSON object can be deserialized to an object of the respective programming language and then processed further.

Although the latter approach is preferable, it also makes signature verification more problematic. To perform this step, the IoTAG object must be serialized to a string again after extraction to calculate the hash sum. However, this serialization produces different results depending on the software used, and thus ultimately results in different hash values. A signature check based on the respective hash sums would thus fail, although the information remained unchanged.

To counter this problem, a way must be found to transfer the IoTAG data set within a JSON object in such a way that it can be extracted by deserialization without affecting the formatting. This can be achieved by treating the serialized IoTAG data for transmission as a string rather than as an object. In this case, all JSON control characters within this string must be replaced by appropriate escape sequences before transmission to ensure error-free interpretation. However, these must also be removed by the receiver before the hash calculation in order not to falsify the result.

Instead, preference is given to another approach. Here, the transmission of the IoTAG data as a string is retained, but the character string resulting from its serialization is first base64 encoded. The result of this process is then set as the value of the IoTAG attribute. This enables the recipient of the data to parse the received JSON object and decode the information it contains, which ultimately results in the same form as it was processed by the sender.

IV. Conclusion

With IoTAG, a fast and easy solution for the security management of IoT networks is described. The proposed standard includes the necessary information for a risk analysis and the possibility to monitor all devices, regarding to their running software version, protocols and the encryption algorithms.

The implementation can be realized with little effort and the security of the whole network can be improved easily. However, this proposed standard must be implemented and integrated into products by all manufacturers.

This standard can also help attackers to gain information about the devices in the network, but with an improved overview over the devices and their security state, it helps more than it brings new risks.

As a next step, IoTAG can be discussed as a standard or an existing standard can be extended with the features of IoTAG. For this purpose, the signature process must also be adopted to ensure data integrity.

We are currently working on implementation examples to help getting started with IoTAG. With these different implementations, it is also possible to evaluate the best methods and libraries for the signature and the JSON serialization.

References

[1] Federal Office for Information Security (Germany), "SYS.4.4: Allgemeines IoT-Gerät," IT-Grundschutz-Kompendium 2. Version 2019, Cologne, Bundesanzeiger Verlag GmbH, 2019, p. 3.

[2] European Telecommunications Standards Institute, "Draft ETSI EN 303 645 V2.0.0 (2019-11)," 2019.

[3] S. Fischer, K. Neubauer, L. Hinterberger, B. Weber, and R. Hackenberg, "IoTAG: An Open Standard for IoT Device IdentificAtion and RecoGnition," The Thirteenth International Conference on Emerging Security Information, Systems and Technologies, IARIA, 2019, pp. 107-113.

[4] World Wide Web Consortium, "Web of Things (WoT) Thing Description," Apr. 2018. [Online]. Available from: https://www.w3.org/TR/wot-thing-description/ [accessed: 2020-07-20].

[5] A. E. Khaled, A. Helal, W. Lindquist, and C. Lee, "IoT-DDL—Device Description Language for the "T" in IoT," IEEE Access, Nr. 6, pp. 24048-24063, Apr. 2018.
[6] U.S. Department of Commerce und National Institute of Standards and Technology, "Secure Hash Standard (SHS)," 2015.
[7] Internet Engineering Task Force, "RFC 4648 - The Base16, Base32, and Base64 Data Encodings," Oct. 2006. [Online]. Available from: https://tools.ietf.org/html/rfc4648. [accessed: 2020-07-20].
[8] National Institute of Standards and Technology, "NIST Policy on Hash Functions - Hash Functions — CSRC," May 2019. [Online]. Available from: https://csrc.nist.gov/Projects/Hash-Functions/NIST-Policy-on-Hash-Functions. [accessed: 2020-07-20].
[9] R. K. Dahal, J. Bhatta, and T. N. Dhamala, "Performance Analysis of SHA-2 and SHA-3 Finalists," International Journal on Cryptography and Information Security (IJCIS), Sept. 2013, pp.720-730.
[10] U.S. Department of Commerce und National Institute of Standards and Technology, "SHA-3 Standard: Permutation-Based Hash and Extendable-Output Functions," 2015.
[11] J. Vermillard, "Sicherheit für IoT-Geräte," Linux Magazin, Oct. 2015.
[12] A. S. Tanenbaum, "Moderne Betriebssysteme," Hallbergmoos: Pearson Deutschland GmbH, 2009, pp. 720-721.
[13] Internet Engineering Task Force, "RFC 3986 - Uniform Resource Identifier (URI): Generic Syntax," Jan. 2005. [Online]. Available from: https://tools.ietf.org/html/rfc3986. [accessed: 2020-07-20].
[14] International Organization for Standardization, "ISO 8601:2004: Data elements and interchange formats — Information interchange — Representation of dates and times," 2004.
[15] Internet Engineering Task Force, "RFC 5656 - Elliptic Curve Algorithm Integration in the Secure Shell Transport Layer," Dec. 2009. [Online]. Available from: https://tools.ietf.org/html/rfc5656. [accessed: 2020-07-20].
[16] A. Healey, "GET 802(R) Standards," [Online]. Available from: https://ieeexplore.ieee.org/browse/standards/get-program/page/series?id=68. [accessed: 2020-07-20].
[17] Bluetooth SIG, Inc., "Bluetooth Core Specification, Revision 5.2," 2019.
[18] ZigBee Alliance, "ZigBee Specification," 2015.
[19] P. Kraft and A. Weyert, "Network Hacking," Franzis Verlag GmbH, 2015, pp. 345-360.
[20] J. Erickson, "Hacking," dpunkt.verlag GmbH, 2009, pp. 472-488.
[21] ECMA International, "The JSON Data Interchange Syntax," 2017.
[22] Internet Engineering Task Force, "RFC 8259 - The JavaScript Object Notation (JSON) Data Interchange Format," Dec. 2017. [Online]. Available from: https://tools.ietf.org/html/rfc8259. [accessed: 2020-07-20].
[23] N. Nurseitov, M. Paulson, R. Reynolds, and C. Izurieta, "Comparison of JSON and XML data interchange formats: A case study," International Conference on Computer Applications in Industry and Engineering, CAINE, 2009, pp.157-162.
[24] U.S. Department of Commerce and National Institute of Standards and Technology, "Recommendation for Key Management," 2015.
[25] Internet Engineering Task Force, "RFC 8017 - PKCS #1: RSA Cryptography Specifications Version 2.2," Nov. 2016. [Online]. Available from: https://tools.ietf.org/html/rfc8017. [accessed: 2020-07-20].
[26] International Telecommunication Union, "Recommendation ITU-T X.509," 2016.
[27] Internet Engineering Task Force, "RFC 2459 - Internet X.509 Public Key Infrastructure Certificate and CRL Profile," Jan. 1999. [Online]. Available from: https://tools.ietf.org/html/rfc2459. [accessed: 2020-07-20].
[28] National Institute of Standards and Technology, "NIST Policy on Hash Functions - Hash Functions — CSRC," May 2019. [Online]. Available from: https://csrc.nist.gov/Projects/Hash-Functions/NIST-Policy-on-Hash-Functions. [accessed: 2020-07-20].
[29] Internet Engineering Task Force, "RFC 5246 - The Transport Layer Security (TLS) Protocol Version 1.2," Aug. 2008. [Online]. Available from: https://tools.ietf.org/html/rfc5246. [accessed: 2020-07-20].
[30] Internet Engineering Task Force, "RFC 7540 - Hypertext Transfer Protocol Version 2 (HTTP/2)," May 2015. [Online]. Available from: https://tools.ietf.org/html/rfc7540. [accessed: 2020-07-20].
[31] Internet Engineering Task Force, "RFC 2616 - Hypertext Transfer Protocol – HTTP/1.1," June 1999. [Online]. Available from: https://tools.ietf.org/html/rfc2616. [accessed: 2020-07-20].
[32] Internet Engineering Task Force, "RFC 7468 - Textual Encodings of PKIX, PKCS, and CMS Structures," Apr. 2015. [Online]. Available from: https://tools.ietf.org/html/rfc7468. [accessed: 2020-07-20].
[33] International Telecommunication Union, "Recommendation ITU-T X.690," 2015.

A Study about the Different Categories of IoT in Scientific Publications

Sebastian Fischer
Secure Systems Engineering
Fraunhofer AISEC
Berlin, Germany
email:
sebastian.fischer@aisec.fraunhofer.de

Katrin Neubauer
Dept. Computer Science and Mathematics
Ostbayerische Technische Hochschule
Regensburg, Germany
email:
katrin1.neubauer@oth-regensburg.de

Rudolf Hackenberg
Dept. Computer Science and Mathematics
Ostbayerische Technische Hochschule
Regensburg, Germany
email:
rudolf.hackenberg@oth-regensburg.de

Abstract—**The Internet of Things (IoT) is widely used as a synonym for nearly every connected device. This makes it really difficult to find the right kind of scientific publication for the intended category of IoT. Conferences and other events for IoT are confusing about the target group (consumer, enterprise, industrial, etc.) and standardisation organisations suffer from the same problem. To demonstrate these problems, this paper shows the results of an analyses over IoT publications in different research libraries. The number of results for IoT, consumer, enterprise and industrial search queries were evaluated and a manual study about 100 publications was done. According to the research library or search engine, different results about the distribution of consumer-, enterprise- and industrial- IoT are visible. The comparison with the results of the manual evaluation shows that some search queries do not show all desired publications or that considerably more, unwanted results are returned. Most researchers do not use the keywords right and the exact category of IoT can only be accessed via the abstract. This shows major problems with the use of the term IoT and its minor limitations.**

Keywords–Internet of Things; IoT; publications; consumer; industrial; enterprise; categorization.

I. INTRODUCTION

The Internet of Things is defined in ISO/IEC 20924:2018 page 9 as "[...] infrastructure of interconnected entities, people, systems and information resources together with services, which processes and reacts to information from the physical world and virtual world." [1] This definition is very broad and includes all possible devices that are connected to other devices via a network (not necessarily the Internet), like smartphones, personal computers, connected vehicles, airplanes, smart grid components, smart home devices, connected environment sensors, eHealth hardware, wearables and many more. The ISO/IEC definition is not the only one using this range of devices, also researchers are using IoT to describe all kind of products and prototypes. This leads to difficult situations where conferences or other events focus on IoT and the attendees do not know if the presentations are in their field of interest.

Searching for IoT scientific publications can be difficult as well. With only IoT, a too wide range of topics are returned. Restrictions, such as "consumer" or "enterprise" can help, but a lot of researchers do not use it. For example, the publication "Smart Charger Based on IoT Concept" [2] is about a consumer product, but the title and the keywords (Smart Charger, Arduino, Phone Charger, Battery Charger) are only containing "IoT" and "Smart Charger". A search for "IoT" and "consumer" will not include the publication.

In this study, we want to show the different problems of IoT as a general term. We start with some related work in Section II and the first part of research (Section III) consists of the different numbers of IoT publications in selected research libraries. The second part (Section IV) shows the results of a manual review of 100 publications according to their IoT category. In Section V, the results were then compared and evaluated to show the problems with the term IoT in research. At the end, a short conclusion and our future work are given in Section VII.

II. RELATED WORK

There is no recent study about current research on IoT publications, which includes the different categories "consumer", "industrial" and "enterprise". Some publications, like a study from Mishra et.al. [3] are covering the years from 2000 to 2015 or another study about the IoT trends reaches from 1992 to 2015 [4].

Some newer bibliometric studies from 2019 and 2020 are restricted to Blockchain [5] or Industrial 4.0 [6]. They are both showing the increasing amount of IoT publications, but no current overview of the whole situation of the last two years.

This study was inspired by the approach of the publications mentioned above, although the focus is different. The used academic search libraries differ in many point. For example, the target group and the type of search are different. IEEE Xplore targets technical publications, while Google Scholar and Semantic Scholar are universal. A 2018 paper examined the sizes of different libraries and identified Google Scholar as the largest [7]. Semantic Scholar, on the other hand, uses an algorithm that is based on artificial intelligence and is therefore supposed to provide very precise results [8]. In the course of this paper, the differences with respect to IoT will become clear again.

III. IOT PUBLICATIONS IN RESEARCH LIBRARIES

The aim of this study is to find out whether it is possible to find publications on specific areas of IoT without getting too many results and limit the great diversity of IoT, but also

TABLE I. NUMBER OF RESULTS PER SEARCH QUERY

Search term:	Springer Link	IEEE Xplore	ScienceDirect	ACM digital library	Google Scholar	Semantic Scholar
iot	16,545	10,996	7,203	3,027	44,800	56,000
iiot	529	398	359	74	4,730	2,230
smart home iot	4,096	615	1,954	814	20,000	11,300
automotive iot	1,277	117	639	155	8,270	2,830

TABLE II. NUMBER AND PERCENTAGE OF THE RELEVANT IOT CATEGORIES

Search term:	Springer Link	IEEE Xplore	ScienceDirect	ACM digital library	Google Scholar	Semantic Scholar
iot	16,545	10,996	7,203	3,027	44,800	56,000
industrial iot	5,780	1,197	3,281	735	20,400	16,000
consumer iot	3,738	545	2,010	1,316	17,100	9,620
enterprise iot	3,272	157	1,712	424	14,200	6,780
% of iot search:						
industrial iot	34.9 %	10.9 %	45.6 %	24.3 %	45.5 %	28.6 %
consumer iot	22.6 %	5.0 %	27.9 %	43.5 %	38.2 %	17.2 %
enterprise iot	19.8 %	1.4 %	23.8 %	14.0 %	31.7 %	12.1 %
Sum of %	77.3 %	17.3 %	97.2 %	81.8 %	115.4 %	57.9 %

without overlooking relevant publications. For this goal, we started with "IoT" as a search query in our manual study (Section IV) and after analysing the publications, we came up with three categories "industrial", "consumer", "enterprise", as most of the devices can be classified into these (see Table III).

To find research about used encryption methods in consumer IoT devices, for example, the first search approach would be "consumer IoT encryption". However, some researcher are not restrict their publications about encryption and just use the term IoT. The previous query will not find this work. If we just use "IoT encryption", there are too many results (compared to the restricted). Research about encryption in vehicles, industrial environment, etc. are included as well.

To prove this statement we started with different research libraries and different queries and collected the numbers of results.

Overall, six libraries / search engines were used:

- Springer Link
- IEEE Xplore
- ScienceDirect
- ACM digital library
- Google Scholar
- Semantic Scholar

These libraries / search engines are the most common ones and widely used in computer science. Because of their different search algorithms (as seen in the results), data from all of them are shown. For example, IEEE Xplore finds a lot of results for "IoT" alone, but not much with "IoT" and other words combined. The words are all combined the same way over all search engines with the "AND" operator to find only publications with both words in it (e.g., "IoT AND consumer").

The search was done with some word combinations to investigate the different areas of IoT. However, only a few words yielded many results. A precise search for a specific area is thus very well possible (e.g., automotive), as can be seen in Table I. However, the abbreviation IIoT for industrial IoT is not very common. All the results in this paper are only with new publications from the years 2019 and 2020, to show a current overview of the research in the field of IoT.

To get a better separation, for example of the whole 44,800 IoT results of Google Scholar, we used the three search terms in addition to "IoT": "industrial", "consumer" and "enterprise". The results are shown in Table II. In our example from Google Scholar, we get about 45.5 % for "industrial", 38.2 % for "consumer" and 31.7 % for "enterprise". The sum is over 100 % because some of the publications can include more than one of them. This shows (in the case of Google Scholar) a good idea of how to find the right IoT category for a research (see Table II).

IV. IoT PUBLICATIONS STUDY

Because of the big differences in the search results and therefore in the search type, we made a manual study with 100 publications about their category of IoT. We want to know exactly, which publication belongs to industrial, consumer, enterprise or is not related to IoT at all. For this study, we needed 100 full publications most random as possible. Because we do not know the algorithms behind the different search engines, we decided to use Semantic Scholar with the option "has PDF". This adds a bit randomness and makes it easier to get the full text. All the search parameters are:

- Keyword: iot
- Language: english
- Publication date: 2019 and 2020
- Option: "has PDF"
- Sort by Relevance

This search leads to 11,800 results. We downloaded the first 100 publications [2], [9]–[107] and determined the categories. For a better evaluation of the results, it was also noted whether the category of the IoT devices in the publication can already be identified in the title, the abstract or only in the text. Additionally, it was evaluated whether the category can already be extracted from the keywords.

Table III shows the result of the manual review. First, the total number of publications. Not specified publications are referring to IoT in general. For example, the publication about "Security on IoT Devices with Secure Elements" [30] can be applied to consumer, enterprise and industrial IoT devices. The category "consumer" consists of devices, which are meant to be used by consumers, not professional people. "Enterprise" describes the category for devices used by companies or installed / assembled by a professional service. The last category "industrial" are IoT devices for production. Overall, the different areas for each category were assigned as follows:

Consumer

- Smart Home devices
- Wearables
- Connected home automation and alarm systems

Enterprise

- Smart city devices
- Environment sensors (for big buildings or fields)
- Medical devices
- Vehicles (transportation)
- Sensors for bigger buildings
- Alarm systems (for business)

Industrial

- Machine sensors
- Machine control systems
- Industrial sensors
- Industrial devices with network connection

The lists above are not exhaustive. Medical and transportation devices can be used by consumer, but they have to be installed by a professional. Therefore, they are assigned to enterprise.

The remaining columns in Table III are showing the difficulty of assigning the publications to the categories. If the category can be be determined by the title, the publication is added to column t. If it is only in part possible, it is added to column (t). For example, the title "IoT based home automation using Raspberry Pi" [23] is clearly for consumer, because home automation is one of the consumer parts. In this case the publications is added to column t. Another title "IoT-Enabled Door Lock System" [28] is not clear, because a door lock system can be for the smart home market or just for business buildings. In this case the publication is added to column (t) as the product is in the title, but the main category can only be recognized in the abstract. Therefore, the publication is added to column a as well. The procedure is the same for the columns a and (a). If it is not possible to recognize the category from the title or abstract at all, the publication is added to the text column. If the category is already determined by the title, it will not be counted to the abstract or text, but it can be added to the keywords.

There are only 9 publications in the keywords column, because only clear keywords like "industrial" count. If the keywords are not clearly about the category, like "door lock", they do not count.

TABLE III. RESULT OF THE MANUAL REVIEWED PUBLICATIONS

		title		abstract			
	total	**t**	**(t)**	**a**	**(a)**	**text**	**keywords**
not specific	30	2	6	17		6	
industrial	14	1	3	8		2	1
consumer	22	4	8	9	1	3	5
enterprise	33	10	15	5		4	3
not IoT	1						
sum	100	17	32	39	1	15	9

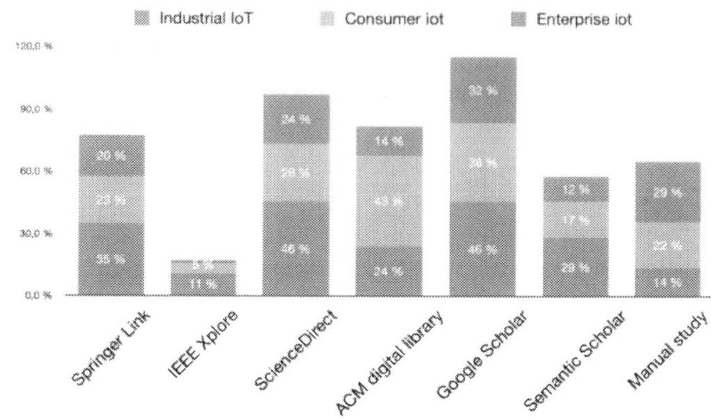

Figure 1. Result of the search in research libraries

There are 30 publications for IoT in general, 22 for consumer devices, 33 for enterprise, 14 for industrial and one publication, which is not related to IoT, but has some serial number with iot in the title. Most of the time, the publications for enterprise can be categorized with the title alone, 10 directly and 15 not clearly with related words. Overall, the most publications can be categorized without reading the whole text (but not without reading the abstract), in only 15 cases, further reading is needed. The keywords usage is not good, as only 9 are clearly categorizeable.

V. RESULTS

All results are from the previous research in early April 2020 as described in Sections III and IV. Figure 1 shows the percentage of the different categories according to the search results for only the term "IoT" in the different research libraries, compared with the manual study.

In the manual study, about 65 percent of all publications can be categorized. Semantic Scholar and Springer Link are near to this number with 58 and 77 percent. But with different weightings of the categories. This may be due to the limited number of samples in the manual study of 100.

IEEE Xplore shows a significantly lower number of results if the search term is expanded with the categories. This is due to the search method of IEEE Xplore, since only the metadata (title, abstract and keywords) are searched by default. This procedure has advantages and disadvantages, as will be shown in Section VI.

The other three libraries, ScienceDirect, ACM digital library and Google Scholar are over 82 percent (Google with

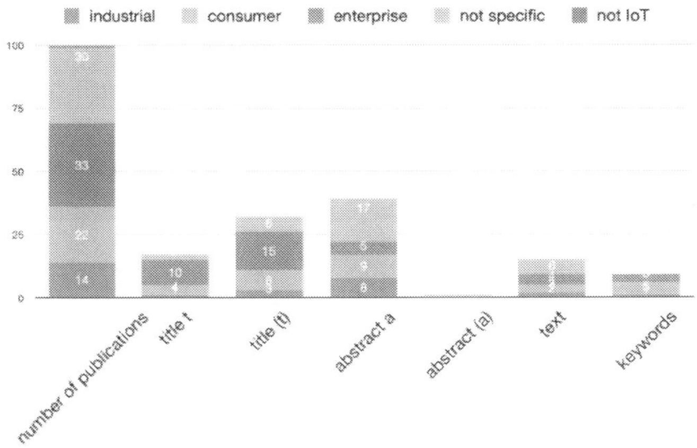

Figure 2. Result of the manual publications study

115 percent even over 100). This is the case, because some publications containing more than one of the three search words. This is useful, because general publications about IoT are still included in the restricted search queries, but for example, Google Scholar finds a lot of publications with "iot AND consumer" which are not consumer related. The high number of search results is because of the comprehensive search method. Even text inside the publication is found. For example, the two search results are in the first 100 results from google (search term: "iot AND consumer"): "A review of Internet of Things (IoT) embedded sustainable supply chain for industry 4.0 requirements" [108] and "Beyond IoT Business" [109].

A big difference in all libraries are the weights between the categories. For example, the technical library IEEE Xplore has more industrial publications as a percentage than all the others. This should be considered by a search for only one category.

The results of the manual study from Section IV are shown in Figure 2. This figure shows the difficulty by categorizing IoT research. Only 17 publications can clearly be assigned with the title and 15 of them only via the text. The keywords are often not used and only useful in 9 cases. The different search approach from IEEE Xplore can only find results from column t and a, but most of the time, there is not a clear "consumer" or "industrial" in the title or the abstract and the library can not include the publication. Some assignments can only be done if, for example, it is possible to relate smart home to consumer.

Only with the results from Figure 1, it seems that IoT can be clearly delimited to the three categories (Google Scholar with over 100 percent together in all 3 categories). However, the manual study shows that there is research in IoT that is suitable for all areas ("not specific" in figure 2). But it is not easy to find the research that is relevant for your own field. Depending on the research library, different numbers of results are found and the weighting of the categories also varies greatly. The search for publications in the field of IoT is therefore associated with many problems, which will be described in more detail in Section VI.

VI. PROBLEMS

Since IoT is a comprehensive term, some problems arise when searching for scientific publications. Some of them are described in more detail in this section on the basis of the previous study.

We use the same example from Section III: searching for an encryption method for consumer IoT devices, like a smart home sensor. If we use "IoT AND consumer AND encryption", we get a lower number of search results, but missing general IoT solutions for encryption, which do not include "consumer" in their text. If we change the search term to "IoT AND encryption AND NOT enterprise AND NOT industrial" we might miss some general research, too, but not as much as before. But also publications about production line encryption will be included, because they often miss the term "industrial IoT" or IIoT. Therefore, all unwanted terms must be excluded.

It takes less effort, to search for more specific term like "smart home" instead of IoT to get fewer results. However, by doing that, one misses a lot of publications or has to search for a lot of specific words. A Keyword search would be the best solution, but only a small subset would be returned. A restriction to categories is almost impossible, regardless of the fact that the keywords exists exactly for this purpose.

One of the biggest problems, with the large amount of search results is the difficulty to determine, if the publication is relevant. The results of the manual publications study shows, most of the time the abstract is necessary to get the information. This should be easier if the title or the keywords are better.

Another problem are the different ways in which the search engines work. Depending on the library, a restriction of IoT is useful or not (fewer results from IEEE Xplore with the category).

As a last issue, it is not clear how many publications in total from one category have been published in 2019 and 2020 because every search engine differs in the number of results and some are showing publications in more than one category. Therefore, this research question cannot be answered by this study.

VII. CONCLUSION AND FUTURE WORK

IoT is a too broad term. Nearly every device can be counted as an Internet of Things devices. Therefore, a scientific search about IoT returns thousand of results. No categorization or other distinction is used by many researchers. In this study we only presented results about the big three categories "consumer", "enterprise" and "industrial". The more detailed results are not necessary for the biggest problems with IoT and not shown in this paper.

Some weak points about this study are the limitation of 100 papers from only one research library and no further research about the quality of the publications. Nevertheless, the study shows the need of clear categories and a strict use of them. The best way is to include them into the keywords and avoid using words from other categories in the whole publication, as the most search engines including the whole text. In some publications, the term IoT is not necessary at all (e.g., smart home or smart vehicles).

As future work, we are trying to find suitable categories and additional characteristics to build a categorization for every IoT device. Because not only researchers are struggling with the term IoT, standardisation organisations have the same problem, too. They have to decide, which product should be included in a new standard and which restrictions can be applied to all the included ones. They use very broad definitions like in ETSI EN 303 645, consumer devices are defined to be used typical in the home or as wearables, but they can be included in enterprise IoT environments as well: "Consumer IoT devices are commonly also used in business contexts. These devices remain classified as consumer IoT devices." [110]

REFERENCES

[1] "Information technology Internet of Things (IoT) Vocabulary," International Organization for Standardization, Geneva, CH, Standard, Dec. 2018.

[2] M. H. bin Husin, "Smart charger based on iot concept," International Journal of Education, Science, Technology and Engineering, vol. 2, 2019, pp. 39–44.

[3] D. Mishra et al., "Vision, applications and future challenges of internet of things: A bibliometric study of the recent literature," Ind. Manag. Data Syst., vol. 116, 2016, pp. 1331–1355.

[4] H.-H. Tsai, "A case study of research trends of internet of things." ICEB, 2015.

[5] M. Kamran, H. U. Khan, M. W. Nisar, M. Farooq, and S.-U. Rehman, "Blockchain and internet of things: A bibliometric study," Comput. Electr. Eng., vol. 81, 2020, p. 106525.

[6] A. Ahmi, H. Elbardan, and R. H. R. M. Ali, "Bibliometric analysis of published literature on industry 4.0," 2019 International Conference on Electronics, Information, and Communication (ICEIC), 2019, pp. 1–6.

[7] M. Gusenbauer, "Google scholar to overshadow them all? comparing the sizes of 12 academic search engines and bibliographic databases," Scientometrics, vol. 118, 2018, pp. 177–214.

[8] S. N. Fricke, "Semantic scholar," Journal of the Medical Library Association : JMLA, vol. 106, 2018, pp. 145 – 147.

[9] Z. B. Celik, G. Tan, and P. D. McDaniel, "Iotguard: Dynamic enforcement of security and safety policy in commodity iot," in NDSS Symposium, 2019.

[10] M. E. SUtIOT, "Exiopol-development and illustrative analyses of a detailed global mr ee sut / iot," 2019.

[11] J. Koo, S.-R. Oh, and Y.-G. Kim, "Device identification interoperability in heterogeneous iot platforms ," Sensors (Basel, Switzerland), vol. 19, 2019.

[12] I. Arpithashankar, "Iot based industrial pollution monitoring system," International Journal of Innovative Research in Technology, vol. 6, 2019, pp. 327–332.

[13] J. S. R. Dr and V. A. J. Ms, "Automation using iot in greenhouse environment," Journal of Information Technology and Digital World, vol. 1, 2019, pp. 38–47.

[14] M. Alhaisoni, "Iot energy efficiency through centrality metrics," Annals of Emerging Technol. in Com., vol. 3, no. 2, 2019, pp. 14–21.

[15] C. Nguyen and D. B. Hoang, "S-manage protocol for provisioning iot applications on demand." JTDE, Vol 7, No 3, Article 185, 2019.

[16] P. Radanliev et al., "Cyber risk in iot systems." Preprints, 2019.

[17] P. Manjunathmin and P. G. Shah, "Machine to machine metamorphosis to the iot," 2019.

[18] D. Johnson and M. Ketel, "Iot: Application protocols and security," I.J. Computer Network and Information Security, 4, 2019, pp. 1–8.

[19] D. Bilgeri, H. Gebauer, E. Fleisch, and F. Wortmann, "Driving process innovation with iot field data," MIS Q. Executive, vol. 18, 2019, p. 5.

[20] D. Sethuramalingam, N. V. Brindha, and S. Balamurugan, "Security for smart vehicle in iot," The IoT and the Next Revolutions Automating the World, 2019, pp. 289–296.

[21] E. Borelli et al., "Habitat: An iot solution for independent elderly," Sensors (Basel, Switzerland), vol. 19, 2019.

[22] A. Mavrogiorgou, A. Kiourtis, K. Perakis, S. Pitsios, and D. Kyriazis, "Iot in healthcare: Achieving interoperability of high-quality data acquired by iot medical devices," Sensors (Basel, Switzerland), vol. 19, 2019.

[23] A. Sinha and R. Tatikonda, "Iot based home automation using raspberry pi," International Journal of Advance Research, Ideas and Innovations in Technology, vol. 5, 2019, pp. 558–560.

[24] N. Walee et al., "An iot based smart parking system," 2019.

[25] L. C. Booth and M. Mayrany, "Iot penetration testing: Hacking an electric scooter," 2019.

[26] R. Pierdicca, M. Marques-Pita, M. Paolanti, and E. S. Malinverni, "Iot and engagement in the ubiquitous museum," Sensors (Basel, Switzerland), vol. 19, 2019.

[27] K. Ma, A. B. Bagula, C. N. Nyirenda, and O. Ajayi, "An iot-based fog computing model," Sensors (Basel, Switzerland), vol. 19, 2019.

[28] T. Adiono, S. Fuada, S. F. Anindya, I. G. Purwanda, and M. Y. Fathany, "Iot-enabled door lock system," International Journal of Advanced Computer Science and Applications, vol. 10, 2019.

[29] A. Singh, U. Sinha, and D. Sharma, "Cloud-based iot architecture in green buildings," Green Building Management and Smart Automation, 2020, pp. 164–183.

[30] T. Schläpfer and A. Rüst, "Security on iot devices with secure elements," 2019.

[31] S. Giordano et al., "Uprise-iot: User-centric privacy & security in the iot," 2019.

[32] M. Ansgariusson and A. Wihlborg-Rasmusen, "Robust header compression for cellular iot," 2019.

[33] Ragula, "Waste management in iot-enabled smart cities," 2019.

[34] L. Nóbrega, P. Gonalves, P. Pedreiras, and J. Pereira, "An iot-based solution for intelligent farming ," Sensors (Basel, Switzerland), vol. 19, 2019.

[35] H. A. Abdul-Ghani and D. Konstantas, "A comprehensive study of security and privacy guidelines, threats, and countermeasures: An iot perspective," J. Sensor and Actuator Networks, vol. 8, 2019, p. 22.

[36] D. Minoli and B. Occhiogrosso, "Practical aspects for the integration of 5g networks and iot applications in smart cities environments," Wireless Communications and Mobile Computing, vol. 2019, 2019, pp. 5 710 834:1–5 710 834:30.

[37] Y. B. Zikria, S. W. Kim, O. Hahm, M. K. Afzal, and M. Y. Aalsalem, "Internet of things (iot) operating systems management: Opportunities, challenges, and solution," Sensors (Basel, Switzerland), vol. 19, 2019.

[38] E. C. Reilly, M. Maloney, M. Siegel, and G. Falco, "A smart city iot integrity-first communication protocol via an ethereum blockchain light client," 2019.

[39] R. H. Putra, F. T. Kusuma, T. N. Damayanti, and D. N. Ramadan, "Iot: smart garbage monitoring using android and real time database," TELKOMNIKA Telecommunication Computing Electronics and Control, vol. 17, 2019, pp. 1483–1491.

[40] D. Krcmarik, M. Petru, and R. Moezzi, "Innovative iot sensing and communication unit in agriculture," European Journal of Electrical Engineering, vol. 21, 2019, pp. 273–278.

[41] T. Alam and B. Rababah, "Convergence of manet in communication among smart devices in iot," International Journal of Wireless and Microwave Technologies, vol. 9, 2019, pp. 1–10.

[42] G. Yoon, D. Choi, J. Lee, and H. Choi, "Management of iot sensor data using a fog computing node," J. Sensors, vol. 2019, 2019, pp. 5 107 457:1–5 107 457:9.

[43] S. K. Lo, C. S. Liew, K. S. Tey, and S. Mekhilef, "An interoperable component-based architecture for data-driven iot system," Sensors (Basel, Switzerland), vol. 19, 2019.

[44] I. Bica, B.-C. Chifor, tefan Ciprian Arseni, and I. Matei, "Multi-layer iot security framework for ambient intelligence environments," Sensors (Basel, Switzerland), vol. 19, 2019.

[45] S. Rathore, Y. Pan, and J. H. Park, "Blockdeepnet: A blockchain-based secure deep learning for iot network," Sustainability, vol. 11, 2019, p. 3974.

[46] W. Ejaz, M. A. Azam, S. Saadat, F. Iqbal, and A. Hanan, "Unmanned aerial vehicles enabled iot platform for disaster management," Energies, vol. 12, 2019, p. 2706.

[47] N. Kherraf, "Provisioning of edge computing resources for heterogeneous iot workload," 2019.

[48] A. Márkus and J. Dombi, "Multi-cloud management strategies for simulating iot applications," Acta Cybernetica, vol. 24, 2019, pp. 83–103.

[49] I. Sittón-Candanedo, R. S. Alonso, Ó. García, L. Muñoz, and S. Rodríguez, "Edge computing, iot and social computing in smart energy scenarios," Sensors (Basel, Switzerland), vol. 19, 2019.

[50] A. M. Zarca et al., "Enabling virtual aaa management in sdn-based iot networks ," Sensors (Basel, Switzerland), vol. 19, 2019.

[51] M. Marchese, A. Moheddine, and F. Patrone, "Iot and uav integration in 5g hybrid terrestrial-satellite networks," Sensors (Basel, Switzerland), vol. 19, 2019.

[52] B. W. Nyamtiga, J. C. S. Sicato, S. Rathore, Y. Sung, and J. H. Park, "Blockchain-based secure storage management with edge computing for iot," Electronics, vol. 8, 2019, p. 828.

[53] M. El-hajj, A. Fadlallah, M. Chamoun, and A. Serhrouchni, "A survey of internet of things (iot) authentication schemes ," Sensors (Basel, Switzerland), vol. 19, 2019.

[54] L. Jiang, X. Lou, R. Tan, and J. Zhao, "Differentially private collaborative learning for the iot edge," in EWSN, 2019.

[55] E. N. Ganesh, "Implementation of digital notice board using raspberry pi and iot," Oriental journal of computer science and technology, vol. 12, 2019, pp. 14–20.

[56] H. Miyajima and N. Shiratori, "Proposal of fast and secure clustering methods for iot," 2019.

[57] A. Brezulianu et al., "Iot based heart activity monitoring using inductive sensors," Sensors (Basel, Switzerland), vol. 19, 2019.

[58] S.-R. Oh, Y.-G. Kim, and S. Cho, "An interoperable access control framework for diverse iot platforms based on oauth and role ," Sensors (Basel, Switzerland), vol. 19, 2019.

[59] H. Muccini, C. Arbib, P. Davidsson, and M. T. Moghaddam, "An iot software architecture for an evacuable building architecture," in HICSS, 2019.

[60] N. T. Kamatham, "Quality and energy aware services selection for iot," International Journal of Scientific Research in Science and Technology, 2020, pp. 93–98.

[61] Y.-S. Seo and J.-H. Huh, "Automatic emotion-based music classification for supporting intelligent iot applications," Electronics, vol. 8, 2019, p. 164.

[62] H. M. A. Islam, D. Lagutin, A. Ylä-Jääski, N. Fotiou, and A. V. Gurtov, "Transparent coap services to iot endpoints through icn operator networks ," Sensors (Basel, Switzerland), vol. 19, 2019.

[63] S. Taj, U. Asad, M. Azhar, and S. Kausar, "Interoperability in iot based smart home: A review," 2019.

[64] N. Surantha, C. Adiwiputra, O. Kurniawan, S. Muhamad, and B. Soewito, "Iot system for sleep quality monitoring using ballistocardiography sensor," International Journal of Advanced Computer Science and Applications, vol. 11, 2020.

[65] A. Pravin, P. Jacob, and G. Nagarajan, "A comprehensive survey on edge computing for the iot," 2019.

[66] S. Awadallah, A. D. Moure, and P. Torres-González, "An internet of things (iot) application on volcano monitoring," Sensors (Basel, Switzerland), vol. 19, 2019.

[67] D. A. F. Saraiva et al., "Prisec: Comparison of symmetric key algorithms for iot devices," Sensors (Basel, Switzerland), vol. 19, 2019.

[68] J. M. Waworundeng, N. C. Suseno, and R. R. Y. Manaha, "Automatic watering system for plants with iot monitoring and notification," 2019.

[69] G. Cerutti, R. Prasad, A. Brutti, and E. Farella, "Neural network distillation on iot platforms for sound event detection," in INTERSPEECH 2019, 2019.

[70] J. M. Ceron, K. Steding-Jessen, C. Hoepers, L. Z. Granville, and C. B. Margi, "Improving iot botnet investigation using an adaptive network layer," Sensors (Basel, Switzerland), vol. 19, 2019.

[71] E. Odat, "Traffic monitoring and mac-layer design for future iot systems," 2019.

[72] K. Kost'al, P. Helebrandt, M. Bellus, M. Ries, and I. Kotuliak, "Management and monitoring of iot devices using blockchain ," Sensors (Basel, Switzerland), vol. 19, 2019.

[73] N. Kumar, S. N. Panda, P. Pradhan, and R. K. Kaushal, "Iot based hybrid system for patient monitoring and medication," EAI Endorsed Trans. Pervasive Health Technol., vol. 5, 2019, p. e1.

[74] F. Zantalis, G. E. Koulouras, S. Karabetsos, and D. Kandris, "A review of machine learning and iot in smart transportation," Future Internet, vol. 11, 2019, p. 94.

[75] T. R. Mauldin, A. H. H. Ngu, V. Metsis, M. E. Canby, and J. Tesic, "Experimentation and analysis of ensemble deep learning in iot applications," OJIOT, vol. 5, 2019, pp. 133–149.

[76] A. L. Golande, P. Sorte, V. A. Suryawanshi, U. Yermalkar, and S. Satpute, "Smart hospital for heart disease prediction using iot," 2019.

[77] C. Kamienski et al., "Smart water management platform: Iot-based precision irrigation for agriculture ," Sensors (Basel, Switzerland), vol. 19, 2019.

[78] X. Yuan and M. Elhoseny, "Intelligent data aggregation inspired paradigm and approaches in iot applications," Journal of Intelligent and Fuzzy Systems, vol. 37, 2019, pp. 3–7.

[79] E. Jovanov, "Wearables meet iot: Synergistic personal area networks (spans)," Sensors (Basel, Switzerland), vol. 19, 2019.

[80] C. Robberts and J. Toft, "Finding vulnerabilities in iot devices : Ethical hacking of electronic locks," 2019.

[81] J. Lee, S. Yu, K. Park, Y. Park, and Y. Park, "Secure three-factor authentication protocol for multi-gateway iot environments," Sensors (Basel, Switzerland), vol. 19, 2019.

[82] S. Ghosh, R. Misoczki, and M. R. Sastry, "Lightweight post-quantum-secure digital signature approach for iot motes," IACR Cryptology ePrint Archive, vol. 2019, 2019, p. 122.

[83] M. U. Ali, S. Hur, and Y. Park, "Wi-fi-based effortless indoor positioning system using iot sensors," Sensors (Basel, Switzerland), vol. 19, 2019.

[84] D. Stiawan et al., "Investigating brute force attack patterns in iot network," J. Electrical and Computer Engineering, vol. 2019, 2019, pp. 4 568 368:1–4 568 368:13.

[85] S. Sidhu, B. J. Mohd, and T. Hayajneh, "Hardware security in iot devices with emphasis on hardware trojans," J. Sensor and Actuator Networks, vol. 8, 2019, p. 42.

[86] F. Chiti, R. Fantacci, and L. Pierucci, "Energy efficient communications for reliable iot multicast 5g/satellite services," Future Internet, vol. 11, 2019, p. 164.

[87] Y. Pu et al., "Two secure privacy-preserving data aggregation schemes for iot," Wireless Communications and Mobile Computing, vol. 2019, 2019, pp. 3 985 232:1–3 985 232:11.

[88] D. Dinculeana and X. Cheng, "Vulnerabilities and limitations of mqtt protocol used between iot devices," Applied Sciences, vol. 9, 2019, p. 848.

[89] N. Mora et al., "Iot-based home monitoring: Supporting practitioners assessment by behavioral analysis," Sensors (Basel, Switzerland), vol. 19, 2019.

[90] F. Kamaruddin et al., "Iot-based intelligent irrigation management and monitoring system using arduino," TELKOMNIKA Telecommunication Computing Electronics and Control, vol. 17, 2019, pp. 2378–2388.

[91] H. Alaiz-Moretón et al., "Multiclass classification procedure for detecting attacks on mqtt-iot protocol," Complexity, vol. 2019, 2019, pp. 6 516 253:1–6 516 253:11.

[92] M. Khapne and N. A. Chavhan, "Secured and reliable urban area applications based on iot," International Journal of Scientific Research in Science and Technology, vol. 6, 2019, pp. 701–703.

[93] K. Jung, J. Gascon-Samson, and K. Pattabiraman, "Oneos: Iot platform based on posix and actors," in HotEdge, 2019.

[94] B. Mataloto, J. Ferreira, and N. Cruz, "Lobemsiot for building and energy management systems," Electronics, vol. 8, 2019, pp. 1–27.

[95] A. D. Dwivedi, G. Srivastava, S. Dhar, and R. Singh, "A decentralized privacy-preserving healthcare blockchain for iot," Sensors (Basel, Switzerland), vol. 19, 2019.

[96] M. P. Doan, V. T. Tran, H. H. Huynh, and H. X. Huynh, "A scalable iot video data analytics for smart cities," EAI Endorsed Trans. Context-aware Syst. and Appl., vol. 6, 2019, p. e3.

[97] S. Janakiraman, S. Rajagopalan, and R. Amirtharajan, "Reliable medical image communication in healthcare iot: Watermark for authentication," 2019.

[98] H. He, Y. Zhang, and S. Wang, "Design of intelligent meter reading technology based on nb-iot," 2019.

[99] A. F. Santamaria, P. Raimondo, M. Tropea, F. D. Rango, and C. Aiello, "An iot surveillance system based on a decentralised architecture," Sensors (Basel, Switzerland), vol. 19, 2019.

[100] M. Chanson, A. Bogner, D. Bilgeri, E. Fleisch, and F. Wortmann, "Blockchain for the iot: Privacy-preserving protection of sensor data," J. AIS, vol. 20, 2019, p. 10.

[101] C. Akasiadis, V. Pitsilis, and C. D. Spyropoulos, "A multi-protocol iot platform based on open-source frameworks," Sensors (Basel, Switzerland), vol. 19, 2019.

[102] J. Rubio-Aparicio, F. Cerdan-Cartagena, J. S. Muro, and J. Ybarra-Moreno, "Design and implementation of a mixed iot lpwan network architecture," Sensors (Basel, Switzerland), vol. 19, 2019.

[103] Y. Kortesniemi, D. Lagutin, T. Elo, and N. Fotiou, "Improving the privacy of iot with decentralised identifiers (dids)," Journal Comp. Netw. and Communic., vol. 2019, 2019, pp. 8 706 760:1–8 706 760:10.

[104] C. Arbib, D. Arcelli, J. Dugdale, M. T. Moghaddam, and H. Muccini, "Real-time emergency response through performant iot architectures," in ISCRAM, 2019.

[105] Y. Wang et al., "Modeling and building iot data platforms with actor-oriented databases," in EDBT, 2019.

[106] M. Nekrasov, R. Allen, I. Artamonova, and E. M. Belding-Royer, "Optimizing 802.15.4 outdoor iot sensor networks for aerial data collection," Sensors (Basel, Switzerland), vol. 19, 2019.

[107] J.-N. Luo and M.-H. Yang, "An improved single packet traceback scheme for iot devices," Journal of Internet Technology, vol. 20, 2019, pp. 887–901.

[108] E. Manavalan and K. Jayakrishna, "A review of internet of things (iot) embedded sustainable supply chain for industry 4.0 requirements," Computers & Industrial Engineering, vol. 127, 2019, pp. 925–953.

[109] H. Kortelainen et al., "Beyond iot business," 2019.

[110] CYBER, "EN 303 645 - V2.1.1 - CYBER; Cyber Security for Consumer Internet of Things: Baseline Requirements," European Telecommunications Standards Institute, Jun. 2020, p. 10.

Threat Analysis of Industrial Internet of Things Devices

Simon Liebl*, Leah Lathrop*, Ulrich Raithel†, Matthias Söllner* and Andreas Aßmuth*

*Technical University of Applied Sciences OTH Amberg-Weiden, Amberg, Germany,
Email: {s.liebl | l.lathrop | m.soellner | a.assmuth}@oth-aw.de
†SIPOS Aktorik GmbH, Altdorf, Germany, Email: ulrich.raithel@sipos.de

***Abstract*—As part of the Internet of Things, industrial devices are now also connected to cloud services. However, the connection to the Internet increases the risks for Industrial Control Systems. Therefore, a threat analysis is essential for these devices. In this paper, we examine Industrial Internet of Things devices, identify and rank different sources of threats and describe common threats and vulnerabilities. Finally, we recommend a procedure to carry out a threat analysis on these devices.**

Keywords*—*Threat analysis; Industrial Internet of Things; low-power devices; Cloud.

I. Introduction

Approximately 20 billion Internet of Things (IoT) devices are in use today [1], and this number could double in the next five years [2]. The steadily increasing number of devices also raises the interest of attackers. During the first half of 2019, the overall number of cyberattacks increased by more than 350% compared to the previous six months [3]. The majority of attacks either aim to infect IoT devices or to launch attacks using them, such as Distributed Denial of Service (DDoS) attacks.

The increasing number of attacks also affects Industrial Internet of Things (IIoT) devices. These are IoT devices specialized on industrial applications and used in Industrial Control Systems (ICSs) for holistic monitoring and analysis using cloud computing. A common approach is to integrate the IIoT functionality into existing low-power Operational Technology (OT) devices. This can be recognized by the number of OT devices connected to a network. While about 60% of OT equipment was connected to the network in 2016, the figure had risen to almost 78% by 2018 [4].

ICSs are a frequent target for attacks. Recently, Microsoft security researchers discovered that the hacker group APT33 focuses specifically on manufacturers, suppliers and maintainers of ICS components [5]. OT devices installed in an ICS can cause extensive damage, since they control physical processes. The impact can be severe, especially in critical infrastructures, where this can result in a breakdown of power or water supply, for example. The increasing number of OT devices connected to the network, however, increases the attack surface of ICSs. As a result, it becomes easier for hackers to attack, successfully exploit OT devices and cause damage to ICSs.

Furthermore, the takeover of IIoT devices can also have an impact on cloud computing. In addition to the previously mentioned DDoS attacks on cloud servers, false data can be injected [6]. For example, ICS operators can be selectively supplied with incorrect information, e.g., abnormally high temperature values, to cause erroneous reactions, such as an emergency stop.

As a consequence of the increasing threats, IIoT manufacturers must secure their devices to prevent such incidents. This requires awareness of the risks. It is important to understand who is interested in exploiting their device and what motivates attackers to do so. In this paper, we aim to identify the threats specific to IIoT devices, describe how attackers could proceed and support IIoT manufacturers in conducting a threat analysis for their devices. The paper is structured as follows: in Section II, the differences between IoT, IIoT and OT devices are clarified and the use of IIoT devices in ICSs are described. Different types of threat sources and their respective intentions are introduced in Section IV. In Section V, several threats and vulnerabilities for IIoT devices are presented. A list of steps for a successful threat analysis follows in Section VI. The paper concludes in Section VII with an outlook on further work.

II. The Industrial Internet of Things

After a term differentiation, three potential setup options for a connection from IIoT devices to the cloud are described.

A. IoT, IIoT, OT and ICS

The IoT is a network of connected devices, which are sensors and/or actuators fulfilling a specific application [7]. Via the network they can, for instance, mutually exchange data or store and process data centrally and feed back the gained knowledge. This can be supported by cloud services. These have the advantage that there are already many semifinished solutions that simplify the integration of different devices. The number of devices or the required storage capacity can also be easily adapted, i.e., scalability. The use cases can be grouped in several categories, such as consumer applications (e.g., Smart Home), commercial (e.g., Medical and Healthcare) or infrastructure applications (e.g., Smart Grid). This paper focuses on industrial applications for which the already introduced term IIoT has been established. The main difference between IIoT and most IoT applications, such as consumer IoT, is that IoT services are human-centered and IIoT services are machine-oriented [8].

The use of IIoT devices can have various advantages, such as boosting productivity, avoiding plant downtimes through predictive maintenance and reducing energy consumption. Furthermore, the IIoT should also enable products to be manufactured only after the order has been placed, i.e., build to order, and to be tracked by the customer during production and delivery. IIoT devices are usually part of the OT. OT can be found, for example, in industrial factories to monitor and control physical processes. The term was introduced to emphasize the significant difference to IT, such as field of application and used communication protocols. Some examples for OT/IIoT sensors are temperature probes or bar code scanners, actuators are, for instance, valves or power converter. The primary security challenges for IoT devices are privacy and confidentiality, e.g., human health data. However, IIoT devices focus additionally on safety and the impact on environment and society [9]. They can potentially cause injury, death, damaged production equipment or environmental disasters. This can also affect large parts of the population through critical infrastructures, such as food or health.

An ICS is usually structured into several layers. The lower levels are made up of OT devices and Programmable Logic Controllers (PLCs). The middle layers contain, for example, Human Machine Interfaces (HMIs) and engineering workstations. The top levels provide servers for services and backups. An increase in security can be achieved by dividing the ICS into multiple layers so that more protection can be provided to the lowest level, which is especially safety-critical. This concept is known as defense in depth. Another approach is air gapping, isolating the entire ICS network from the Internet or even corporate network. It has been demonstrated that particularly the latter does not provide sufficient security. Nevertheless, both measures result in more complex and expensive attacks. First, the IT network must be compromised (e.g., via email intrusion), then malware must be transferred to the OT network (e.g., via USB sticks) and, lastly, malicious code must be transferred to the PLCs [10]. Once this is achieved, systems be controlled, damaged or spied on. However, these approaches conflict with the IIoT functionality of OT devices, as the lowest level requires Internet access. As a result, the architecture of ICS networks is affected by IIoT devices.

B. Cloud Connection Setups

Several IoT/IIoT architectures have already been proposed to implement segmented and logically structured networks [11]. In reality, however, these architectures can differ significantly. Therefore, different setups are only considered in an abstract way. The characteristics of a device, the task it performs and the level it is located on are important for the threat analysis.

Figure 1 illustrates three possible setups. In small ones, each device can be connected separately to clouds. This could be, for example, a small, remote hydroelectric power plant connected to the Internet via mobile networks. The proprietary firmware of valves has been extended by a network stack for this purpose. The devices are connected to the operator's cloud for centralized monitoring and controlling and to the device manufacturer's cloud service for installing remote firmware updates.

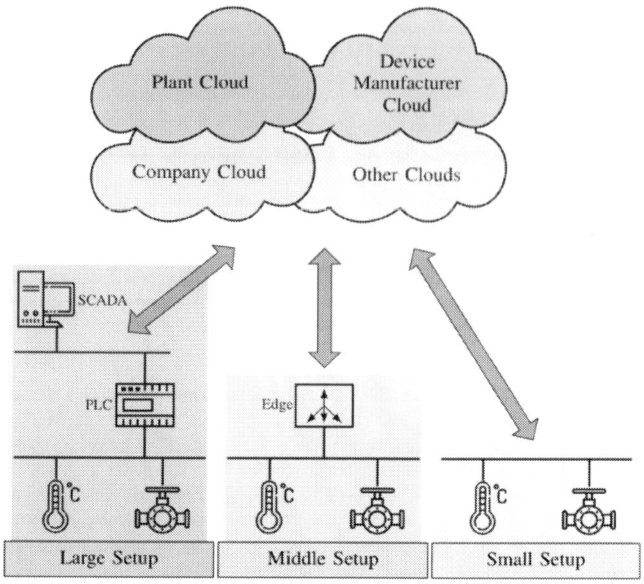

Figure 1. Three possible setups for connections from IIoT devices to clouds.

In the middle setup, devices are connected to the cloud via an edge gateway. It is not unusual for industrial devices to be older than ten years. They were not designed to send data to the cloud. Therefore, gateways collect data from several devices over mostly proprietary protocols, such as CAN or Modbus. Compared to low-power field devices, gateways have a more powerful processor and often a Linux-based operating system.

Even entire Supervisory Control And Data Acquisition (SCADA) systems are outsourced to the cloud in large industrial factories. Flexible web interfaces for desktops and mobile devices allow remote monitoring and control of the entire plant. In this scenario, many more connections to the cloud are possible, e.g., when the numerous field devices connect to their manufacturer's cloud or when all plants are combined in a company cloud.

III. Related Work

Since many IoT device manufacturers often prioritize functionality and time to market, security is neglected or not considered. This has been recognized by researchers and governmental institutions, leading to active research on the threats, necessary security requirements and mitigation techniques.

The German Federal Office for Information Security (BSI) releases annually an Information Security Management System (ISMS), the so-called IT-Grundschutz Compendium, that covers, among others, technical and organizational aspects of information security [12]. The aspects are divided into several modules. For example, embedded devices (SYS.4.3), IoT devices (SYS.4.4) and ICS components (IND.2.1) are modules concerning threats and the resulting requirements.

In [13], Abomhara et al. evaluate IoT device attacks, vulnerabilities, assets and possible intruders. Although industrial systems, such as SCADA systems, are mentioned, the special characteristics of ICSs are not described in depth. In [14], Wurm et al. conducted a security analysis on a consumer IoT and an IIoT device and demonstrated how these devices could be exploited. However, the procedure is too specific and cannot be adapted to other devices.

So far, manufacturers are assisted by standards and scientific papers in conducting a threat analysis for any system. However, there are no mandatory international guidelines on how the analysis should be carried out. In addition, computer-based threat modeling tools are not suitable for the special conditions of IIoT devices.

IV. Threat Sources and Motives

To protect IoT devices from unauthorized access, it is helpful to know who is interested in using them, i.e., the threat sources. Depending on application and device characteristics, the sources can be different. For instance, IIoT applications in critical infrastructures are more likely to be attacked by Advanced Persistent Threat (APT) groups, whereas IoT devices with open Telnet or SSH ports are favored by botnet operators. Generally, there are also threats caused by natural disasters or unintentional misuse by employees, but these will not be considered in this paper. We have classified the sources based on two characteristics. First, to what extent the attack targets were selected arbitrarily or intentionally. Second, what capabilities attackers have, i.e., how many skills and financial resources are available to them. Figure 2 classifies nine threat sources accordingly. In the following section, each source is described in detail.

A. Targeted attacks and capable attackers

a) Government-Sponsored: The most serious threat arises when an ICS is the target of attackers who are supported by a government or agency. Examples include the attacks on the Iranian nuclear program (Stuxnet) [15] or on the Ukrainian power grid [16], both of which are suspected to have been supported by foreign governments. The attacks were targeted and only possible at high expense due to their complexity. The motives to conduct such attacks are usually political or economical.

b) Industrial Espionage: Economic reasons are generally a major motive. Targeted attacks aim, for example, to sniff production figures, customer data and know-how, or simply cause financial loss to competitors. In recent years, there were several espionage attacks on German companies of the DAX (German stock index), including the ICS component manufacturer Siemens [17].

B. Less targeted attacks, but capable attackers

a) Organized Crime: Organized cybercriminals try to blackmail their victims by encrypting sensitive data. The recently discovered ransomware EKANS seems to be specifically intended for ICSs because it terminates several common ICS-specific software processes [18].

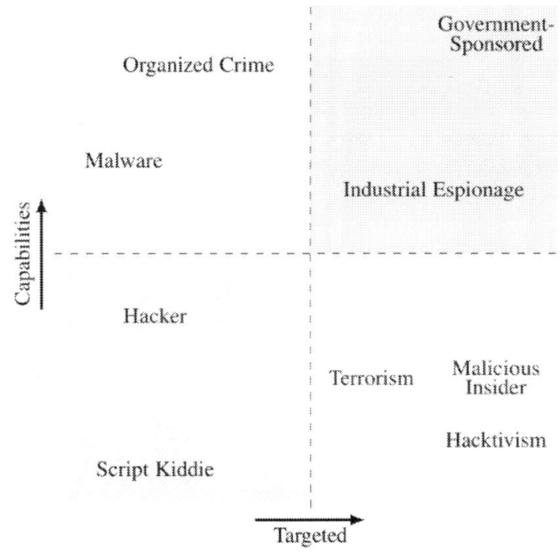

Figure 2. Threat Sources.

b) Malware: Malware is often designed to infect as many devices as possible, for instance, to build botnets. Mirai and its many variants demonstrated that millions of IoT devices are vulnerable to malware attacks [19].

C. Targeted attacks, but less capable attackers

a) Terrorism: Threats from terrorism can be considered from two perspectives. There is a threat from extremist organizations. Although they are theoretically capable of carrying out attacks, few attacks are known in practice [20]. Additionally, terrorism can also be sponsored by states. Attacks on critical infrastructures, such as energy or water, affect the general civilian population. Therefore, they are a kind of terrorism. Since government-sponsored threats are already covered, the capabilities of terrorism is rated low.

b) Malicious Insider: Insider attacks by (former) employees or contractors cause an average annual loss of more than eight million dollars [21]. Employees, for example, could sell confidential data for personal financial gain or sabotage machines due to hostility towards the employer. They also possess specialist knowledge, which is particularly required for attacks on IIoT devices. Insider attacks are the major threat to OT [22], especially for ICSs in critical infrastructures, as identified by an evaluation of US hydropower dams [23].

c) Hacktivism: The number of attacks by hacktivists is increasing and should therefore not be neglected. The attacks are targeted, but have not frequently been effective so far. Besides DoS attacks, attempts are made to steal data. This could affect, for instance, oil and gas companies or companies that make politically controversial decisions. The latter happened to heavy machinery maker Caterpillar Inc. as a result of the sale of bulldozers to Israel [24].

D. Less targeted attacks and less capable attackers

a) Hacker and Script Kiddie: The last two threat sources we identified are hackers and script kiddies. The source code of malware, e.g., Mirai, is frequently published on code sharing platforms like Github or hacker forums. As a result, many people want to try them out for themselves. Compared to script kiddies, experienced hackers can build on this code and develop their own variants.

V. Threats, Vulnerabilities and their Impact

Several threats were already mentioned in the listing of threat sources. In the following section, the threats are summarized briefly and common vulnerabilities are described. Possible attack vectors on IIoT devices are illustrated afterwards. Table I provides an overview of frequent threats and vulnerabilities for IIoT devices.

TABLE I. Common threats and vulnerabilities.

Threats	Vulnerabilities
Abuse	Code execution
Denial of Service	Communication manipulation
Destruction	Design flaws and bugs
Espionage	Memory manipulation
Intellectual property theft	Misconfiguration
Maloperation	Physical manipulation
Ransomware	Privilege escalation
Repudiation	Repudiation
Spoofing	Web-based vulnerabilities

A. Threats

a) Abuse: The source of this threat could be malware or employees. The former utilizes IIoT devices as part of a botnet for DoS attacks, mining cryptocurrencies or for spreading spam. The latter could use the device for private purposes.

b) Denial of Service: For ICS operators, the availability of all devices is most important because a single temporary breakdown can potentially lead to a production stop. Therefore, the failure of a device could have financial consequences for operators. A denial of service can be achieved not only by flooding devices with network requests but also by changing their configuration. Multiple devices could also be utilized to stop cloud servers. This would not only block one plant from its cloud services but all other plants of a large company.

c) Destruction: The destruction of a device is also a form of denial of service, more precisely a permanent denial of service. The attack can be either on hardware or software. An example of the latter is BrickerBot, which destroyed more than ten million IoT devices [25]. Furthermore, the actuators of an OT device can be incorrectly triggered, destroying components, such as engines. The consequences are far more serious than a normal DoS attack. If there is no backup device that takes over immediately, the plant is out of operation. Additionally, data saved on the device may be lost.

d) Espionage: Espionage was already introduced in Section IV. Stealing production data, process procedures or even user data is often easy because many industrial communication protocols are not encrypted at all.

e) Intellectual property theft: OT devices are usually specialized on one specific task. Manufacturers invest a lot of effort into their product in order to be better than competitors. As a result, leading manufacturers struggle with plagiarism and cloned, cheaply replicated hardware that runs their original firmware.

f) Maloperation: Starting or stopping machines unexpectedly or making them work in slightly different ways is not a theoretical issue anymore. Two recent examples are TRITON [26] and Industroyer [27] that were specifically created for OT devices and protocols. The latter supports four industrial communication protocols and is capable of controlling switches and circuit breakers in electricity substations.

g) Ransomware: If, in addition to the IT network, the OT network is also affected by a ransomware attack, some machines in the plant may no longer be available. As a result, the ICS must be shut down. This incident happened recently to a pipeline operator, who had to shut its operation down for two days, according to a report by the US Cybersecurity and Infrastructure Security Agency (CISA) [28].

h) Repudiation: In case of an error in an ICS, it should be possible to reconstruct the exact procedure with logs. Attackers could manipulate or delete them in order to remain undetected.

i) Spoofing: IIoT devices must be uniquely identifiable. Attackers could masquerade as the device and send false data to PLCs or cloud services. The latest firmware could also be obtained by cloning original devices and spoofing their identity.

B. Vulnerabilities

a) Code execution: Arbitrary code execution is the goal of every attacker. Attacks can be either local or remote. Since the firmware of IIoT devices is mostly written in C/C++, they are vulnerable to memory attacks, such as buffer overflows.

b) Communication manipulation: Message senders or receivers, measured values or commands can be easily manipulated due to unencrypted communication.

c) Design flaws and bugs: Many industrial devices and protocols were not designed with security in mind. Even if this is the case, bugs can still occur. An example of this is the encrypted OPC UA protocol, which contained numerous flaws [29]. This is particularly critical in ICSs because the firmware of the countless devices is rarely or never updated.

d) Memory manipulation: By manipulating the memory, incorrect configurations can be loaded, faulty data can lead to inappropriate reactions and features that would be subject to additional costs can be unlocked illicitly.

e) Misconfiguration: Misconfigurations enable many attacks. Common mistakes are unchanged default passwords, disabled firmware patches and open but unused ports.

f) Physical manipulation: Attackers with physical access to IIoT devices can alter the hardware, e.g., sensors or actuators but also microcontrollers or memories.

g) Privilege escalation: Some actions should only be executed with higher privileges. For IIoT devices it is often simple to obtain these due to standard or company-wide passwords or backdoors of the developers. Furthermore, most industrial protocols do not support authentication. Therefore, it is not possible to verify authorization for them.

h) Repudiation: The aforementioned threat is also a vulnerability, since insufficient logging and monitoring hinders the detection and verification of threats. Due to lack of identification mechanisms, actions can be easily repudiated.

i) Web-based vulnerabilities: IIoT devices often run a web server for configuration, maintenance, monitoring or control of the devices. But this exposes them to web-based attacks. According to OWASP, the greatest risks include injection, broken authentication and cross-site scripting (XSS) among others [30].

C. Attack Vectors

IIoT devices are becoming increasingly complex. As a result of the IoT, new communication interfaces are being integrated that were previously rarely or never used in OT. In any case, they provide typically several interfaces for specific requirements. For better illustration, we have structured the various interfaces into zones in Figure 3. Zones 0 and 1 describe the hardware and software of a device. In zones 2 to 4, established communication protocols are listed in the left-hand column while systems that interact with them are listed in the right-hand column.

In the following section, three possible attack vectors are introduced. Examples are used to illustrate how attackers from the different zones could proceed or how they could have an impact on other devices in these zones.

a) Device attacks: In zone 0, device components can be physically manipulated. This may be intentional or accidental. In the latter case, a burnt-out circuit board or a defective engine could be replaced by a spare part that was not purchased from the original manufacturer for price reasons. Compatibility of hardware or software is not guaranteed for these components causing faulty operation, DoS and even destruction to result.

As discussed in Section IV, IIoT devices are especially threatened by highly capable actors. Attacks with high complexity and effort should consequently not be ignored. Costly invasive hardware attacks, such as probing, or rather cheaper non-invasive attacks, such as side-channel analysis, enable access to secret data, e.g., cryptographic keys. Attackers can also directly access the flash memory or EEPROM via interfaces from zone 2, e.g., JTAG. First, this allows them to read the memory to retrieve the firmware, i.e., intellectual property theft. Second, data or configurations can be modified, e.g., access data. Third, firmware can be exchanged so that arbitrary code can be executed. Attacks of this kind are complex, but they can cause considerable damage. In case the necessary knowledge is lacking, there are appropriate service providers for this (e.g., www.break-ic.com).

The popular USB interface also enables multiple attacks. USB sticks can be used, for example, to load malware or destroy badly protected power and data lines, i.e., kill USB sticks. With bad usb devices, such as Hak5's rubber duckies, it is also possible to execute arbitrary commands and thus manipulate the device.

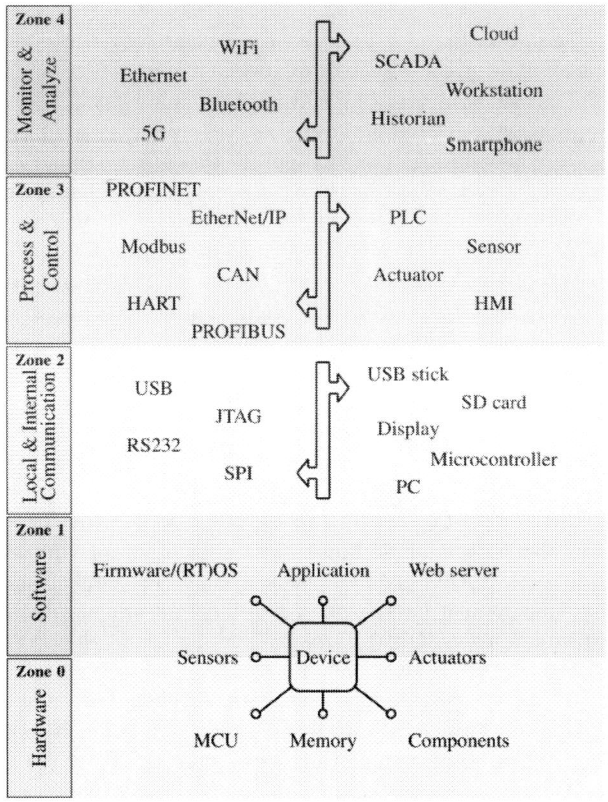

Figure 3. Different zones of a device and their respective interfaces with interaction systems.

b) Application attacks: The process of a production plant can be interrupted or stopped if the application of IIoT devices do not work properly. An attacker might change the configuration or move an actuator incorrectly via its display. The devices are often misconfigured as they still have the default or a trivial password. Many IIoT devices can also be programmed using a PC-based configuration tool. A common design flaw is that users must not be authorized to carry out these changes. As a result, it is often possible to reconfigure, update or reset a device by connecting to it via a cable or network. When such a vulnerability is exploited, it is difficult to reconstruct and verify the incident, as the devices often do not support user identification.

Wrong commands can also originate from the devices of zone 3. The source can be either an already compromised PLC or a completely different device. Since messages of the most proprietary protocols are not authenticated, a different sender address can be spoofed. Reversely, incorrect information can also be sent to PLCs or HMIs. For example, PLCs from the manufacturer Schneider can be stopped using a simple command via the Modbus protocol [31]. The consequences of this abrupt stop may be catastrophic. Faulty commands or sensor data can also be sent to systems in zone 4, e.g., the SCADA system or the cloud. Since more decisions will be made by a data-driven Artificial Intelligence (AI) in the future, wrong choices may result.

Due to the more widespread network protocols in zone 4, vulnerabilities can also be exploited remotely. Such vulnerabilities can be located in the firmware/operating system or the application. An example of the former are the Treck TCP/IP stack vulnerabilities called Ripple20 that allow remote code execution, which were recently discovered [32]. Vulnerabilities in the application can be caused by a web server that allows SQL injection, for instance. Once they have successfully exploited a vulnerability, process operations can be sabotaged.

c) Network attacks: The vulnerabilities just mentioned also allow an infection of botnets. If several devices in a network are infected and the botnet operator launches a DDoS attack, internal network traffic can be delayed. This can, for example, interrupt the connection of PLCs to the SCADA system. In case the attack is targeted at the own global company cloud, other plants might be affected as well.

If the device is a network node, such as an edge device, this also results in multiple threats. Besides sniffing or tampering with messages, they can also be delayed or blocked. Especially for systems that have to meet real-time constraints, this can become a major threat.

The network is also useful for spreading an infection. Especially the systems in zone 4 are targeted either for monetary gain through a ransomware attack or to obtain as much control as possible. Workstations with Win 7 or Win XP are not rare in ICSs, and thus this is often not much effort for an attacker.

VI. Recommended Procedure

Finally, we summarize all the previously discussed aspects to define a recommended procedure for the threat analysis.

1) Know your device: It is important to know the IIoT device in depth. Which operating system and third party libraries are utilized? Does it include actuators and sensors and/or is it collecting data from other devices (i.e., edge device)? How is the setup? What other equipment is connected to it? Is it connected to the Internet directly or through a gateway? Is it installed in critical infrastructures? What additional (PC-)tools are available for the device?

2) Creation of a network diagram: A network diagram including all interfaces of the device can help identify which other systems it interacts with. The authorization should be specified for each entry and exit point, i.e., which actions can be performed and by whom. This is especially important for industrial protocols, such as PROFINET. While most IoT applications allow to implement security measures manually, it is not possible with these proprietary protocols.

3) Identification and ranking of assets: Which security goal is the most important one? Is the focus on maximum availability, authenticity of actions or privacy of user data? First, this is important to prioritize the exploration of vulnerabilities, and second, to subsequently find an appropriate mitigation measure. The latter is particularly relevant when safety must be guaranteed, as real-time behavior and encryption may not be feasible on a low-power IIoT device.

4) Identification of threat sources: Who is interested in attacking the device and what are their motives? This is useful for deliberately including or excluding types of attacks. For IIoT devices in critical infrastructures, the more complex invasive and non-invasive hardware attacks should be addressed.

5) Identification of threats and vulnerabilities: The next step is to identify threats and vulnerabilities. Table I serves as a kick-off aid. In general, we can consider attacks on identification and authentication, authorization, availability, system, data and communication integrity, data confidentiality, privilege escalation and repudiation. Penetration testing can be used to discover additional vulnerabilities, but also to verify those already identified and show their severity.

Using attack scenarios, attacks can be better reconstructed in retrospect. For example, the threat *setting an invalid communication configuration* results in a *denial of service*. The attack vector is that the *web server* is accessible via the *Ethernet* interface. The action *changing of communication parameter* has the consequence that the *connection to PLCs is terminated.* The utilized vulnerability is a *default password* that results in a *privilege escalation*. Additional notes, such as *default password can be found in the manual*, can also be useful.

6) Vulnerability and risk assessment: To rate a vulnerability, all threats and their consequences from the different attack scenarios should be considered. Using the Common Vulnerability Scoring System (CVSS), the severity of vulnerabilities can be expressed by a number. For risk assessment, it is advisable to consider not only the severity of the vulnerability but also its likelihood and impact.

VII. Conclusion and Further Work

Compared to IoT equipment, IIoT devices are at increased risk, since they are part of the OT that controls physical processes. Beside high availability, safety is also particularly important in these applications. In addition to destroying a production facility, people can be injured and a population can even be cut off from the power grid.

Several threat sources and their motives were presented and ranked using examples. It turned out that the most serious threat originates from government-sponsored actors, who often target critical infrastructures. Afterwards, numerous threats and vulnerabilities were listed, which exist among other reasons, because security was ignored in the industrial sector for decades. Among the threats, destruction caused by moving parts and intellectual property theft must be highlighted, while the vulnerabilities include manipulation of the hardware and the frequently insecure communication. Lastly, we provided a procedure for identifying and assessing threats and vulnerabilities that emphasizes the specialties of IIoT devices. In order to prevent these, we intend to develop countermeasures for low-power IIoT devices as the next step.

Acknowledgment

The research project "Intelligent Security for Electrical Actuators and Converters in Critical Infrastructures (iSEC)" is a collaboration of SIPOS Aktorik GmbH, Grass Power Electronics GmbH and OTH Amberg-Weiden. It is supported and funded by the Bavarian Ministry of Economic Affairs, Regional Development and Energy.

REFERENCES

[1] M. Hung, "Leading the IoT: Gartner Insights on How to Lead in a Connected World," Gartner, White Paper, 2017.

[2] IDC Corporate USA, "The Growth in Connected IoT Devices Is Expected to Generate 79.4ZB of Data in 2025, According to a New IDC Forecast," June 18th, 2019. [Online]. Available: https://www.idc.com/getdoc.jsp?containerId=prUS45213219 [accessed: 2020-08-25]

[3] F-Secure, "Attack Landscape H1 2019," 2019. [Online]. Available: https://blog-assets.f-secure.com/wp-content/uploads/2019/09/12093807/2019_attack_landscape_report.pdf [accessed: 2020-08-25]

[4] J. Santagate, R. Glaisner, and R. Westervelt, "Operational Cybersecurity for Digitized Manufacturing: Emerging Approaches for the Converged Physical-Virtual Environment," IDC, 2019. [Online]. Available: https://www.fortinet.com/content/dam/fortinet/assets/white-papers/wp-idc-operational-cybersecurity-for-digitized-manufacturing.pdf [accessed: 2020-08-25]

[5] A. Greenberg, "A Notorious Iranian Hacking Crew Is Targeting Industrial Control Systems," Wired, November 20th, 2019. [Online]. Available: https://wired.com/story/iran-apt33-industrial-control-systems/ [accessed: 2020-08-25]

[6] B. Bostami, M. Ahmed, and S. Choudhury, "False Data Injection Attacks in Internet of Things," in Performability in Internet of Things, F. Al-Turjman, Ed. Cham: Springer International Publishing, 2019, pp. 47–58.

[7] B. Dorsemaine, J.-P. Gaulier, J.-P. Wary, N. Kheir, and P. Urien, "Internet of Things: A Definition & Taxonomy," in 2015 9th International Conference on Next Generation Mobile Applications, Services and Technologies, Cambridge, United Kingdom, 2015, pp. 72–77.

[8] E. Sisinni, A. Saifullah, S. Han, U. Jennehag, and M. Gidlund, "Industrial Internet of Things: Challenges, Opportunities, and Directions," IEEE Trans. Ind. Inf., vol. 14, no. 11, pp. 4724–4734, Nov. 2018, DOI: 10.1109/TII.2018.2852491.

[9] A. Hahn, "Operational Technology and Information Technology in Industrial Control Systems," in Cyber-security of SCADA and Other Industrial Control Systems, 2016, pp. 51–68, DOI: 10.1007/978-3-319-32125-7_4.

[10] Symantec, "Internet of Things: Protecting Against Industrial Cyber Attacks," 2018. [Online]. Available: https://www.symantec.com/content/dam/symantec/docs/brochures/internet-of-things-protecting-against-industrial-cyber-attacks-en.pdf [accessed: 2020-08-25]

[11] H. P. Breivold, "A Survey and Analysis of Reference Architectures for the Internet-of-things," in The Twelfth International Conference on Software Engineering Advances, 2017, pp. 132-138.

[12] Federal Office for Information Security, Ed., "IT-Grundschutz Compendium" (IT General Protection Compendium), 2019.

[13] M. Abomhara and G. M. Køien, "Cyber security and the internet of things: Vulnerabilities, threats, intruders and attacks," Journal of Cyber Security and Mobility, vol. 4, no. 1, pp. 65–88, 2015.

[14] J. Wurm, K. Hoang, O. Arias, A. Sadeghi, and Y. Jin, "Security analysis on consumer and industrial IoT devices," 2016 21st Asia and South Pacific Design Automation Conference (ASP-DAC), Macau, 2016, pp. 519-524, DOI: 10.1109/ASPDAC.2016.7428064.

[15] E. Nakashima and J. Warrick, "Stuxnet was work of U.S. and Israeli experts, officials say," The Washington Post, June 2nd, 2012. [Online]. Available: https://www.washingtonpost.com/world/national-security/stuxnet-was-work-of-us-and-israeli-experts-officials-say/2012/06/01/gJQAlnEy6U_story.html [accessed: 2020-08-25]

[16] R. Lee, M. Assante, and T. Conway, "Analysis of the Cyber Attack on the Ukrainian Power Grid," E-ISAC, 2016. [Online]. Available: https://ics.sans.org/media/E-ISAC_SANS_Ukraine_DUC_5.pdf [accessed: 2020-08-25]

[17] H. Tanriverdi, S. Eckert, J. Strozyk, M. Zierer, and R. Ciesielski, "Attacking the Heart of the German Industry," BR, July 24th, 2019. [Online]. Available: https://web.br.de/interaktiv/winnti/english/ [accessed: 2020-08-25]

[18] A. Greenberg, "Mysterious New Ransomware Targets Industrial Control Systems," Wired, February 3rd, 2020. [Online]. Available: https://wired.com/story/ekans-ransomware-industrial-control-systems/ [accessed: 2020-08-25]

[19] C. Cimpanu, "A decade of malware: Top botnets of the 2010s," Wired, December 3rd, 2019. [Online]. Available: https://www.zdnet.com/article/a-decade-of-malware-top-botnets-of-the-2010s/ [accessed: 2020-08-25]

[20] S. Sin, E. Asiamah, L. Blackerby, and R. Washburn, "Determining Extremist Organisations' Likelihood of Conducting Cyber Attacks," presented at the 8th International Conference on Cyber Conflict, Tallinn, 2016.

[21] Ponemon Institute, "2018 Cost of Insider Threats: Global," April, 2018. [Online]. Available: https://153j3ttjub71nfe89mc7r5gb-wpengine.netdna-ssl.com/wp-content/uploads/2018/04/ObserveIT-Insider-Threat-Global-Report-FINAL.pdf [accessed: 2020-08-25]

[22] Siemens, "Caught in the Crosshairs: Are Utilities Keeping Up with the Industrial Cyber Threat?," 2019. [Online]. Available: https://assets.new.siemens.com/siemens/assets/api/uuid:35089d45-e1c2-4b8b-b4e9-7ce8cae81eaa/version:1572434569/siemens-cybersecurity.pdf [accessed: 2020-08-25]

[23] U.S. Department of the Interior Office of Inspector General, "U.S. Bureau of Reclamation Selected Hydropower Dams at Increased Risk from Insider Threats," June, 2018. [Online]. Available: https://www.hsdl.org/?view&did=829751 [accessed: 2020-08-25]

[24] K. Fazzini, "Rising Hacktivist Attacks Take Companies By Surprise," Dow Jones, April 4th, 2017. [Online]. Available: https://dowjones.com/insights/rising-hacktivist-attacks-take-companies-surprise/ [accessed: 2020-08-25]

[25] radware, "'BrickerBot' Results In PDoS Attack," 2018. [Online]. Available: https://security.radware.com/ddos-threats-attacks/brickerbot-pdos-permanent-denial-of-service/ [accessed: 2020-08-25]

[26] S. Miller, N. Brubaker, D. Kapellmann Zafra, and D. Caban, "TRITON Actor TTP Profile, Custom Attack Tools, Detections, and ATT&CK Mapping," FireEye, April 10th, 2019. [Online]. Available: https://www.fireeye.com/blog/threat-research/2019/04/triton-actor-ttp-profile-custom-attack-tools-detections.html [accessed: 2020-08-25]

[27] A. Cherepanov and R. Lipovsky, "Industroyer: Biggest threat to industrial control systems since Stuxnet," welivesecurity, June 12th, 2017. [Online]. Available: https://www.welivesecurity.com/2017/06/12/industroyer-biggest-threat-industrial-control-systems-since-stuxnet/ [accessed: 2020-08-25]

[28] Cybersecurity and Infrastructure Security Agency (CISA), "Ransomware Impacting Pipeline Operations," February 18th, 2020. [Online]. Available: https://www.us-cert.gov/ncas/alerts/aa20-049a [accessed: 2020-08-25]

[29] Kaspersky, "Kaspersky Lab discovers critical vulnerabilities in popular industrial protocol, affecting products from multiple vendors," May 10th, 2018. [Online]. Available: https://www.kaspersky.com/about/press-releases/2018_kaspersky-lab-discovers-critical-vulnerabilities-in-popular-industrial-protocol [accessed: 2020-08-25]

[30] OWASP, "OWASP Top 10 - 2017," 2017. [Online]. Available: https://owasp.org/www-pdf-archive/OWASP_Top_10-2017_(en).pdf.pdf [accessed: 2020-08-25]

[31] C. E. Bodungen, B. L. Singer, A. Shbeeb, S. Hilt, and K. Wilhoit, Hacking exposed, industrial control systems: ICS and SCADA security secrets & solutions. New York Chicago San Francisco: Mc Graw Hill Education, 2017, p.146.

[32] M. Kol and S. Oberman, "Ripple20," JSOF, White Paper, 2020. [Online]. Available: https://www.jsof-tech.com/wp-content/uploads/2020/06/JSOF_Ripple20_Technical_Whitepaper_June20.pdf [accessed: 2020-08-25]

Development of a Process-oriented Framework for Security Assessment of Cyber Physical Systems

Katrin Neubauer
Dept. Computer Science and Mathematics
Ostbayerische Technische Hochschule
Regensburg, Germany
email: katrin1.neubauer@oth-regensburg.de

Rudolf Hackenberg
Dept. Computer Science and Mathematics
Ostbayerische Technische Hochschule
Regensburg, Germany
email: rudolf.hackenberg@oth-regensburg.de

***Abstract*—Cloud Computing and Internet of Things (IoT) influence the constantly growing networking of systems. Both belong to Cyber Physical Systems (CPS) are highly networked systems. The increasing establishment of CPS creates new challenges and further security and data protection aspects arise. Existing frameworks for security assessment are not suitable for CPS. The requirement criteria for CPS are scalability, real-time, performance, functional safety and volatility. Data security has so far been evaluated by the two-level trust model (secure and insecure). This trust model is not suitable for CPS. The reasons for this are the large amount of data and the wide variety of data types. This paper presents the required criteria for security assessment of CPS, the development of the Process-oriented Framework for Security Assessment of Cyber Physical Systems and the application of the security model. The Process-oriented Framework for Security Assessment of Cyber Physical Systems includes the steps analysis of the application, security, scalability and real-time assessment and automated mapping of security measures.**

Keywords*—*Cyber Physical System; security assessment; security analysis; Internet of Things; Smart Grid.

I. INTRODUCTION

Cyber Physical Systems (CPS) are the next generation of engineered systems. Cloud Computing and Internet of Things (IoT) have an impact on networking in industrial environments and daily life. The digital age is influenced by SMAC technologies. Social, mobile, analytics and Cloud Computing are the SMAC technologies. Digitalization describes the socioeconomic process and digitization means the technical process [1]. CPS results from the networking of SMAC technologies.

The digitalization of the economy and industry is progressing continuously. One example is the digitalization of the energy sector. The implementation of intelligent electricity meters (so-called smart meters) is creating the necessary communication infrastructure. The most important component is the gateway (Smart Meter Gateway, SMGW), which serves as the central communication unit [2]. Cost and benefit analyses have shown that the construction and operation of this infrastructure are too expensive for the application "smart metering" [3]. For this reason, the infrastructure is being opened up for other divisions and services, such as value-added services. The networking of everyday life in your own home is summarized under the term Smart Home. By networking different sensors and devices, daily life is supported. IoT describes sensors and devices which have a connection to the internet. For example, value-added services can represent the connection of Smart Home or Ambient Assisted Living (AAL) services. Services like Smart Home and AAL are made possible by IoT devices.

By mapping value-added services to the Smart Grid infrastructure, the topics IoT and Smart Grid are linked. This combination creates a highly scalable and volatile system. This leads to a higher volume of data of varying quality, devices and users supplying and accessing data and a high number of participants. One challenge is that the structure of existing architectures is changing and/or expanding. If the existing architectures grow into a highly scalable and volatile system, they must be reconsidered in terms of security.

The existing process models are limited to the analysis of information systems in companies or are models for the development of software under the aspect of security. The consideration and analysis (security modeling and assessment) of highly scalable, volatile systems are not carried out within this frameworks. For future systems, which have the property of being highly scalable and volatile, an appropriate framework for security modeling must be developed. This means, data security according to the requirements of scalability, real-time and a consideration of the overall-process should be represented by the new framework. The aim is the development of a Process-oriented Framework for Security Assessment of Cyber Physical Systems.

The paper is structured as follows. Section II covers the related work. In Section III, we describe the CPS and discuss the topic of security. In the next session, the development of a Process-oriented Framework for Security Assessment of Cyber Physical Systems is performed and Section V, describes the application example. Finally, the conclusion and future work are given.

II. RELATED WORK

The state of the art is examined with regard to the following question: Which approaches or frameworks are available for security modeling of processes in highly scalable, volatile systems or in CPS.

There are best practice approaches for security assessment. These are ISO/IEC 27000:2018 [8] or the BSI-Standards (BSI-Standards 200-1, 200-2 and 200-3 [5]–[7]). Main focus of this security frameworks are the assessment of the business process of a company.

The security modeling is based on a two-level trust model. This means, there are two categories of data: worthy of protection and no worthy of protection [13].

In [9]–[12], security is considered during the development process of software. Another approach are security by design and privacy by design. Security and data protection are already considered during the development process.

Security and privacy considerations for Smart Grid extended by value-added service (e.g., AAL, IoT devices), with a focus on survey and research challenges are shown in [14] and [15]. In [16]–[18], the security and communication analysis of an extended Smart Grid infrastructure are shown.

A survey of literature on security and privacy of CPS is done in [19]. The publication provides an overview of the fields of application and identifies threats and vulnerabilities. In [20], the security analysis is shown on the basis of the different layers (perception layer, transmission layer, application layer).

In summary, these models for security modeling as well as the two-level trust model are not suitable for CPS and high scalable, volatile systems. The models for the security assessment shown, the business process of a company, the software development process and sub-processes of a company are considered. The security and privacy assessment of CPS are open questions.

III. Cyber Physical Systems

CPS are systems in which computing, communication, and control technologies are integrated [21]. There are different types of CPS. In this publication, CPS is described as follows. In CPS, information and software components are combined with mechanical components. The data transfer, data exchange, monitoring and control takes place via the internet and is done in real time. Components are mobile and movable installations, devices and machines, embedded systems and networked objects (IoT). CPS can be described by the following characteristics [22].

- Direct connection between physical world and digital world
- Innovative system functions through information, data and function integration
- Functions integration: multi-functionality
- Soft to hard time requirements
- Extensive interaction networks of sensors or actuators
- Networking within the systems and externally
- Dedicated user interfaces: Strong integration in action sequences
- Use under often difficult physical boundary conditions
- Long-term operation
- Automation, adaptivity and autonomy
- High requirements to:
  - Functional security
  - Access security and data security
  - Reliability
  - High cost pressure

The application field of CPS are production, logistics, mobility, energy and distribution. Smart Grid is a variant of CPSs. The characteristics of future systems are highly scalable, volatile, high data volume and different types of data. For example, the use case "data logging electricity" shows us that the data flaw from final consumers to the energy supplier. This means for high scalability, two million participants and 192 million consumption values per day. If we have a look inside the communication, there is a data transfer every 15 minutes. This describes the volatility. The next characteristic is high data volume. For example, two million participants generating 22 gigabyte data per day. Different types of data means the diversity of data, like customer data, power consumption or IP address. Further field of application of the Smart Grid infrastructure are Smart Home, gas, water and value-added service.

Security must also be considered by CPS. Until now, the focus has been on robustness and performance. CPSs are fast-growing systems in which personal and sensitive data are also transferred. Furthermore, existing systems and architectures are extended by this. These systems are difficult to define. Security assessment already carried out must be renewed. The requirement criteria for security assessments of CPS are the following.

- Data security
- Scalability
- Real-time
- Performance
- Functional safety
- Volatility

The security assessment of CPS must be developed according to this requirement criteria.

IV. Development of a Process-oriented Framework for Security Assessment of Cyber Physical Systems

In the first step, the requirement criteria data security (DS), scalability (SC) and real-time (RT) are focused. In the context of security modeling of CPS, all three must be considered. The security assessment results from the description of the process by this criteria and is defined as follows: $usecase_{process} = (DS, SC, RT)$. The result of the security assessment depends from the description of the process. The framework for the security assessment is as follows. At first, the analysis of the process and infrastructure and also the data and information. The next step is the security assessment against the criteria DS, SC and RT. The last step is the automated mapping

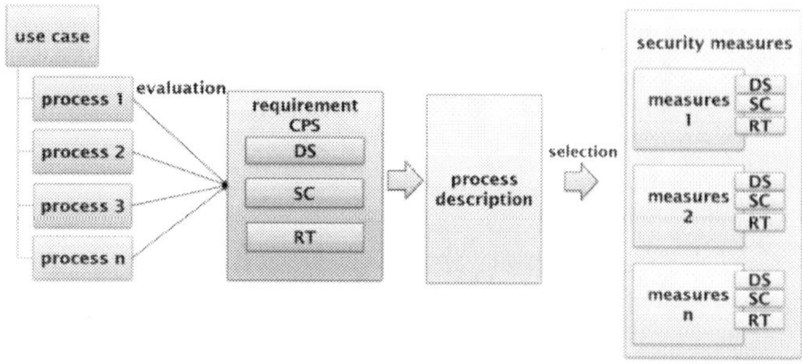

Figure 1. Process-oriented Framework for Security Assessment of Cyber Physical Systems

of the model based on the use case process and assignment of security measures. Further requirements are performance, functional safety, volatility and connectivity. These are not yet considered in the current work status. Figure 1 describes the Process-oriented Framework for Security Assessment of Cyber Physical Systems. The use case is divided into processes. The process is evaluated against the criteria DS, SC and RT. A process description is derived and an automated selection of security measures is possible. The security measures are evaluated by the criteria DS, SC and RT. In the following subsections, the individual characteristics of the tuple are described.

A. *Data security*

The 4-Level-Trust-Model for safety-critical systems is a model for security assessment of CPS. Classically, the data are divided into two categories - secure and insecure. This describes the classical security model. The 4-Level-Trust-Model for safety-critical systems is one option of the role-based trust model for safety-critical systems [23]. In the new 4-Level-Trust-Model for safety-critical systems the data are categorized in 4 categories. The categorization depends on the requirements analysis for CPS. The 4-Level-Trust-Model for safety-critical systems are defined as follows.

1) Category: non sensitive data
   - All data that do not contain any personal reference or have been made anonymous.
   - There are no effects of damage or damage that has occurred for the affected person.
   - The security level is low.
2) Category: high sensitive data I
   - All data which, through the combination of several data in category 2 and 3, have a personal reference, but do not have a direct reference themselves (e.g., network status data).
   - The damage effects are limited and manageable. Any damage that has occurred is relatively easy to heal for the affected person.
   - The security level is minimal.
3) Category: high sensitive data II
   - All data which, through the combination of a further data in categories 2 and 3, have a personal reference, but do not have a direct reference themselves (e.g., status data of a meter).
   - The impact of the damage can be assessed as significant by one person. Damage that has occurred for the person affected can be healed with increased effort.
   - The security level is intermediate.
4) Category: high sensitive data III (personal data)
   - All data that are personal data or data worth protecting according to the Federal Data Protection Act (e.g., name, address).
   - The effects of the damage have reached an existentially threatening, catastrophic extent. Damage that has occurred to the affected person cannot be healed.
   - The security level is high.

The division into four categories is due to the fact that different data are transferred. Data are transferred which are anonymised or does not allow any personal reference (non sensitive data). Furthermore, data are transmitted which are personal data or sensitive data (high sensitive data III). In addition, there is a further database, which is to be classified in two categories (high sensitive data I and high sensitive data II). Table I shows the 4-Level-Trust-Model for safety-critical systems with the coding and the security level. The 4-Level-Trust-Model for safety-critical systems permits to consider the security assessment of data.

TABLE I. EVALUATION CRITERIA DATA SECURITY

category	description	security level	coding
1. Category	non sensitive data	low	0
2. Category	high sensitive data I	minimal	1
3. Category	high sensitive data II	intermediate	2
4. Category	high sensitive data III	high	3

With the 4-Level-Trust-Model it is possible to evaluate data and information of use case in CPS with regard to security. By subdividing the data worthy of protection, a further gradation between personal data and sensitive data is made. With this model, appropriate security measures can be selected.

B. *Scalability*

The next criteria is SC. SC describes the number of participants. Participants are understood as users and devices. The scalability is divided in 4 categories (compare Table II).

TABLE II. EVALUATION CRITERIA SCALABILITY

description	coding
≤ 1	0
$2 \leq 100$	1
$101 \leq 10.000$	2
≥ 10.001	3

The selection of the criteria is based on the Smart Grid use case. "$\leq$ 1" corresponds to one participant and "2 $\leq$ 100" corresponds to a networked household. A residential unit is mapped with the values "101 $\leq$ 10.000". The entire network is described with the value from "$\geq$ 10.001".

C. Real-time

Another criteria is RT. The RT capability of a system means that a system must react to an event within a given time frame. Table III shows the division into 4 categories.

TABLE III. EVALUATION CRITERIA REAL-TIME

description	coding
$\leq$ 1 sec	0
2 sec $\geq$ 1 min	1
1 min $\geq$ 15 min	2
$\geq$ 15 min	3

The time specifications correspond to the requirements from the Smart Grid use case. Critical values are the requirement for real time ($\leq$ 1 sec) as well as the transmission of measurement data in 15 minute intervals.

D. Summary

With the Process-oriented Framework for Security Assessment of Cyber Physical Systems it is possible to evaluate the process of use case in CPS regard to DS, SK and RT. With the achievement of this result, the appropriate security measures can be selected.

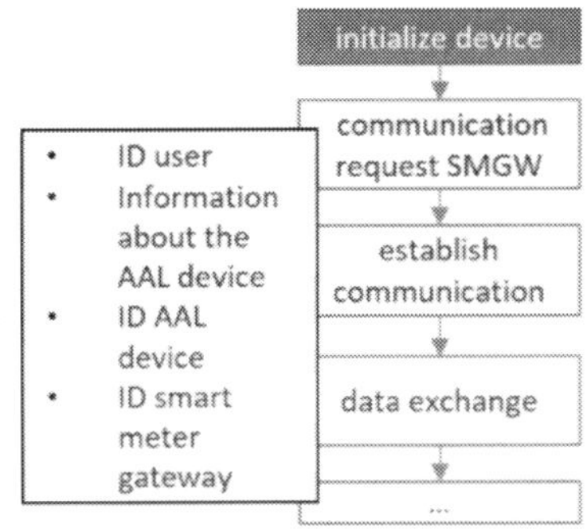

Figure 2. Process 1: Initialize device

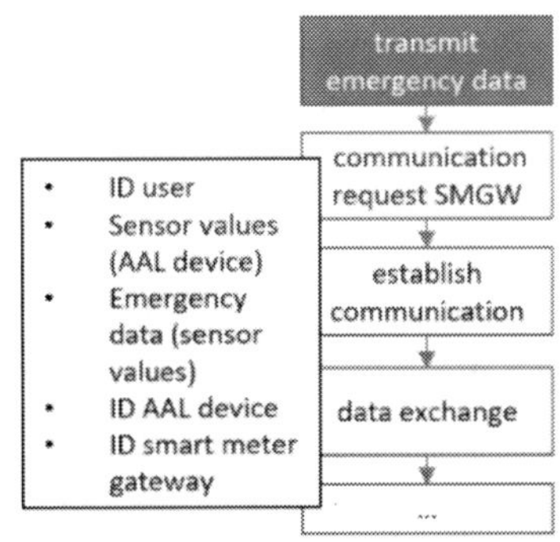

Figure 3. Process 5: Transmit emergency data

V. USE CASE EXAMPLE

Secure Gateway for Ambient Assisted Living (SEGAL) is a publicly funded research project and describes a value-added service. The aim of the project is the development of the SEGAL service, based on the use of AAL devices (IoT devices) and the Smart Grid infrastructure. AAL data collected within an AAL environment are recorded manually and automatically by sensors and forwarded to an external control center for processing. The AAL environment consists of digital assistants (Alexa or Google Home Mini, etc.), AAL-Devices (sphygmomanometer, heart rate monitor, etc.) or Smart Home devices (smoke detector, thermostat etc.). The communication takes place via a SMGW. The SMGW is connected to the AAL-Hub. The AAL-Hub connects the sensors, managed the communication with the gateway and the resulting data are aggregated.

A. Analysis of the application

The first step is the analysis of process, infrastructure, data and information. The use case SEGAL is divided into the following process:

- Process 1: Initialize device
- Process 2: Delete device
- Process 3: Update
- Process 4: Transmit data
- Process 5: Transmit emergency data

In the context of further analysis, we regard to the processes "process 1: initialize device" and "process 5: transmit emergency data". In case of "process 1: initialize device", the following data are transmitted (compare Figure 2).

- ID user
- Information about the AAL device
- ID AAL device
- ID SMGW

In case of "process 5: transmit emergency data", the following data are transmitted (compare Figure 3).

- ID user
- Sensor values (AAL device)
- Emergency data (sensor values)
- ID AAL device
- ID SMGW

B. Security assessment

The next step is the security assessment. The security assessment is divided in DS, SK and RT.

1) Data security: The data security assessment for process 1: initialize device is the third category "high sensitive data" (compare Table IV). ID user, information about the AAL device, ID AAL device and ID SMGW are no personal data, but data which have in combination of a further data in categories 2 and 3, have a personal reference, but do not have a direct reference themselves.

The data security assessment for process 5: transmit emergency data is the third category "high sensitive data" (compare

Table IV). ID user, sensor values, emergency data, ID AAL device and ID SMGW are no personal data, but data which have in combination of a further data in categories 2 and 3, have a personal reference, but do not have a direct reference themselves.

TABLE IV. OVERVIEW: DATA SECURITY

process	category	description	security level	coding
1	3. Category	high sensitive data II	intermediate	2
5	3. Category	high sensitive data II	intermediate	2

2) Scalability: If we consider the scalability in process 1: initialize device, we find out that we have between 2 and 100 participants (compare Table V). The coding of the criteria scalability for the process 1: initialize device is "1".

The scalability of process 5: transmit emergency data is "1" (compare Table V). There are participants between 2 and 100 participants.

TABLE V. OVERVIEW: SCALABILITY

process	description	coding
1	$2 \leq 100$	1
5	$2 \leq 100$	1

3) Real-time: The requirement real-time of "process 1: initialize device" is not given and the coding is "2" (compare Table VI).

In case of "process 5: transmit emergency data" the requirement real-time is given (compare Table VI). The coding of process 5 is "0".

TABLE VI. OVERVIEW: REAL-TIME

process	description	coding
1	1 min $\geq$ 15 min	2
5	$\leq$ 1 sec	0

4) Summary: The result of the assessment is the following description of the respective processes.

- $SEGAL_{process1}$ = (2,1,2)
- $SEGAL_{process5}$ = (2,1,0)

The evaluation provides a statement about how security critical the process is and a statement about SC and RT requirements. The example of the use case SEGAL illustrates that the difference can be seen in the RT requirement, while maintaining the same level of DS and SC. This must be taken into account when selecting suitable security measures.

C. Automated mapping of security measures

The last step is the automated assignment of the appropriate security measures. The security measures are also evaluated according to the CPS requirement criteria. The evaluation of security measures using the example of authentication is work in progress.

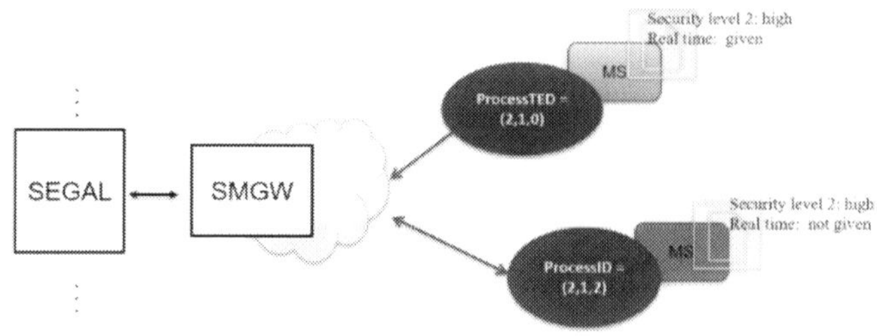

Figure 4. Use case SEGAL

D. Summary

With this example, it can be shown that the evaluation of DS and SC is the same. The difference between the use cases is the RT requirement. With the result obtained, appropriate security measures can be selected for the use case. Security measures, such as authentication, must be selected based on the real-time requirement criterion (compare Figure 4).

VI. CONCLUSION AND FUTURE WORK

In this paper, we presented the problem of security in future highly scalable and volatile systems. Based on the requirement criteria we developed the Process-oriented Framework for Security Assessment of Cyber Physical Systems. The model consists of the following steps: analysis of the application, security assessment, automated mapping of security measures. We showed the application of the model using the SEGAL use case. The use case showed us the necessity, different evaluation of security in CPS.

The Process-oriented Framework for Security Assessment of Cyber Physical Systems is a new framework for security assessment of CPS. With this model it is possible to evaluate use cases and processes in highly scalable, volatile systems and to select security measures such as authentication in a targeted manner. The model is intended to provide practical assistance in the evaluation of processes and use cases in highly scalable, volatile systems. The next steps are the automation of the framework, the definition of the security measures and the extension of the framework with the criterion performance, functional safety and volatility.

REFERENCES

[1] C., Legner, et al., Digitalization: Opportunity and Challenge for the Business and Information Systems Engineering Community, Bus Inf Syst Eng 59, pp. 301–308, 2017.
[2] M. Irlbeck, Digitalisierung und Energie 4.0 – Wie schaffen wir die digitale Energiewende?, Springer Fachmedien Wiesbaden GmbH, pp. 135-148, 2017.
[3] Ernst u. Young GmbH, Kosten-Nutzen-Analyse fuer einen flaechendeckenden Einsatz intelligenter Zaehler, 2013.
[4] ISO/IEC Information Technology Task Force, ISO/IEC 27000:2018 Information technology — Security techniques — Information security management systems — Overview and vocabulary, 2018.
[5] Federal Office for Information Security (Germany), BSI-Standard 100-1 Managementsysteme fuer Informationssicherheit (ISMS), 2008, [Online]. Available from: https://www.bsi.bund.de/SharedDocs/Downloads/DE/BSI/Publikationen/ITGrundschutzstandards/BSI-Standard_1001.pdf?__blob=publicationFile&v=2 [retrieved: 08, 2020].

[6] Federal Office for Information Security (Germany), BSI-Standard 200-2 IT-Grundschutz Methodology, 2017. Available from: https://www.bsi.bund.de/SharedDocs/Downloads/DE/BSI/Grundschutz/International/bsi-standard-2002_en_pdf.pdf?__blob=publicationFile&v=1 [retrieved: 08, 2020].
[7] Federal Office for Information Security (Germany), BSI Standard 200-3: Risk Analysis based on IT Grundschutz, 2017. Available from: https://www.bsi.bund.de/SharedDocs/Downloads/DE/BSI/Grundschutz/International/bsi-standard-2003_en_pdf.pdf?__blob=publicationFile&v=2 [retrieved: 08, 2020].
[8] ISO/IEC Information Technology Task Force, ISO/IEC 27000:2018 Information technology — Security techniques — Information security management systems — Overview and vocabulary, 2018.
[9] R. Matulevičius, et al., Adapting Secure Tropos for Security Risk Management in the Early Phases of Information Systems Development, International Conference on Advanced Information Systems Engineering, pp. 541-555, 2008.
[10] P. Bresciani, A. Perini, P. Giorgini, F. Giunchiglia, and J. Mylopoulos, Tropos: An Agent-Oriented Software Development Methodology, Autonomous Agents and Multi-Agent Systems 8, pp. 203–236, 2004.
[11] D. Mellado, C. Blanco, and L. Sanchez, A systematic review of security requirements engineering, Computer and Standards & Interfaces, Volume 32, Issue 4, pp. 153 – 165, 2010.
[12] L. Compagna, P. El Khoury, A. Krausová, F. Massacci, and N. Zannone, How to integrate legal requirements into a requirements engineering methodology for the development of security and privacy patterns, Artif Intell Law 17, pp. 1–30, 2008.
[13] K. Boroojeni, M. Amini, and S. Iyengar, Smart Grids: Security and Privacy Issues, Springer International Publishing, 2017.
[14] F. Dalipi and S. Y. Yayilgan, Security and Privacy Considerations for IoT Application on Smart Grids. Survey and Research Challenges, IEEE 4th International Conference on Future Internet of Things and Cloud Workshops (FiCloudW), pp. 63-68, 2016.
[15] M. Yun and B. Yuxin, Research on the architecture and key technology of Internet of Things (IoT) applied on smart grid, International Conference on Advances in Energy Engineering, pp. 69-72, 2010.
[16] B. Genge, A. Beres, and P. Haller, A survey on cloud-based software platforms to implement secure smart grids, 49th International Universities Power Engineering Conference (UPEC),pp. 1-6, 2014.
[17] S. Bera, S. Misra, and J. Rodrigues, J.P.C: Cloud Computing Applications for Smart Grid. A Survey, IEEE Trans. Parallel Distrib. Syst. 26 (5), pp. 1477-1494, 2015.
[18] Y. Simmhan, A. G. Kumbhare, B. Cao, and V. Prasanna, An Analysis of Security and Privacy Issues in Smart Grid Software Architectures on Clouds, IEEE 4th USENIX International Conference on Cloud Computing (CLOUD), pp. 582-589, 2011.
[19] A. Humayed, J. Lin, F. Li, and B. Luo, Cyber-Physical Systems Security—A Survey, IEEE Internet of Things Journal, vol. 4, no. 6, pp. 1802-1831, 2017.
[20] Y. Ashibani and Q. H. Mahmoud, Cyber physical systems security: Analysis, challenges and solutions, Computers & Security, Volume 68, Pages 81-97, 2017.
[21] K. Kim and P. R. Kumar, Cyber–Physical Systems: A Perspective at the Centennial, Proceedings of the IEEE, vol. 100, no. Special Centennial Issue, pp. 1287-1308, 2012.
[22] M. Broy, Cyber-Physical Systems — Wissenschaftliche Herausforderungen Bei Der Entwicklung, Cyber-Physical Systems acatech DISKUTIERT, pp. 17-32, 2010.
[23] K. Neubauer, S. Fischer, and R. Hackenberg, Work in Progress: Security Analysis for Safety-critical Systems: Smart Grid and IoT, ARCS Workshop, 32nd International Conference on Architecture of Computing Systems, pp. 1-6, 2019.

Securing the Internet of Things from the Bottom Up Using Physical Unclonable Functions

Leah Lathrop*, Simon Liebl*, Ulrich Raithel†, Matthias Söllner* and Andreas Aßmuth*

*Technical University of Applied Sciences OTH Amberg-Weiden, Amberg, Germany,
Email: {l.lathrop | s.liebl | m.soellner | a.assmuth}@oth-aw.de
†SIPOS Aktorik GmbH, Altdorf, Germany, Email: ulrich.raithel@sipos.de

***Abstract*—Cyberattacks that target hardware are becoming increasingly prevalent. These include probing attacks that aim at physically extracting sensitive information including cryptographic keys from non-volatile memory. Internet of Things devices that communicate with the Cloud are susceptible to such attacks. Therefore, the integrity of data and ability to authenticate devices are threatened. Physical Unclonable Functions (PUFs) offer a countermeasure to such attacks. A market analysis of products containing PUFs was carried out. An extract of the market analysis and the inferences that were drawn from it is provided. The analysis showed that although many different types of PUFs have been integrated into a variety of devices, most of them are still used in very rudimentary ways.**

Keywords–Cloud; Physical Unclonable Function; Critical Infrastructure; Internet of Things; Hardware Security.

I. Introduction

The Internet of Things (IoT) has engulfed many aspects of industrial sectors and the lives of private individuals. The number of actively connected IoT devices is forecast to grow to 22 billion by 2025 [1]. The Industrial IoT (IIoT) is the subset of the IoT that is used in industrial applications, e.g., healthcare, energy supply, transportation, and manufacturing. IIoT devices provide many advantages for traditional systems including making their management more efficient. The number of IIoT devices has risen from 3.96 billion in 2018 to 5.81 billion in 2020 [2].

Many IoT devices are constrained by power consumption and computational resources. The role of IoT devices can be leveraged through a symbiotic relationship with cloud computing to carry out data storage, analysis, and monitoring. In healthcare, storage and analysis of patient data collected by IIoT devices in the Cloud can be used to avoid preventable deaths, e.g., by hospital error; real-time monitoring enables emergency response when necessary [3]. Cloud computing is also used for the identification and authentication of actuators according to Molle [4]. The actuators are IIoT devices that can, e.g., be used to open and close valves to control the water supply.

The number of opportunities for cyberattacks grows with the number of IoT devices. The integrity of the data the Cloud and the IIoT device receive from each other is contingent upon the security of these devices. The examples in the previous paragraph showed that IIoT devices are even being used in healthcare and water supply, which are considered critical infrastructures in most countries. Compromise or failure of these systems could harm a society. Attacks that target both hardware and software threaten these devices. Hardware security is becoming increasingly important. An example of a hardware attack is the probing attack, which aims to extract sensitive data from a device's non-volatile memory. Physical Unclonable Functions (PUFs) are a countermeasure to these attacks.

The motivations for the use of PUFs are elaborated in Section II. A detailed explanation of PUF technology is given in Section III. An explanation of the applications for which PUFs can be used in IIoT devices specifically are provided in Section IV. An extract of a market analysis, which was carried out on PUFs, is presented in Section V. The paper is concluded in Section VI.

II. Motivation

Probing attacks can be used to extract sensitive information including cryptographic keys from non-volatile memory. The casing of an Integrated Circuit (IC) is removed, and the internal wires of a security critical module are accessed to retrieve the data. A Focused Ion Beam (FIB) uses ions at high beam currents to remove or deposit chip material with nanometer resolution. The attacker can use a FIB to deposit conducting paths that may serve as electrical probe contacts [5]. Tarnovsky carried out an attack to probe the firmware of the Infineon SLE 66CX680P/PE security/smart chip by probing the buses of the chip using an FIB [5] [6]. An informative introduction on probing attacks can be found in chapter 10 of a book on hardware security by Bhunia and Tehranipoor [5].

Hardware attacks, such as probing attacks, may need more knowledge, time, and monetary resources than software related attacks. However, they must still be considered a valid threat. The attacks are more accessible than some may assume. An FIB can be purchased on the resale market relatively inexpensively or rented at an hourly rate. Furthermore, there are parties for which the above stated factors are not a hindrance. Politically motivated attacks including cyberwarfare must be taken into consideration when evaluating the security of IIoT devices employed in critical infrastructures. Such attacks have occured in the past and may be state-sponsored, eliminating time and financial resources as obstacles. Examples of attacks on critical infrastructures include two attacks that resulted in power outages in the Ukraine. In December 2015, a cyberattack on three Ukrainian energy companies rendered approximately 225,000 people without power for several hours [7]. Ukraine's top law enforcement claimed this was a cyberattack by Russia. Investigations following the attack showed evidence to support the claim [8]. A second attack took place almost exactly a year later [9]. The attacks on the power supply in the Ukraine were not caused by hardware attacks on IIoT devices. However, IIoT devices are employed to take on various roles in energy supply. If attackers retrieve a cryptographic key from such a device, they may be able to eavesdrop onto the communication with the Cloud. This can help them gain information that will aid them in an attack.

A malevolent faction may go about an incursion on critical infrastructures with so much exertion because of the considerable amount of damage that can be caused. Denial of Service (DoS) attacks on power supply, which is usually also considered a critical infrastructure, can have detrimental effects on the economy. The authors of [10] created blackout-simulator.com, a tool that provides an estimate of the economic damage caused by power outages in Europe. The user can specify the start time, date, and the length of a power outage, and the region in which the power outage is taking place and receives an estimate of the economic damage. For example, the tool estimated the damages caused by a hypothetical six hour power outage in the state of Bavaria starting at 8 am on February 24th, 2020 to be approximately 660 million euro [11]. Furthermore, other critical infrastructures, such as healthcare, would also break down, causing deaths. This provides another reason why it is important to defend against all cyberattacks on IIoT devices, especially those that are used in critical infrastructures.

Some may also consider the shrinking size of integrated circuits with time a limiting factor. However, FIBs are also used for the failure analysis in ICs and will therefore continue to be developed and researched to accommodate the size of hardware [5].

A recent study shows that hardware- and silicon level security are becoming a reality for many companies. Forrester Consulting was commissioned to carry out a study to evaluate the needs of companies managing breaches to their hardware- and silicon-level devices and supply chains. The survey was carried out recently — between March 2019 and May 2019 — and included decision makers in 307 companies. The study showed that 63% of companies had experienced data compromise or breach due to an exploited vulnerability in hardware or silicon level security at least once within the last 12 months; 70% of the surveyed companies consider silicon-level security as critically important or very important [12]. The broad spectrum of invasive and non-invasive hardware attacks were implied by this study. These also include probing attacks.

IIoT devices are particularly susceptible to hardware attacks for several reasons. Man-At-The-End (MATE) attacks happen from the inside when an adversary gains "physical access to a device and compromises it by inspecting or tampering with the hardware itself or the software it contains" [13]. Several different third parties, some of which are trusted, have unhampered access to IIoT devices at various points in their life cycle. Companies have their IC designs manufactured in semiconductor fabrication plants. There are some cases in which the manufacturer must place information including cryptographic keys into non-volatile memory during production. The manufacturers may try to extract the information and keep it. During operation, (I)IoT devices are often employed in remote areas without supervision giving attackers unlimited access to the device.

III. Physical Unclonable Functions

PUFs offer a countermeasure against probing attacks. Analogous to biometrics, such as fingerprint detection or a retinal scan, a probabilistic characteristic of a physical object is used to derive a unique cryptographic secret. Semiconductor components in electrical devices contain production tolerances, which are usually unwanted and cannot be controlled. Although these tolerances are only visible on a microscopic level, they manifest themselves in small differences in physical sizes, e.g., two voltages may be slightly different. Therefore, devices which are constructed in exactly the same way can be individualized. PUFs that derive their fingerprints from tolerances from the semiconductor production process, e.g., random fluctuations in the dopant concentration or doping profiles, are called silicon PUFs.

A wide variety of different PUFs have emerged including the arbiter PUF. Figure 1 shows how a single bit can be derived to illustrate the principle of the arbiter PUF. A chain of electrical components, each having two inputs and outputs, is formed resulting in two race tracks for electrical signals. When applying an electrical signal to both inputs at exactly the same time, the signals should theoretically arrive synchronously. Contrary to what might be expected, the arrival times of the electrical signals are minutely different, due to tolerances from the semiconductor production process. The outputs are encoded as a "0" or a "1," and the bits for the keys can be derived based on which output the signal arrived at first. The output of a PUF is called the response [14]. A third input allows for configuration of the paths; each electrical component can either be configured as straight or switched. Different configurations for PUFs are called challenges. Pairs of challenges and responses are called Challenge-Response Pairs (CRPs).

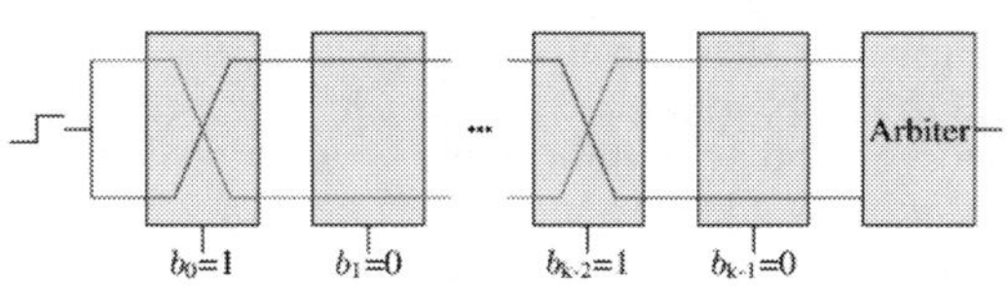

Figure 1. Arbiter PUF [14].

The SRAM PUF, first introduced by Guajardo in [15], offers another method of deriving a cryptographic key from a stochastic process. SRAM cells are constructed in a way that enables easy writing making them prone to intrinsic fluctuations. This does not affect the SRAM cells in any way during normal operation when an externally exerted signal is applied to them. However, when the memory cells are in an undefined state, they take on disparate values. Since SRAM is a form of volatile memory, such a state is achieved during power-up. The cryptographic secret can be extracted from the device during that time. The response is retrieved from the states of the memory cells of the SRAM.

The SRAM and arbiter PUFs can both be considered silicon PUFs. Although they share this similarity, these PUF types can also be distinguished in several different ways. The nature of the probabilistic behavior is different. PUF principles that are derived from similar processes can be separated into different categories. The SRAM PUF belongs to the category of memory-based PUFs which are derived from a type of memory. The arbiter PUF belongs to a category of PUFs that rely on delays of signals called delay-based PUFs. The second large difference lies in the amount of challenges which can be applied to a PUF instance. A PUF which has very few or only one challenge is called a Physically Obfuscated Key (POK) in PUF literature. A PUF that has many challenges is called a PUF or strong PUF. The SRAM PUF is an example of a POK because it only has one challenge whereas the arbiter PUF has many challenges and can therefore be considered a strong PUF. The difference is important when considering how they are integrated into security protocols.

Many formal definitions have been introduced in literature. The definitions provided by Rührmair are best suited for IIoT devices because of the consideration that the adversary has access to the device for a long time [16]. The source provides formal definitions for both POKs and strong PUFs. Assuming an adversary has access to a PUF for a set amount of time and can retrieve CRPs from it. A PUF is strong if the adversary can not collect enough CRPs, to deliver the correct response to a randomly chosen challenge with a probability greater than 90%. The probability must be greater than 50% to allow systems with binary outputs to be strong PUFs. However, whether that value is 90% or 75% is somewhat arbitrary. The key derived from a system may be called obfuscating PUF or POK if it derived at least in part from random, uncontrollable manufacturing variations. It must also be infeasible for an attacker to guess each digit in the key with a probability greater than 90% when given the device for a specified amount of time [16].

IV. Applications of PUFs

A PUF key can be used to hide a cryptographic key, thereby eliminating the risk of a probing attack. PUF keys are not stored in the device but are generated on demand when they are needed and subsequently deleted. A cryptographic secret can be derived from a PUF and used directly to substitute one which was stored in non-volatile memory. The PUF response can alternatively be used as a Key Encryption Key (KEK) to encrypt sensitive information stored in non-volatile memory including cryptographic keys. In the former scenario, an attacker would no longer find the cryptographic secret in the device when it is powered off. A probing attack in the latter scenario would be futile because the data is encrypted. A POK is well-suited for this because there is no need to store a challenge. Security protocols that are not specifically designed for PUFs can then be used.

Several protocols that harness the specific advantages offered by PUFs have also been designed that offer improvements upon traditional security protocols. These include protocols for authentication and authenticated execution for a variety of different devices on a spectrum of capabilities regarding power consumption and computing power. A protocol, which is based on the principle of the Controlled PUF (CPUF), was introduced by Gassend in [17]. A CPUF can only be accessed through an algorithm that is physically linked to the PUF in an inseperable way. The algorithm can be used to restrict challenges or limit information about responses. The algorithms with which the PUF can be accessed in this particular protocol are shown in Figure 2. The owner of the PUF has one CRP that was extracted from the PUF before it was employed. This CRP was extracted by applying a pre-challenge to get a response. The actual challenge can then be computed by calculating the hash value of the combination of the pre-challenge and a hash

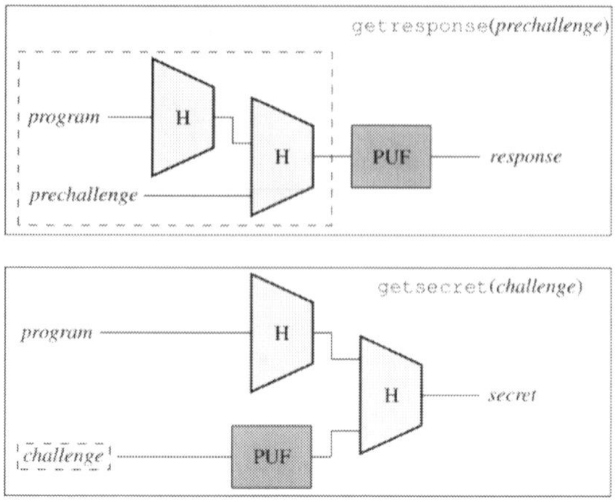

Figure 2. Algorithms to access the CPUF [17].

value of the program, as shown in the box with the dotted line. This allows the owner to calculate the same secret the PUF calculates using `getsecret`(*prechallenge*) later on. In IoT devices this protocol could, e.g., be used to authenticate a measurement taken by a sensor. The execution program is sent to the PUF. The first instruction of the program is to calculate `getsecret`(*prechallenge*). The secret can then be used by the device to generate a Message Authentication Code (MAC). The owner of the PUF can also generate the secret because he has the CRP and can use it to verify the result. Even if attackers extract the challenge from the program, they will still not be able to use it because they need the pre-challenge to calculate the response. This is impossible because it would require them to reverse the hash functions.

Although this paper focuses on the use of PUFs to secure (I)IoT devices communicating with a cloud, there are also many other cloud applications in which PUFs can be used. A Field-Programmable Gate Array (FPGA) can be used to accommodate hardware to accelerate certain algorithms, e.g., in cryptography. They can be reprogrammed offering flexibility. There are services that offer their customers to carry out their work on FPGA boards in the Cloud. These services include Amazon Web Service's EC2 F1 Instances and services offered by the company reconfigure.io. The CPUF could be used to authenticate the results of the computations of the FPGA boards.

V. Available PUF Technologies

Several PUF technologies have emerged on the market. An extensive analysis of available PUF technologies was carried out. An extract of the results of the market analysis is provided below. The PUF technologies that were included in the extract were chosen because they best illustrate the insights gained in the market analysis. Most companies that integrate a PUF into their products buy the technology from a vendor as Intellectual Property (IP). The IP vendors were researched and mapped to the companies that integrate them into their products. In this way, a better idea could be gained of all available PUF technologies because not all IPs have been integrated into products that are available for public purchase. An insight could also be gained into what companies license their technologies from the same vendor.

When contemplating the integration of technologies with PUFs into IIoT devices, there are several challenges that must be considered. For example, IIoT devices can sometimes have longer lifespans in comparison to regular IoT devices. Therefore, it is even more important that these can be flexibly updated because it is far more likely that changes in security may occur over a span of ten years than over a span of two to three years.

The IP vendor Intrinsic ID designs a PUF IP that uses the SRAM PUF technology as described in Section III. The technology can either be integrated into a product as a hardware IP (QuiddiKey) [18] or software IP (BroadKey) [19]. BroadKey can even be integrated into devices that have already been employed such as IoT devices [20]. The company Renesas has a family of Microcontroller Units (MCUs) called Synergy. Renesas offers a free version of BroadKey called DemoKey which can be tested on Synergy MCUs [21]. Several vendors of electrical components have integrated the hardware IP QuiddiKey into their products. These include NXP's LPC5500 series of MCUs [22] and the LPC540XX family of MCUs [23]. NXP also includes the PUF in two families of i.MX RT crossover processors — the i.MX RT600 [24] and the i.MX RT1170 [25]. Crossover processors combine the advantages of high end MCUs and application processors to meet the needs of IoT devices [26]. The NXP products use the PUF to encrypt data in memory and as a KEK to secure cryptographic keys in non-volatile memory [24] [27]. Microsemi also uses the SRAM PUF technology in several products including the PolarFire FPGA Boards to secure non-volatile memory [28].

Two different PUF technologies are based on the principle of the current mirror circuit shown in Figure 3, the current mirror PUF by Invia and ChipDNA by Maxim Integrated. The black portion of the circuit shows a current mirror as it can be found in many electrical circuits as a constant current source. The gate and the drain of MOSFET M_1 are connected. Therefore, the MOSFET stays in saturation and the current I_1 will stay constant.

The gates of M_1 and M_2 are connected causing their potentials to be equal. Equation (1) can be used to calculate the drain current of a MOSFET [29]. W and L are the width and length of the channel of the MOSFET, V_{Th} is the threshold voltage, V_{GS} is the gate-source voltage, C_{ox} is the gate oxide capacitance per unit area, and μ_n is the charge carrier effective mobility. If the MOSFETs that are used for M_1 and M_2 are of the same type and from the same manufacturer, the values of these variables should theoretically be the same. Therefore, I_{ref} and I_1 should also be the same. In practice, there will be small tolerances from the production process, that can affect any of the variables in (1) and cause miniscule differences between the two currents. The blue part of the circuit shows, that a second constant current source can simply be added by including another MOSFET M_3. Small production tolerances in the MOSFETs will also affect the currents I_1 and I_2.

$$I_D = \frac{1}{2}\mu_{\mathrm{n}} C_{\mathrm{ox}} \frac{W}{L}(V_{\mathrm{GS}} - V_{\mathrm{Th}})^2 \quad (1)$$

The company Invia has developed a PUF as a hardware IP that utilizes the principle of the current mirror. The PUF consists of a matrix of cells that each contain two MOSFETs producing two constant current sources. The matrix consists of 128 elements — 8 rows and 16 columns. Figure 4 shows how the value of each element is evaluated; only the first row of the matrix is depicted. The two resulting currents are compared. The result will depend on which current is larger. There are

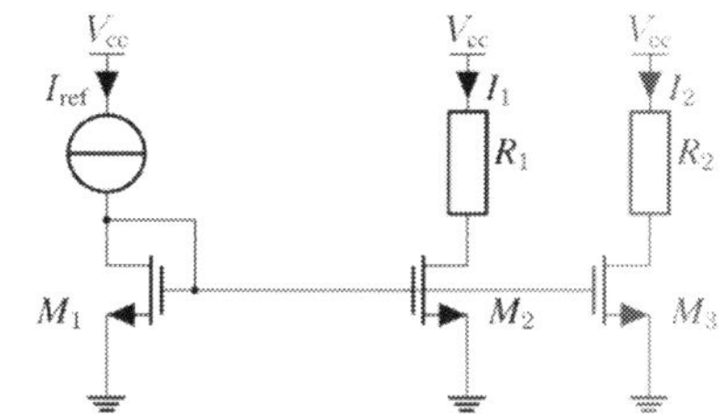

Figure 3. Current mirror as a constant current source.

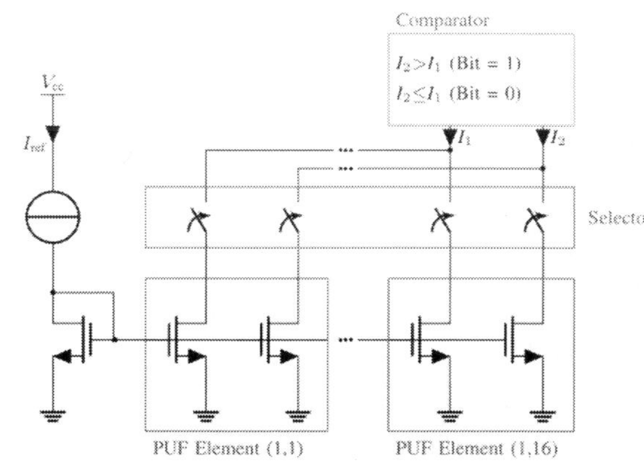

Figure 4. Current mirror PUF by Invia [30].

currently no products available for purchase to the public that contain this hardware IP.

Maxim Integrated is a vendor of electrical components. Rather than purchasing their PUF as a hardware IP, they have designed their own technology called ChipDNA, shown in Figure 5. The PUF also makes use of the principle of the current mirror. It consists of a matrix of 256 elements — 16 rows and 16 columns. As Figure 5 shows, each cell contains two MOSFETs, a p-channel MOSFET M_1 and an n-channel MOSFET M_2. The left part of the circuit and M_1 of each element of the matrix form a current mirror, providing a constant current source. The gate and the drain of MOSFET M_2 are connected causing the MOSFET to stay in the saturation region and switched on. When a MOSFET is switched on, it conducts current but has a resistance $R_{\mathrm{DS,on}}$ so there is a voltage drop across the component. These voltages will vary slightly depending on production tolerances of the MOSFETs used for the current mirror and for the voltage drop. Therefore, they can be compared in order to derive a value. In a diagram of the PUF provided by Maxim Integrated, the gate and drain of M_{ref} are not connected [31]. The assumption is made that this is a mistake because the circuit would cease to function if this would not be the case. The 256 elements of the array are combined into 128 pairs to achieve higher stability [31]. Maxim Integrated is the assignee of a patent that describes an algorithm in which matrix elements are paired [32]. It is likely that this algorithm is used to create the pairs mentioned in [31].

ChipDNA has been integrated into several electrical components, including the DS2477 [33] and DS28E50 [34], which can be used for authentication. Authentication is carried out using a challenge-response protocol. The shared secrets needed for the challenge-response protocol can be stored on the components. Only one secret can be stored on the DS28E50,

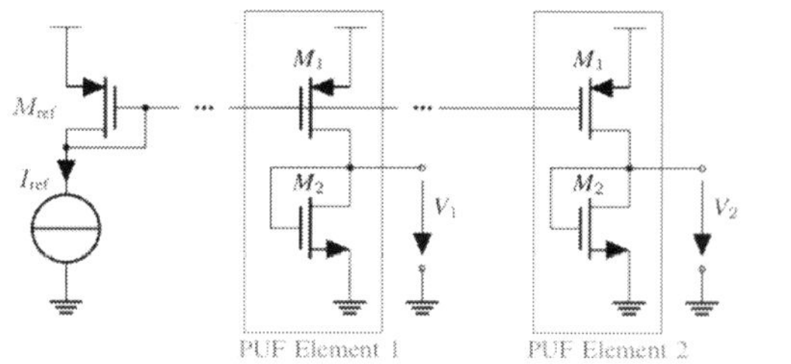

Figure 5. ChipDNA PUF Technology by Maxim Integrated [31].

and multiple secrets can be stored on the DS2477. The key generated by the ChipDNA is used to "cryptographically secure" all data stored on the device including the secret for the challenge-response protocol. The electrical components both contain a True Random Number Generator (TRNG) and a SHA-3 engine, which can be used to create a Hash-based Message Authentication Code (HMAC) for the challenge-response protocol. Maxim Integrated sees great potential in the integration of these devices into medical equipment among other applications. They also offer an MCU with a PUF — MAX32520 [35]. The PUF can be used for internal flash encryption, device authentication, and to generate a public and private key pair. The associated public key can be exported and signed by a certification authority.

According to several sources, the PUF that is integrated into Xilinx products is sourced from the IP designer Verayo [36]. The PUF technology that Xilinx integrates into their Zync UltraScale+ products is a Ring Oscillator PUF (ROPUF) [37]. It can therefore be deduced that Verayo develops an ROPUF. Srini Devadas who founded Verayo supervised the masters thesis in which the ROPUF was introduced [38] and was involved in a publication in which a variation of the ROPUF is proposed [39]. In the Zync UltraScale+ products, the PUF is utilized as a KEK to encrypt a user key. The user key can be used to encrypt the boot image [37] [40, pg. 270]. The Zync UltraScale+ products include multi processor system on chips (MPSoC).

Figure 6 shows a diagram of the ROPUF. An asynchronously oscillating loop is formed by inverting the output of a digital delay line and feeding it back to the input. The frequency of the oscillator is determined by the delay line, which is influenced by the manufacturing tolerances of the electrical components. Consequently, the instances of the circuit have distinct frequencies. The edges of the signal are counted using a digital counter to derive a PUF response. The function $n(t)$ is the edge count as a function of time. The input *challenge* can be used to configure the delay line [41]. In [39], a variation of the ROPUF is introduced to reduce the influence of environmental variations like temperature. The counters of two instances of the ROPUF circuit are compared to derive the bit, instead of using the counter as a response directly. The exact version of the ROPUF that is used in the Zync UltraScale+ products is not specified in the datasheet. It is safe to assume that a variation of the ROPUF is used that does not require a challenge as there is no mention of this in the data sheet [40].

Several important insights were gathered from the market analysis. A variety of different PUF technologies (e.g., current mirror PUF, SRAM PUF, ROPUF) are incorporated into a diverse group of devices (e.g., FPGA, MCU, MPSoC). PUFs

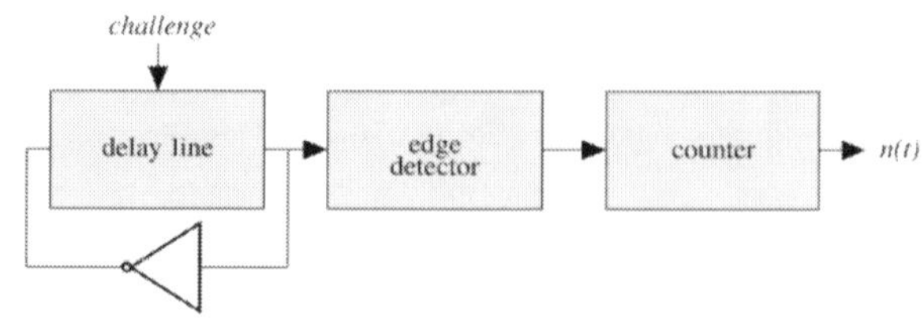

Figure 6. Ring Oscillator PUF [41].

contribute to the security of a diversity of applications, e.g., flash encryption and secure boot processes. However, most are used in a similar way: to encrypt data on the device or replace a cryptographic key stored in non-volatile memory. Most of the technologies still use the PUF in a very rudimentary way, not taking advantage of the specific PUF properties such as the CPUF protocol. All of the technologies, which were found in the analysis, were POKs. Although the ROPUF can potentially have multiple challenges, no mention of these were made in the datasheet of the product leading to the assumption that the ROPUF was implemented without them [40].

VI. Conclusion and Future Work

Hardware attacks including probing attacks are a surging problem to which PUFs offer an attainable countermeasure. Many different PUF technologies have been integrated into a variety of products on the market. Most PUF technologies available on the market are only used to secure keys which are then used in traditional security protocols. Based on all the sources found in the market analysis, most products currently available on the market for public purchase do not leverage a protocol that exploits the specific advantages offered by PUFs and all used PUF technologies are POKs. It will be interesting to observe the future developments of the PUF market.

Acknowledgement

The research project "Intelligent Security for Electrical Actuators and Converters in Critical Infrastructures (iSEC)" is a collaboration of SIPOS Aktorik GmbH, Grass Power Electronics GmbH and OTH Amberg-Weiden. It is supported and funded by the Bavarian Ministry of Economic Affairs, Regional Development and Energy.

References

[1] K. L. Lueth, "State of the IoT 2018: Number of IoT devices now at 7B – Market accelerating," 2018, URL: https://iot-analytics.com/state-of-the-iot-update-q1-q2-2018-number-of-iot-devices-now-7b/ [accessed: 2020-07-27].

[2] "Gartner Says 5.8 Billion Enterprise and Automotive IoT Endpoints Will Be in Use in 2020," 2019, URL: https://www.gartner.com/en/newsroom/press-releases/2019-08-29-gartner-says-5-8-billion-enterprise-and-automotive-io [accessed: 2020-07-27].

[3] M. S. Hossain and G. Muhammad, "Cloud-assisted industrial internet of things (iiot) - enabled framework for health monitoring," *Computer Networks*, vol. 101, pp. 192–202, 2016.

[4] M. Molle, U. Raithel, D. Kraemer, N. Graß, M. Söllner, and A. Aßmuth, "Security of cloud services with low-performance devices in critical infrastructures," in *The Tenth International Conference on Cloud Computing, GRIDs, and Virtualization – CLOUD COMPUTING 2019*, 2019, pp. 88–92.

[5] M. Tehranipoor and S. Bhunia, *Hardware Security A Hands-On Learning Approach*. Elsevier, 2019.

[6] C. Tarnovsky, "Security Failures in Secure Devices," 2008, URL: https://www.blackhat.com/presentations/bh-dc-08/Tarnovsky/Presentation/bh-dc-08-tarnovsky.pdf [accessed: 2020-07-27].

[7] "Analysis of the Cyber Attack on the Ukrainian Power Grid," 2016, URL: https://ics.sans.org/media/E-ISAC_SANS_Ukraine_DUC_5.pdf [accessed: 2020-07-27].

[8] J. Pagliery, "Scary questions in Ukraine energy grid hack," 2016, URL: https://money.cnn.com/2016/01/18/technology/ukraine-hack-russia/ [accessed: 2020-07-27].

[9] P. Polityuk, O. Vukmanovic, and S. Jewkes, "Ukraine's power outage was a cyber attack: Ukrenergo," 2017, URL: https://www.reuters.com/article/us-ukraine-cyber-attack-energy-idUSKBN1521BA [accessed: 2020-07-27].

[10] M. Schmidthaler and J. Reichl, "Assessing the socio-economic effects of power outages ad hoc," *Computer Science - Research and Development*, vol. 31, pp. 157–161, 03 2016.

[11] "Blackout Simulator 2.0," URL: http://blackout-simulator.com/ [accessed: 2020-07-27].

[12] "BIOS Security – The Next Frontier for Endpoint Protection," 2019, URL: https://www.dellemc.com/ja-jp/collaterals/unauth/analyst-reports/solutions/dell-bios-security-the-next-frontier-for-endpoint-protection.pdf [accessed: 2020-07-27].

[13] M. Jakubowski, P. Falcarin, C. Collberg, and M. Atallah, "Software protection," *IEEE Software*, vol. 28, pp. 24–27, 03 2011.

[14] D. Lim, "Extracting secret keys from integrated circuits," Master's thesis, Massachusetts Institute of Technology, May 2004.

[15] J. Guajardo, S. S. Kumar, G.-J. Schrijen, and P. Tuyls, "Fpga intrinsic pufs and their use for ip protection," in *Cryptographic Hardware and Embedded Systems - CHES 2007*, P. Paillier and I. Verbauwhede, Eds. Berlin, Heidelberg: Springer Berlin Heidelberg, 2007, pp. 63–80.

[16] U. Rührmair, J. Sölter, and F. Sehnke, "On the foundations of physical unclonable functions," *IACR Cryptology ePrint Archive*, June 2009, 2009/277 URL: ia.cr/2009/277 [accessed: 2020-07-29].

[17] B. Gassend, D. Clarke, M. van Dijk, and S. Devadas, "Controlled physical random functions," in *18th Annual Computer Security Applications Conference, 2002. Proceedings.*, 01 2002, pp. 149–160.

[18] "QuiddiKey," URL: https://www.intrinsic-id.com/products/quiddikey/ [accessed: 2020-07-27].

[19] "Bk software," URL: https://www.intrinsic-id.com/products/bk-software/ [accessed: 2020-07-27].

[20] "Intrinsic ID's BROADKEY Secures IoT with Key Management Software Powered by SRAM PUF," 2017, URL: https://www.intrinsic-id.com/intrinsic-ids-broadkey-secures-iot-key-management-software-powered\\-sram-puf/ [accessed: 2020-07-27].

[21] "Secure Key Management Software," URL: https://www.renesas.com/us/en/products/synergy/gallery/partner-projects/intrinsic-id-secure-key-management-software.html [accessed: 2020-07-27].

[22] "LPC5500 Series: World's Arm Cortex-M33 based Microcontroller Series for Mass Market, Leveraging 40nm Embedded Flash Technology," URL: https://www.nxp.com/products/processors-and-microcontrollers/arm-microcontrollers/general-purpose-mcus/lpc5500-cortex-m33:LPC5500_SERIES [accessed: 2020-07-27].

[23] "LPC540XX: Power-Efficient Microcontrollers (MCUs) with Advanced Peripherals Based on Arm Cortex-M4 Core," URL: https://www.nxp.com/products/processors-and-microcontrollers/arm-microcontrollers/general-purpose-mcus/lpc54000-cortex-m4-/power-efficient-microcontrollers-mcus-with-advanced-peripherals-based\\-on-arm-cortex-m4-core:LPC540XX [accessed: 2020-07-27].

[24] "RT600 (Datasheet)," URL: https://www.nxp.com/docs/en/data-sheet/DS-RT600.pdf [accessed: 2020-07-27].

[25] "i.MX RT1170 Crossover MCU Family - First Ghz MCU with Arm Cortex-M7 and Cortex-M4 Cores," URL: https://www.nxp.com/products/processors-and-microcontrollers/arm-microcontrollers/i.mx-rt-crossover-mcus/i.mx-rt1170-crossover-mcu-family-first-ghz-mcu-with-arm-cortex-m7\\-and-cortex-m4-cores:i.MX-RT1170 [accessed: 2020-07-27].

[26] "Crossover Embedded Processors – Bridging the gap between performance and usability," URL: https://www.nxp.com/docs/en/white-paper/I.MXRT1050WP.pdf [accessed: 2020-07-27].

[27] "LPC55S6x (Datasheet)," URL: https://www.nxp.com/docs/en/data-sheet/LPC55S6x.pdf [accessed: 2020-07-27].

[28] "UG0753 User Guide PolarFire FPGA Security," URL: https://www.microsemi.com/document-portal/doc_download/136534-ug0753-polarfire-fpga-security-user-guide [accessed: 2020-07-27].

[29] M. T. Thompson, *Intuitive Analog Circuit Design*. Newnes, 2014, URL: https://www.elsevier.com/books/intuitive-analog-circuit-design/thompson/978-0-12-405866-8 [accessed: 2020-07-27].

[30] V. Telandro and C. Tremlet, "Why should your next secure design be PUF based," 2019, URL: https://www.design-reuse-embedded.com/ipsocdays/ipsocdays2019/china2019/slides/1-Invia%20-%20Why_should_your_next_PUF_based.pptx [accessed: 2020-07-27].

[31] "How ChipDNA Physically Unclonable Function Technology Protects Embedded Systems (Application Note 6767)," URL: https://pdfserv.maximintegrated.com/en/an/ChipDNA-Unclonable-Protects-Embedded-Systems.pdf [accessed: 2020-07-27].

[32] P. Parvarandeh and S. Ung Kwak, "Systems and Methods for Stable Physically Unclonable Functions (US Patent 9,485,094)," 2016.

[33] "DeepCover Secure SHA-3 Coprocessor with ChipDNA PUF Protection," URL: https://www.maximintegrated.com/en/products/embedded-security/secure-authenticators/DS2477.html/tb_tab0 [accessed: 2020-07-27].

[34] "DeepCover Secure SHA-3 Authenticator with ChipDNA PUF Protection," URL: https://www.maximintegrated.com/en/products/embedded-security/DS28E50.html [accessed: 2020-07-27].

[35] "ChipDNA Secure Arm Cortex M4 Microcontroller," URL: https://datasheets.maximintegrated.com/en/ds/MAX32520.pdf [accessed: 2020-07-27].

[36] Design&Reuse, "Verayo puf ip on xilinx zynq ultrascale+ mpsoc devices addresses security demands," URL: https://www.design-reuse.com/news/40875/verayo-puf-ip-xilinx-zynq-ultrascale-mpsoc.html?utm_campaign=40875&utm_content=1&utm_medium=rss&utm_source=designreuse [accessed: 2020-07-27].

[37] E. Peterson, "Developing Tamper-Resistant Designs with Zynq UltraScale+ Devices (XAPP1323)," 2018, URL: https://www.xilinx.com/support/documentation/application_notes/xapp1323-zynq-usp-tamper-resistant-designs.pdf [accessed: 2020-07-27].

[38] B. Gassend, "Physical random functions," Master's thesis, Massechusetts Institute of Technology, February 2003.

[39] G. Suh and S. Devadas, "Physical unclonable functions for device authentication and secret key generation," in *Proc 44th ACM/IEEE Design Automation Conference*, 07 2007, pp. 9–14.

[40] "Zynq UltraScale+ Device Technical Reference Manual," 2019, URL: https://www.xilinx.com/support/documentation/user_guides/ug1085-zynq-ultrascale-trm.pdf [accessed: 2020-07-27].

[41] R. Maes and I. Verbauwhede, "Physically unclonable functions: A study on the state of the art and future research directions," in *Information Security and Cryptography*. Springer Berlin Heidelberg, 2010, pp. 3–37, URL: https://doi.org/10.1007%2F978-3-642-14452-3_1 [accessed: 2020-04-10].

An IoT Crypto Gateway for Resource-Constrained IoT Devices

Ahmed Alqattaa
Department of Electrical Engineering,
Media and Computer Science
OTH – Technical University of Applied Sciences
Amberg, Germany
Email: a.alqattaa@oth-aw.de

Daniel Loebenberger
Department of Electrical Engineering,
Media and Computer Science
OTH – Technical University of Applied Sciences
Amberg, Germany
Email: d.loebenberger@oth-aw.de

***Abstract*—One of the biggest challenges for the Internet of Things (IoT)-Security is to implement high-end asymmetric cryptography while at the same time meeting the requirements of IoT devices due to their constrained resources. Instead of reducing the security level (e.g., by employing lightweight cryptographic primitives), this paper presents a work-in-progress project and specifies the overall architecture of an IoT cryptographic gateway "*IoT crypto gateway*", which sits in-between attached IoT devices and the cloud. The gateway communicates with the cloud implementing the Message Queuing Telemetry Transport (MQTT) protocol over a TLS (Transport Layer Security) connection employing up-to-date asymmetric cryptography at a high security level. On the other hand, the gateway allows the IoT devices to connect to the network by implementing MQTT over the Quick UDP Internet Connections (QUIC) protocol, which is at the moment still being developed by IETF. Since on transport layer, the gateway is fully transparent, the (logical) TLS connection in QUIC between the IoT devices and the gateway may save time, power and computation on the IoT device's side without compromising security.**

Keywords–gateway; IoT; TLS; QUIC; MQTT.

I. Introduction

Through huge technological advances, society is moving towards an "always connected" paradigm. One wide concept associated with the "future Internet" is the *Internet of Things (IoT)*. The IoT is a network where all kinds of electronic devices are connected to each other and provide the capability to interact. The "Thing" in IoT can be any device, for instance a phone or a small sensor node that is able to connect, transfer, receive or exchange data with the network [1].

Developers as well as companies have started to increasingly introduce numerous IoT-based products and services. Furthermore, practitioners increasingly view the IoT as a real business opportunity, and expect that it could grow to USD 949.42 billion by 2025 [2]. The IoT converts the everyday world into a more flexible and accessible one. Thing, place and time do not matter anymore as long as there is access to the Internet. However, if the IoT devices are connected to the Internet without being protected properly, they may become vulnerable to attacks on the devices and the network itself.

Thus, IoT security is a relevant aspect in the design of IoT protocols. For instance, in 2015, the Federal Bureau of Investigation published a public service announcement to warn against the potential vulnerabilities of IoT devices [3]. In addition, the German Federal Office for Information Security (BSI) continuously warns against the potential attacks on the IoT and gives users possible countermeasures at hand in order to limit serious attacks against IoT devices [4] [5] [6].

As an example, Wenxiang et al. presented how to use multiple vulnerabilities to achieve a remote attack on some of the most popular smart speakers. The attack effects include silent listening, control of speaker speaking content, and other demonstrations, while offering no clue to the user that the device has been compromised [7].

This paper is structured as follows: we first discuss in Sections I-A and I-B different security requirements and challenges of the IoT, respectively. Afterwards, in Section II, related work of the past few years is identified and discussed. In Section III, the contribution is stated. Finally, the proposed architecture of this paper is described in Section IV.

A. Security Requirements for the IoT

Various hardware mechanisms and software parameters must be taken in consideration in order to secure IoT devices. We list here the most important cryptographic ones most of which can also be found in the surveys [8] [9] [10].

1) Confidentiality: the tunnel is private. Encryption is used for all messages after a simple handshake. Thus, the data is only visible to the endpoints (end-to-end encryption). A proper encryption mechanism is required to ensure the confidentiality of data in IoT [4] [5].

2) Integrity: the channel is reliable. It ensures that data contained in the device is not changed unnoticed during the transmission. Because of the constrained resources of IoT devices and network, the data, which is stored on an IoT node, could be vulnerable to integrity violation by compromising it [9].

3) Authentication and Authorization: the tunnel is authenticated. A proper implementation of authentication and authorization results in a trustworthy environment, which ensures a secure environment for communication. The variety of authentication mechanisms for the IoT exists mainly because of the different heterogeneous underlying architectures and environments that support IoT devices. These environments pose a challenge for the definition of a global standard protocol for authentication in the IoT [4] [5] [9].

Additionally, there are non-cryptographic requirements for IoT devices, such as availability, which are not addressed here.

B. IoT Security Challenge

IoT devices are often resource-constrained, low-power, and have small storage. Thus, attacks on IoT architectures may result in an increase in energy consumption by flooding the network and exhausting IoT resources through redundant or forged service requests [11]. Moreover, cryptographic functionalities can be realized by implementing one of the two schemes: symmetric key algorithms or public key algorithms. In comparison, public key algorithms offer a totally different set of security features such as digital signatures and key exchange mechanisms, however at higher computational cost. Taking the constrained resources of IoT devices into account, the high overhead of public key cryptography has become a major bottle-neck and triggered the use of lightweight cryptography. This, however, comes at the cost of a reduced security level [12] [13].

In order to understand the overall approach to data security, there is a need to know about the security requirements for all key components of IoT systems, i.e., IoT devices, IoT users, the IoT gateway, communication channels and cloud applications. For instance, public key infrastructure may not be suitable for IoT environments as it becomes a computationally expensive task to calculate ciphertexts because of the high computational cost for asymmetric cryptography. On the other hand, asymmetric cryptography provides additional security functionalities against attacks [13] [14].

II. Related Work

Two years ago, the Internet Engineering Task Force (IETF) finished the development of a new version of TLS, 1.3 [15]. Furthermore, the IETF is recently working on deprecating TLS 1.0 and 1.1 because these versions lack support for current and recommended cipher suites [16]. The primary goal of TLS is to secure the communication between two peers (client and server) by providing three basic properties: confidentiality, integrity and authentication. Note that other requirements, such as privacy, are not addressed by TLS and are typically not met when using TLS for IoT devices [10] [15].

Currently, the IETF is working on developing the security of the QUIC protocol by integrating TLS 1.3 in it [17] [18]. Quick UDP Internet Connections (QUIC) is a transport protocol developed by google, which reduces latency compared to TCP [19]. QUIC is a TCP-like protocol, which supports congestion control and loss recovery. It reduces a number of transport and application layers problems that occur in modern web applications, while requiring little or no modification from application writers [20] [17]. In addition, QUIC was the first protocol that can create a secure connection implementing a 0-RTT handshake between the peers, which has been later adopted in TLS 1.3 with some improvements [15] [18] .

The DTLS protocol is based on TLS and provides security for UDP-based applications. The purpose of DTLS is to make only the minimal changes to TLS required to fix loosing or reordering the packets when implementing TLS over UDP (DTLS) [21]. Currently, IETF is working on developing a new version of DTLS, 1.3 [22]. However, the UDP-Based multiplexed and secure transport (QUIC) is different from DTLS. QUIC combines multiple data streams into a single flow of UDP packets and necessarily has to handle reordering and loosing packets, like TCP [17].

The Message Queuing Telemetry Transport (MQTT) protocol is a lightweight messaging protocol, which works over the transmission protocol TCP/IP and is one of the most used protocols for IoT devices [23] [24]. For embedded devices, MQTT is highly recommended because it can work with limited processor and memory resources. In addition, through the Publish/Subscribe message pattern, the protocol provides one-to-many message distribution. The MQTT protocol itself supports only a username and a password to secure the communication between a server and clients. Any additional security has to be added into the protocol individually by employing a suitable transport protocol [25].

The mitmproxy project is a free and open source interactive HTTPS proxy, which differs from the gateway proposed here in several points, since it has the ability to communicate with different peers using different layer protocols. Furthermore, mitmproxy has been developed for other purposes, such as modifying and intercepting data between the peers [26].

NGINX published the technology preview of HTTP/3 (QUIC+HTTP), which is at the moment still being developed by IETF, at an open source repository [27] [28]. The project is a pre-release software, which is based on the IETF QUIC draft and maintained in a development branch, which is isolated from the stable and mainline branches. The release is an initial development and available for interoperability testing, feedback and code contributions. Notably, QUIC also incorporates TLS as an integral component, not as an additional layer as with HTTP/1.1 and HTTP/2 (see Figure 1) [17] [29]. Moreover, OpenSSL as well as wolfSSL have just started adding QUIC to their libraries [30] [31].

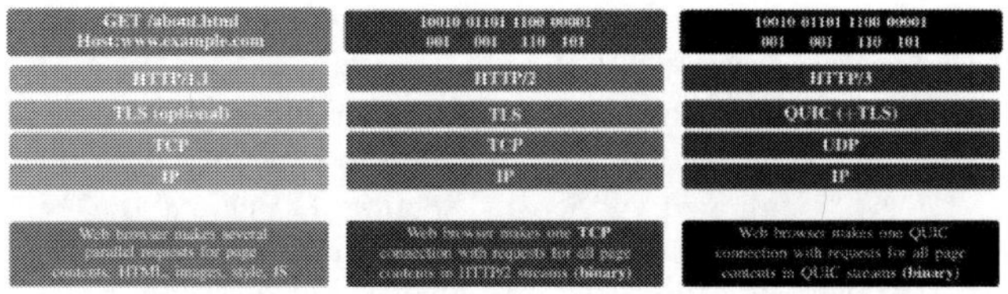

Figure 1. High-level overview of HTTP transport stacks [29].

Recently, many authentication schemes for IoT have been proposed. For instance, Tewari et al. [32] suggested a robust anonymity preserving authentication protocol for IoT devices that provides mutual authentication between tag and reader through the server. This scheme uses Elliptic Curve Cryptography to implement authentication. As a method to provide the user the access to sensors or sensor data, the user is usually authenticated through the gateway.

Research by King et al. [33] attempted to reduce the energy consumption of IoT devices by performing lightweight protocols on the IoT device side and with minimal resource requirements, while heavier tasks are performed in the gateway side. The proposed mechanism utilizes a symmetric encryption for data objects combined with the native wireless security to offer a layered security mechanism between the device and the gateway.

In addition, Razouk et. al. [34] suggested a security middleware architecture based on fog computing and cloud to support resource constrained devices for authentication. The middleware acts as a smart gateway in order to pre-process data at the edge of the network. Thus, data is either processed and stored locally on fog or sent to the cloud for further processing.

As a result, all of the stated approaches either use expensive concepts of public key cryptography in order to establish a high security level or reduce the security level by employing cheaper lightweight methods. As it turns out, constrained IoT devices which communicate through proposed middleware, have access to more computing power and have thus enhanced capabilities to perform secure communications at a high security level [13] [34].

III. Contribution

We present here a work-in-progress IoT crypto gateway, which has the ability to reduce the required security computations for IoT devices based on low-power System-on-a-Chip (SoC). The IoT crypto gateway stands between the cloud and the IoT devices and communicates with the cloud as a client and with the IoT devices as a cloud (see Figure 2).

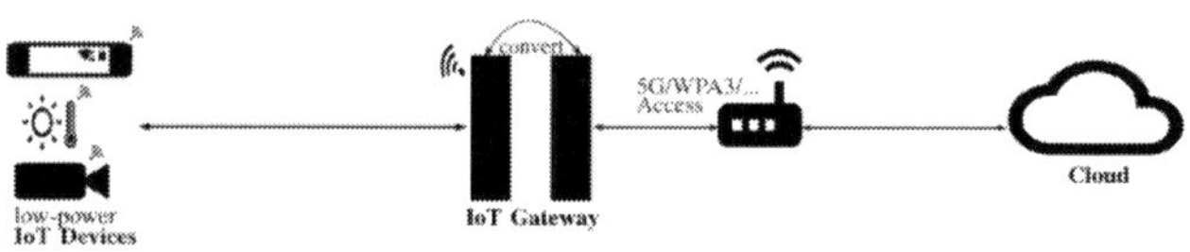

Figure 2. Establishing a connection between the IoT crypto gateway and the IoT device.

Precisely, this project aims to reduce the required security computations for the IoT devices by implementing MQTT over IETF QUIC in the IoT devices and developing an IoT crypto gateway, which has the ability to convert the communication from TCP-TLS-MQTT, which is the actual/common case, to QUIC-MQTT and vice versa.

IV. Proposed Architecture

The gateway developed should perform as a translator between the IoT devices and the cloud using common protocols with the cloud and more efficient/suitable protocols with the IoT devices in order to save energy and improve performance.

As mentioned earlier in Section I, one of the biggest challenge of securely attaching IoT devices to cloud services is to achieve a high security level using only low resources. The storage and processing capabilities of an IoT device are restricted by the resources available, which are, for example, constrained due to size limitation, energy, and computational capability. Thus, these systems rely on IoT middleware to provide needed capabilities [34].

Traditionally, IoT devices may be connected to the cloud implementing two ways (see Figure 3). First, the IoT devices may have the ability to securely communicate via TLS directly with the cloud (see Figure 3(a)). In this way, both peers can perform a direct TLS-handshake between each other. Hence, the data can be secured in the private as well as the public network.

Second, the IoT devices might be connected to the cloud through a TLS (opt. reserve) proxy implementing a web server (e.g., NGINX), which only secures the data before emerging out to the public network (see Figure 3(b)). Thus, the connection between the proxy and the cloud is secured via TLS, and data between the proxy and the IoT devices is transmitted without TLS. The proxy aims to reduce the risks on the IoT devices by securing the data only in the public network and to save the resources of the IoT devices by decrypting the data before emerging in the private network [35].

Both communication scenarios have their drawbacks. By implementing the one in Figure 3(a), the IoT devices have to establish an (expensive) secured tunnel which is – at a high security level – not suitable for constrained IoT devices [15] [36]. Furthermore, by implementing the scheme in Figure 3(b), the connection between the proxy and the IoT devices does not provide the security requirements mentioned in Section I-A. Additionally, some attacks, such as DDoS and MITM, are possible on the network [37] [38].

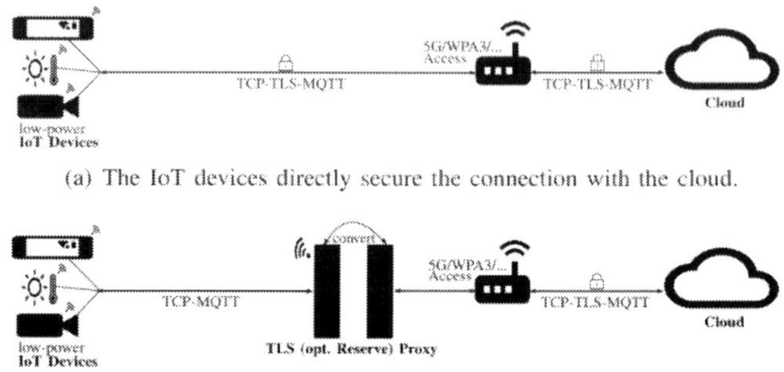

(a) The IoT devices directly secure the connection with the cloud.

(b) A TLS (opt. reserve) proxy between the IoT devices and the cloud.

Figure 3. Illustrations of how IoT devices may secure the connection with a cloud service.

To circumvent both problems, we present the following architecture: the IoT crypto gateway stands between the cloud and the IoT devices and communicates with the cloud as a client and with the IoT devices as a cloud, as shown in Figure 2. When an IoT device attempts to connect to a cloud service in order to send or request some data, it first connects to the Internet using one of the Internet access protocols, such as 5G or WPA3. The IoT crypto gateway creates an Internet connection with the IoT device and starts to establish it in order to receive the data from the IoT device and transmit it to the cloud. Since QUIC does not support all TLS versions, the gateway is restricted to secure the communication with the IoT devices using TLS 1.3 and above. On the other side, the gateway secures the communication implementing TLS 1.2 and above. However, for the reason that the transport layer (TCP-like) and TLS are integrated in QUIC, the IoT devices exchange less packets with the gateway. Hence, the battery life, the CPU computations and the resource usage in the IoT devices side may be better optimized. We summarize the benefits of our approach in TABLE I.

TABLE I. THE PROPOSED IMPLEMENTATION COMPARED WITH TRADITIONAL CONNECTIONS SECURED DIRECTLY WITH TLS.

#	IoT devices secured via QUIC	via TLS directly
Security	high	high
Latency	lower	longer
Resource usage	lower	higher
Battery life	longer	shorter
Computations	lower	higher

The IoT crypto gateway establishes the connection using TCP and communicates with the cloud implementing MQTT over TLS (see Figure 4). At the same time, the IoT crypto gateway communicates with the IoT devices implementing MQTT over IETF QUIC (+ TLS). Thus, the crypto gateway should perform with both peers and transmit the packets almost simultaneously.

Assuming an MQTT-Publish message must be sent from one of the IoT devices to the cloud. Since TLS is integrated in

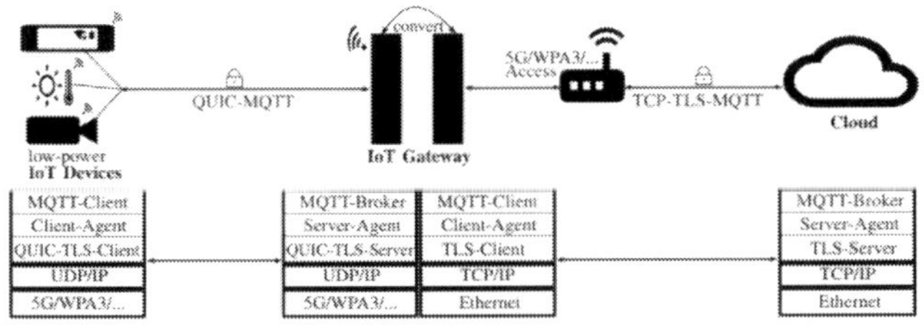

Figure 4. The IoT crypto gateway secures the connection between both peers implementing different layer protocols.

QUIC, the client can start to communicate with the gateway by sending its first packet ClientHello (CH), which is contained in the first QUIC message and should then be resent to the cloud. The gateway initiates establishing a TCP connection with the cloud and sends its CH message. Additionally, the gateway checks the CH packet sent from the client and performs a full TLS handshake if there was no previous connection with the peers before and a resumed TLS handshake using PSKs if the peers have connected with each other before. As a server, the gateway completes establishing the QUIC connection with the IoT device. Furthermore, as a client, the gateway completes the connection with the server implementing TLS over TCP (see Figure 5). The gateway may perform mutual authentication with both peers in order to hand high security for the IoT devices and may frequently use PSKs (TLS-PSK) with the IoT devices in order to optimize their performance. In addition, the gateway communicates with both peers individually and may therefore use different TLS versions, parameters and RTTs at the same time. Finally, the IoT device can communicate MQTT and send its MQTT-Publish message to the gateway, which will be sent to the server.

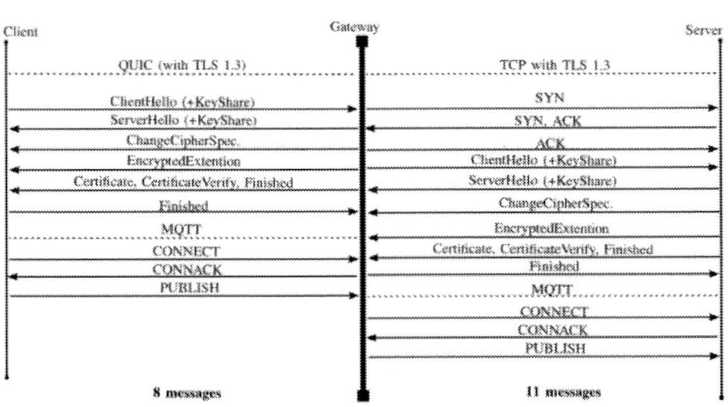

(a) Packets exchange using a full TLS 1.3 handshake.

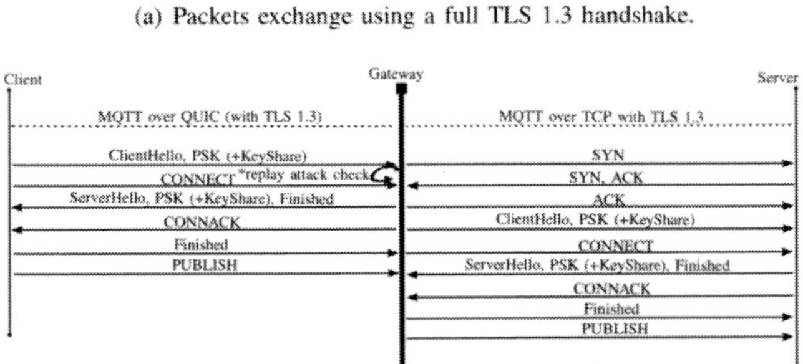

(b) Packets exchange using a TLS-PSK 1.3 handshake.

Figure 5. Illustrations of the IoT crypto gateway packets exchange between the IoT client and the cloud service assuming only one side authentication.

In case of using the TLS-PSK mechanism, the IoT gateway should check if the connection is a replay attack against the cloud and interrupt the connection/return back to a full TLS handshake if it is needed. In order to discover a replay attack, the IoT crypto gateway should implement one of the following three mechanisms: saving the session tickets which can be used once only and rejecting duplicates, recording a unique value (e.g., the random value) derived from the CH packets and refusing duplicates, or refusing old packets by checking the time in the CH packets to efficiently determine whether a CH was sent recently or it was an old packet. Furthermore, the IoT crypto gateway may check the validation of the PSKs, HMACs and signatures and interrupt/retry the connection if it is needed [15] [18].

V. Conclusion and Future Work

This paper proposed a cryptographic gateway between low-power IoT devices and a cloud service, which connects the device to the cloud service with a high security level while at the same time saving considerable resources on the side of IoT devices by using a transparent cryptographic gateway.

The proposed gateway opens in direction of the cloud a fully-fledged authenticated TLS tunnel and in direction of the IoT device a TLS connection using the new (IETF) QUIC protocol which exchanges less packets and employs after the first handshake a PSK. As a result, peers are able to establish a TLS connection with less resources for the IoT devices. Thus, the gateway may save time, power and computation on the IoT device's side without compromising security.

The QUIC protocol is still a work in progress by IETF, which forces adding changes in this project continously and makes the implementation of it difficult. Cases, such as authentication and certificates handling between the peers, are still under research and development. Nevertheless, as a next step, a proof of concept implementation is in plan.

Acknowledgement

This paper is a part of the BMBF-funded project "Lernlabor Cybersicherheit" at Ostbayerische Technische Hochschule (OTH) Amberg-Weiden in cooperation with Fraunhofer AISEC.

References

[1] F. Alkhabbas, R. Spalazzese, M. Cerioli, M. Leotta, and G. Reggio, "On the Deployment of IoT Systems: An Industrial Survey," in 2020 IEEE International Conference on Software Architecture Companion (ICSA-C), May 2020, pp. 17–24, retrieved: August 2020. [Online]. Available: https://ieeexplore.ieee.org/abstract/document/9095740

[2] Research and Markets (The world's largest market research store), "Industrial Internet of Things (IIoT) Market Size, Share & Trends Analysis Report by Component, by End Use (Manufacturing, Energy & Power, Oil & Gas, Healthcare, Logistics & Transport, Agriculture), and Segment Forecasts, 2019 - 2025," June 2019, retrieved: August 2020. [Online]. Available: https://www.researchandmarkets.com/reports/4240418/industrial-internet-of-things-iiot-market-size

[3] Federal Bureau of Investigation, "Internet of Things Poses Opportunities for Cyber Crime," Federal Bureau of Investigation, September 2015.

[4] BSI, "BSI - SYS: IT-Systeme - SYS.4.4 Allgemeines IoT-Gerät," retrieved: August 2020. [Online]. Available: https://www.bsi.bund.de/DE/Themen/ITGrundschutz/ITGrundschutzKompendium/bausteine/SYS/SYS_4_4_Allgemeines_IoT-Ger%C3%A4t.html

[5] BSI, "BSI - IT-Grundschutz-Kompendium - Umsetzungshinweise zum Baustein SYS.4.4 Allgemeines IoT-Gerät," retrieved: August 2020. [Online]. Available: https://www.bsi.bund.de/DE/Themen/ITGrundschutz/ITGrundschutzKompendium/umsetzungshinweise/

SYS/Umsetzungshinweise_zum_Baustein_SYS_4_4_Allgemeines_IoT-Ger%C3%A4t.html

[6] BSI, "Sicherheit von Geräten im Internet der Dinge," retrieved: August 2020. [Online]. Available: https://www.allianz-fuer-cybersicherheit.de/ACS/DE/_/downloads/BSI-CS/BSI-CS_128.pdf?__blob=publicationFile&v=10

[7] W. HuiYu, Q. Wenxiang, and L. Yuxiang, "Breaking Smart Speaker: We are Listening to You," August 2018, Tencent Blade Team.

[8] A. Hameed and A. Alomary, "Security Issues in IoT: A Survey," in 2019 International Conference on Innovation and Intelligence for Informatics, Computing, and Technologies (3ICT), 2019, pp. 1–5, retrieved: August 2020. [Online]. Available: https://ieeexplore.ieee.org/abstract/document/8910320

[9] I. Alqassem and D. Svetinovic, "A Taxonomy of Security and Privacy Requirements for the Internet of Things (IoT)," in 2014 IEEE International Conference on Industrial Engineering and Engineering Management. Selangor Darul Ehsan, Malaysia: IEEE, December 2014, pp. 1244–1248, retrieved: August 2020. [Online]. Available: http://ieeexplore.ieee.org/document/7058837/

[10] S. Oh and Y. Kim, "Security Requirements Analysis for the IoT," in 2017 International Conference on Platform Technology and Service (PlatCon), March 2017, pp. 1–6, retrieved: August 2020. [Online]. Available: https://ieeexplore.ieee.org/abstract/document/7883727

[11] U. Singh and I. Chana, "Enhancing Energy Efficiency in IoT (Internet of Thing) Based Application," in Inventive Computation Technologies, ser. Lecture Notes in Networks and Systems, S. Smys, R. Bestak, and A. Rocha, Eds. Cham: Springer International Publishing, November 2019, pp. 161–173.

[12] Z. Zhang et al., "IoT Security: Ongoing Challenges and Research Opportunities," in 2014 IEEE 7th International Conference on Service-Oriented Computing and Applications, 2014, pp. 230–234, retrieved: August 2020. [Online]. Available: https://ieeexplore.ieee.org/document/6978614

[13] G. Matsemela, S. Rimer, K. Ouahada, R. Ndjiongue, and Z. Mngomezulu, "Internet of Things Data Integrity," in 2017 IST-Africa Week Conference (IST-Africa), November 2017, pp. 1–9, retrieved: August 2020. [Online]. Available: https://ieeexplore.ieee.org/document/8102332

[14] R. Roman, C. Alcaraz, J. Lopez, and N. Sklavos, "Key Management Systems for Sensor Networks in the Context of the Internet of Things," Computers & Electrical Engineering, vol. 37, no. 2, March 2011, pp. 147–159.

[15] E. Rescorla, "The Transport Layer Security (TLS) Protocol Version 1.3," Internet Engineering Task Force, August 2018, RFC 8446, retrieved: August 2020. [Online]. Available: https://tools.ietf.org/html/rfc8446

[16] K. Moriarty and S. Farrell, "Deprecating TLSv1.0 and TLSv1.1," Internet Engineering Task Force, Internet-Draft, January 2020, work in Progress,retrieved: August 2020. [Online]. Available: https://datatracker.ietf.org/doc/html/draft-ietf-tls-oldversions-deprecate

[17] J. Iyengar and M. Thomson, "QUIC: A UDP-Based Multiplexed and Secure Transport," Internet Engineering Task Force, Internet-Draft, June 2020, Work in Progress, retrieved: August 2020. [Online]. Available: https://datatracker.ietf.org/doc/html/draft-ietf-quic-transport-29

[18] M. Thomson and S. Turner, "Using TLS to Secure QUIC," Internet Engineering Task Force, Internet-Draft, June 2020, work in Progress, retrieved: August 2020. [Online]. Available: https://datatracker.ietf.org/doc/html/draft-ietf-quic-tls-29

[19] P. Kumar and B. Dezfouli, "Implementation and analysis of QUIC for MQTT," Computer Networks, vol. 150, February 2019, pp. 28–45.

[20] The Chromium Projects, "QUIC, a multiplexed stream transport over UDP - The Chromium Projects," library Catalog: www.chromium.org, retrieved: August 2020. [Online]. Available: https://www.chromium.org/quic

[21] E. Rescorla and N. Modadugu, "Datagram Transport Layer Security Version 1.2," RFC 6347, Internet Engineering Task Force, June 2012, retrieved: August 2020. [Online]. Available: https://rfc-editor.org/rfc/rfc6347.txt

[22] E. Rescorla, H. Tschofenig, and N. Modadugu, "The Datagram Transport Layer Security (DTLS) Protocol Version 1.3," Internet Engineering Task Force, Internet-Draft, May 2020, work in Progress, retrieved: August 2020. [Online]. Available: https://datatracker.ietf.org/doc/html/draft-ietf-tls-dtls13-38

[23] M. B. Yassein, M. Q. Shatnawi, and D. Al-zoubi, "Application Layer Protocols for the Internet of Things: A Survey," in 2016 International Conference on Engineering MIS (ICEMIS), September 2016, pp. 1–4.

[24] A. Talaminos-Barroso, M. A. Estudillo-Valderrama, L. M. Roa, J. Reina-Tosina, and F. Ortega-Ruiz, "A Machine-to-Machine Protocol Benchmark for eHealth Applications – Use Case: Respiratory Rehabilitation," Computer Methods and Programs in Biomedicine, vol. 129, June 2016, pp. 1–11.

[25] A. Banks and R. Gupta, "MQTT Version 3.1.1," October 2014, retrieved: August 2020. [Online]. Available: http://docs.oasis-open.org/mqtt/mqtt/v3.1.1/os/mqtt-v3.1.1-os.html

[26] Mitmproxy, "mitmproxy - an interactive HTTPS proxy," retrieved: August 2020. [Online]. Available: https://mitmproxy.org/

[27] NGINX, "nginx-quic: log," retrieved: August 2020. [Online]. Available: https://hg.nginx.org/nginx-quic/shortlog

[28] M. Bishop, "Hypertext Transfer Protocol Version 3 (HTTP/3)," Internet Engineering Task Force, Internet-Draft, June 2020, work in Progress, retrieved: August 2020. [Online]. Available: https://datatracker.ietf.org/doc/html/draft-ietf-quic-http-29

[29] NGINX, "Introducing a Technology Preview of NGINX Support for QUIC and HTTP/3," June 2020, library Catalog: www.nginx.com, retrieved: August 2020. [Online]. Available: https://www.nginx.com/blog/introducing-technology-preview-nginx-support-for-quic-http-3/

[30] OpenSSL, "QUIC and OpenSSL," February 2020, retrieved: August 2020. [Online]. Available: https://www.openssl.org/blog/blog/2020/02/17/QUIC-and-OpenSSL/

[31] D. Stenberg, "QUIC with wolfSSL," June 2020, retrieved: August 2020. [Online]. Available: https://daniel.haxx.se/blog/2020/06/18/quic-with-wolfssl/

[32] A. Tewari and B. B. Gupta, "A Robust Anonymity Preserving Authentication Protocol for IoT Devices," in 2018 IEEE International Conference on Consumer Electronics (ICCE), January 2018, pp. 1–5, retrieved: August 2020. [Online]. Available: https://ieeexplore.ieee.org/document/8326282

[33] J. King and A. I. Awad, "A Distributed Security Mechanism for Resource-Constrained IoT Devices," Informatica, vol. 40, no. 1, February 2016, retrieved: August 2020. [Online]. Available: http://www.informatica.si/index.php/informatica/article/view/1046

[34] W. Razouk, D. Sgandurra, and K. Sakurai, "A New Security Middleware Architecture based on Fog Computing and Cloud to Support IoT Constrained Devices," October 2017, pp. 1–8.

[35] NGINX, "Improve IoT Security with NGINX Plus: Encrypt & Authenticate MQTT," March 2017, library Catalog: www.nginx.com, retrieved: August 2020. [Online]. Available: https://www.nginx.com/blog/nginx-plus-iot-security-encrypt-authenticate-mqtt/

[36] O. Rajaee, "IoT, Resource Constrained Devices, Security," February 2017, conference: RSA 2017, at: San Francisco, CA.

[37] S. Andy, B. Rahardjo, and B. Hanindhito, "Attack Scenarios and Security Analysis of MQTT Communication Protocol in IoT System," in 2017 4th International Conference on Electrical Engineering, Computer Science and Informatics (EECSI), 2017, pp. 1–6.

[38] G. Perrone, M. Vecchio, R. Pecori, and R. Giaffreda, "The Day After Mirai: A Survey on MQTT Security Solutions After the Largest Cyber-attack Carried Out through an Army of IoT Devices:," in Proceedings of the 2nd International Conference on Internet of Things, Big Data and Security. Porto, Portugal: SCITEPRESS - Science and Technology Publications, 2017, pp. 246–253.

Reliable Fleet Analytics for Edge IoT Solutions

Emmanuel Raj
AI Center of Excellence
TietoEVRY
Keilalahdentie 2-4, 02150 Espoo, Finland
emmanuelraj7@gmail.com

Magnus Westerlund
Department of Business and Analytics
Arcada University of Applied Sciences
Jan-Magnus Janssonin aukio 1, 00560 Helsinki, Finland
magnus.westerlund@arcada.fi

Leonardo Espinosa-Leal
Department of Business and Analytics
Arcada University of Applied Sciences
Jan-Magnus Janssonin aukio 1, 00560 Helsinki, Finland
leonardo.espinosaleal@arcada.fi

Abstract—**In recent years we have witnessed a boom in Internet of Things (IoT) device deployments, which has resulted in big data and demand for low-latency communication. This shift in the demand for infrastructure is also enabling real-time decision making using artificial intelligence for IoT applications. Artificial Intelligence of Things (AIoT) is the combination of Artificial Intelligence (AI) technologies and the IoT infrastructure to provide robust and efficient operations and decision making. Edge computing is emerging to enable AIoT applications. Edge computing enables generating insights and making decisions at or near the data source, reducing the amount of data sent to the cloud or a central repository. In this paper, we propose a framework for facilitating machine learning at the edge for AIoT applications, to enable continuous delivery, deployment, and monitoring of machine learning models at the edge (Edge MLOps). The contribution is an architecture that includes services, tools, and methods for delivering fleet analytics at scale. We present a preliminary validation of the framework by performing experiments with IoT devices on a university campus's rooms. For the machine learning experiments, we forecast multivariate time series for predicting air quality in the respective rooms by using the models deployed in respective edge devices. By these experiments, we validate the proposed fleet analytics framework for efficiency and robustness.**

Keywords–Fleet Analytics; Edge Computing; Machine Learning; Internet of Things; AI

I. INTRODUCTION

In the last years, we have seen a surge in cloud computing, making it a vital part of businesses and IT infrastructures. The paradigm offers benefits to organizations such as no need to buy and maintain infrastructure, less technical in-house expertise required, scaling, robust services, and pay as you go features. Organizations can now centrally store massive amounts of data and optimize computational resources to deliver on their data processing needs, which depict the change from localized computing (own servers and data centers) to centralized computing (in the cloud). Cloud computing is today an industry that has enabled many new opportunities in terms of computation, visualization, and storage capacities [1]. However, cloud computing has also introduced significant security and data privacy issues and challenges [2]; it is essential to critically assess limitations, alternative designs, and develop an overall understanding of ecosystem design [3].

With the advent of big data, mobile devices (self-driving cars, mobiles, etc.), and industrial IoT, there is now an increasing emphasis on local processing of information to enable instantaneous decision making. We are witnessing a shift in trend from conceptually centralized cloud computing to decentralized computing. Here, *Edge Computing* is the process of performing computing tasks physically close to target devices, rather than in the cloud [4], [5]. It enables extracting knowledge, insights, and making decisions near the data origin quickly, secure, and local, which facilitates decentralized processing. Edge computing also enables data confidentiality and privacy preservation, something that is becoming essential across multiple industries. The growing amount of (IoT) data and the associated limitations of using cloud computing (networking, computation, and storage) are currently drivers for decentralized systems, such as Edge Computing.

To achieve a computing approach that considers resource optimization in terms of energy, efficiency, operational costs, and human resources, we need a shift from pure cloud computing to a more nuanced architecture that provides sustainable computing resources and infrastructure for organizations to run their services [6], [7]. Green IT, where energy and resource optimization are essential, has also been extended to Green IoT [8]. Hence, we see investments from the public and private sectors going towards building smart solutions and cities that enable smart societies [6]. In use-cases where sensitive data is handled or require low latency delays, cloud computing may not be a perfect solution.

With examples such as big data, self-driving cars, and IoT, there is an increasing emphasis on local processing of information to enable instantaneous decision making using AI, also called the Artificial Intelligence of Things (AIoT) [9], [10]. Edge computing can unlock the potential for making real-time decisions or extract knowledge near the data origin in a resource-efficient and secure manner [4]. Edge computing has gradually emerged from the client/server architecture; for example, in the late 1990s [11] showed how resource constrained mobile devices could offload some of their processing needs to servers. Later the Content Delivery Network (CDN) was launched by Akamai [12] and certain notorious peer-to-peer networks. Since then, there have been major developments in cloud computing, edge computing, IoT, and low latency

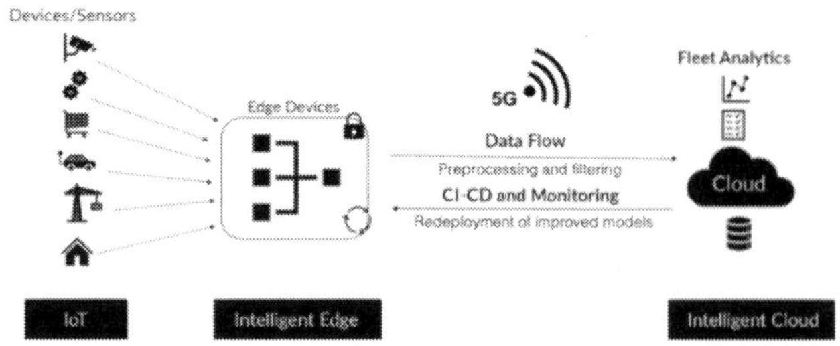

Figure 1. Intelligent edge and Intelligent cloud powered by 5G networks

networks. When Akamai launched its CDN the idea was to introduce nodes at locations geographically closer to the end-user to deliver cached content such as images and videos. Today many companies utilize a similar approach for speech recognition services and other AI-enabled or processing heavy services.

A massive growth in IoT device deployments, as of 2018, there was an estimated 22B devices [13], has not happened without significant security challenges. To manage the scale of IoT device deployments, edge computing will play an important role. The aim is to promote IoT scalability and robustness in order to handle a huge number of IoT devices and big data volumes for real-time low-latency applications while avoiding introducing new security threats. Edge computing is increasingly defined as performing data processing on nearby compute devices that interface with sensors or other data origins [4]. Edge-based IoT solutions must cover a broad scope of requirements while focusing on scalability and robustness through resource distribution.

The structure of the paper is the following. Section II, expounds the design demands for creating Artificial Intelligence of Things. In Section III, we review the AIoT design support methodologies and practices. Section IV, defines our modular design framework for fleet analytics, and in Section V, we discuss a validation of our framework. Section VI concludes the paper with a note about future work.

II. Scalability and Reliability for AIoT

In order to perform computing close to the data source and to offload centralized computing to a decentralized infrastructure, require explicit and well formalized processes. Edge computing means we should apply different machine learning algorithms at the edge, enabling new kinds of experiences and new kinds of opportunities across many industries, ranging from mobility, connected home, security, surveillance, and automotive. Further, edge computing may also enable secure and reliable performance for data processing and coordination of multiple devices [14]. Figure 1 depicts an overview diagram of how a secure and reliable intelligent edge architecture is constructed.

Reliability for distributed systems demands strict protocols that each node adheres to. Reliability, as defined by Adkins *et al.* [15], is considered a distinct topic from security, although sharing several properties. Reliability is a demanding task that must be considered early in the planning phase to capture the emerging properties and continuously capture requirements for achieving reliability that may evolve in time. Reliability for today's landscape involves other considerations than purely technical ones. The main driver for reliable edge solutions may be the increase of regional legislation in the digital space [16].

TABLE I. Design reasons and considerations for utilizing fleet analytics for edge IoT solutions.

Concept	*Description*	*Reference*
Local compliance	Regional regulations e.g. for privacy and security may be easier to implement with localized computing.	[16]
Service level	Meeting service level objectives for IoT networks may require precise measurements at the edge to monitor decision making and feedback loops on the physical plane.	[14]
Ease of use	Building a reliable decoupled system may require a design where data is processed close to the IoT node. Thus, avoiding transferring data to a different backend environment.	[16]
System stability	Stability under heavy load demands scalability and throughput, for distributed systems this means that single point of failure designs must be avoided.	[4]
System safety	Systems that interact with their surroundings may benefit from physical proximity to models and supervising algorithms in order to speed up decision making. This demands well-formed streaming pipelines that consider freshness, correctness, and coverage.	[14]

TABLE II. Design planes for fleet analytics in edge IoT solutions.

Plane	*Description*
Hardware	Telemetry from devices and their sensors may help us monitor the device itself and the environment the device resides in.
AI	The use of machine learning means that the systems must be continuously monitored during their operation.
Service	Operational support methods help to deploy and maintain a reliable fleet analytics solution.

IoT systems' distributed nature means that dependencies between nodes should be avoided while striving for integrating automated redundancy when designing systems. In Table I, we summarize some of the considerations for building edge IoT solutions that include fleet analytics. Fleet analytics is still an emerging field of research, and in the absence of direct references, we provide general references for each topic.

In Table II, we separate the design considerations further into three different planes. First, the hardware plane that the IoT device is implemented on. Here we should note that a multitude of designs exist, some with considerable processing power limited mainly by a thermal dissipation to systems on a chip (SOC) running on battery power. The second plane is represented by the AI models processing the data and interactions that the IoT device captures. These models are susceptible to drift among many other issues, meaning that both the input and output should always be monitored for any statistical abnormalities. Third, is the service plane where decision making and reliability automation come together.

III. Operational Support Methodologies

To understand the need for Fleet analytics is vital to turn an eye to software development practices starting from DevOps to DataOps to MLOps.

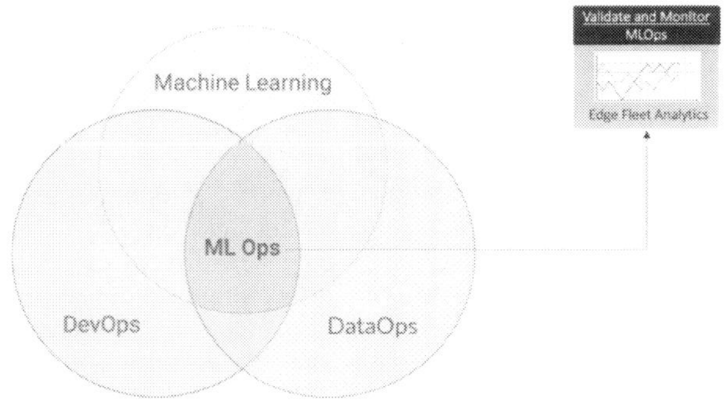

Figure 2. Need for Edge Fleet Analytics Framework

A. DevOps

DevOps extends Agile development practices by streamlining software changes through the build, test, deploy, and delivery stages. DevOps empowers cross-functional teams with the autonomy to execute on their software applications, driven by continuous integration, continuous deployment, and continuous delivery. It encourages collaboration, integration, and automation among software developers and IT operators to improve efficiency, speed, and quality of delivering customer centric software. DevOps provides a streamlined software development framework for designing, testing, deploying, and monitoring production systems. DevOps has made it possible to ship software to production in minutes and keep it running reliably [17].

B. DataOps

DataOps refers to practices centered around data operations that bring speed, agility, and reproducibility for end-to-end data pipelines. The DataOps process considers the entire data life cycle activities and is derived from DevOps. The business aim of DataOps is to achieve data quality from optimized data pipelines by utilizing automated orchestration and monitoring of processes. DataOps practices assume that data will be processed further in various analytics-based setups [18].

C. MLOps

Software development is an interdisciplinary field and is evolving to facilitate machine learning in production use. MLOps is an emerging method to fuse machine learning engineering with software development. MLOps combines Machine Learning, DevOps, and Data Engineering, and aims to build, deploy, and maintain machine learning models in production reliably and efficiently. Thus, MLOps can be expounded by this intersection, as depicted in Figure 2. MLOps was defined in [19] as 1) dealing with continuous training and serving, 2) monitoring solutions, 3) high level of automation, and 4) an orchestrated environment for model validation. MLOps is still only an emerging operational support method. However, the need to establish operational trust towards ML models and integrate machine learning with software development speaks in MLOps favor.

IV. Fleet Analytics for IoT Networked Devices

To manage distributed IoT systems (aka. fleet management), we have implemented a fleet analytics framework that allows us to address the three different operational support methodologies in a unified way. Fleet analytics for distributed IoT systems arises from the necessity to continuously validate and monitor the operational methods whose distributed nature makes them somewhat different from traditional development. Thus, we introduce a robust and reliable fleet analytics framework that can be used in production environments.

Fleet analytics enables validation and monitoring of edge devices (via telemetry data), sensor data, and machine learning models. Fleet analytics provides a continuous holistic and analytical view of the health of the system. The aim has been to automate the monitoring and orchestration of devices. An important goal has been to create a framework for fleet analytics that maintains high reliability for the system. In Figure 3, we propose a modular design framework. We want to acknowledge that the framework is still a work in progress and is not complete. The proposed framework intends to clarify the design components of the proposed system.

A. Framework proposal

The framework proposes a triune approach to fleet analytics for edge computing driven by MLOps. To validate and monitor the edge computing system is vital to monitor the analytics process, supervision (system actions and performance), and device health.

1) Analytics Process: The analytics process is key to driving the decisions and actions of the system. Hence it is vital to monitor the analytics process end-to-end. This means starting from data processing, training the machine learning model, deploying and monitoring the models on edge devices. We have separated the analytics process into three operations: the *modeling approach*, the *decision making*, and the continued upkeep that we refer to as *automated accountability*. To synchronize these three operations, MLOps provides a method for orchestrating the transfer of machine learning models in the system and to devices, while also assisting in the continued monitoring of the system. MLOps empowers data scientists and application developers to develop and bring machine learning models to production, that for an edge setup like ours, means that models may be trained on shared, dedicated machinery. At the same time, the inference is performed at the outermost edge close to the recording sensor or actuator. MLOps thereby enables a systematic approach to track, version control, audit, certify, and re-use every asset in the ML life cycle. By providing orchestration services for infrastructure, MLOps streamlines the life cycle management of edge solutions. To track and monitor the analytics process as part of fleet analytics holistically, we observe these following aspects:

a) Modeling approach: This aspect of the analytics process defines the machine learning model setup and enables training, evaluation, and testing (fitness) for production. In some instances, it may involve ensembles and arranging models logically to specify well formed processing pipelines.

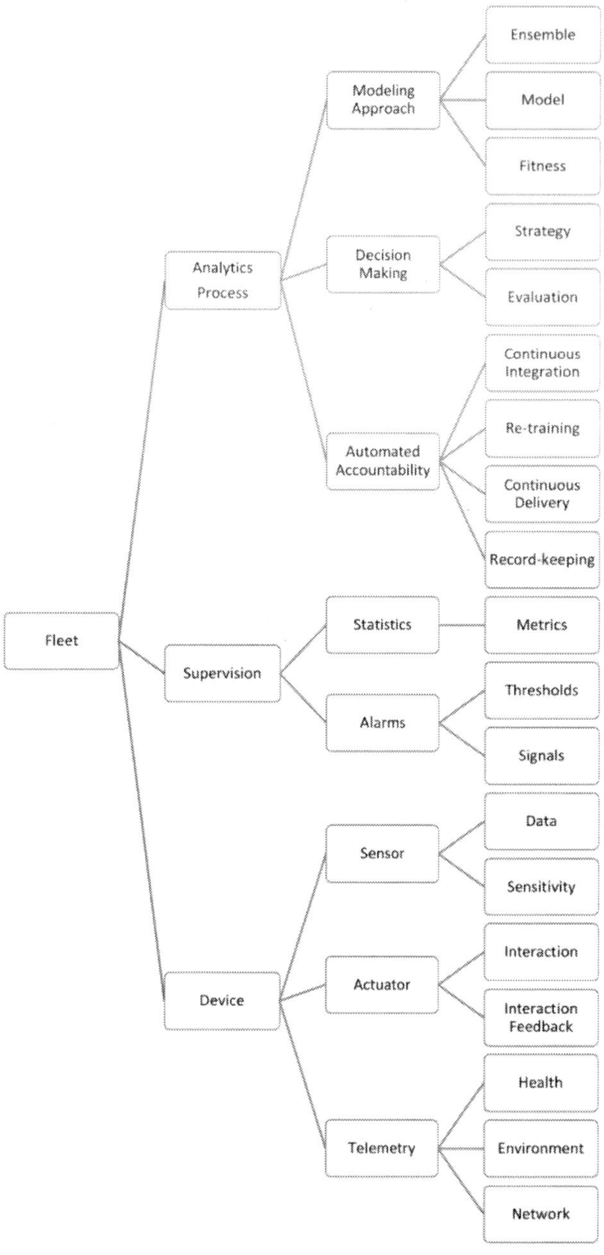

Figure 3. A modular design framework for a fleet analytics system.

b) Decision making: The modeling approach utilizes a set of query inputs and produces inference from experience stored in the knowledge base or training data (used to train the models). The decision making operations enables the system to interact with the environment and to introduce expert knowledge. For high-impact decisions, such as automated system operation, that can impact human well-being or damage property or the environment, it is prudent to introduce fail-safe measures so that the model output is confined within a trusted decision space. The key to good decision making is defining a decision making strategy that includes planning, formulation, implementation of various methods, and workflows. When a decision making strategy is implemented, it is essential to track and monitor the progression over time to ensure an efficient and reliable performance for the complete system.

c) Automated Accountability: When the human element is introduced into the design of decision support systems, entirely new layers of social and ethical issues emerge but are not always recognized as such. Hence, automating operations is intended to reduce these issues and the dependence on human ad-hoc interaction. Some key drivers of automation are continuous integration and continuous deployment because they enable the ability to automate model retraining and deployment of the latest models according to the latest system developments and data. Such practices should reduce the occurrence of human error or need to maintain direct human oversight of system developers. With proper auditing and record-keeping, it is efficient to monitor and debug the system's continued operations.

2) Supervision: Having a reliable supervision strategy in place is vital for the efficient functioning of machine learning driven systems. Systems are supervised statistically using metrics defined to monitor the performance. As decision making is an essential behavior of an analytics-based system, decisions also need to be supervised and monitored to avoid any unnecessary failures and harmful system interactions. System alarms can be created for critical decisions or failures using thresholds and signals. Such alarms can provide human supervisors with an asynchronous method for ensuring robust system performance.

3) Device: There are typically several types of devices in a complete system; here we reduce the types to three different types. Sensors that provide measurement data of the environment, actuators that perform actions, and telemetry data sources that can measure both physical and virtual properties that provide meta information about the functioning system. DataOps practices can be used to automate data collection and provide reproducibility and end-to-end data pipelines.

Monitoring the health and performance of edge and IoT nodes is essential to avoid any system's unexpected failures. Telemetry data from the nodes is an important part of fleet analytics. Telemetry data ensures that the devices are running as intended and that any potential failures can be predicted in advance and addressed before they occur. Telemetry data offers diagnostic insights into the device health, environment, and network. This data provides valuable insight into the health and environment of the IoT devices, actuators, and edge devices, which can be used to automate much of their operation through fleet analytics. As we consider, Fleet analytics is not complete without comprehensive device data in the form of telemetry data for ensuring data quality and integrity. This is also a reason for considering DataOPS as an operational support method for fleet analytics.

V. Experimental Framework Validation

To validate the fleet analytics framework and design, we have implemented a system and conducted a live experiment for 45 days. We use three IoT devices and three edge devices for performing inference from machine learning models to predict the air quality inside three rooms during this process. Each room had one IoT device or sensor that measured the

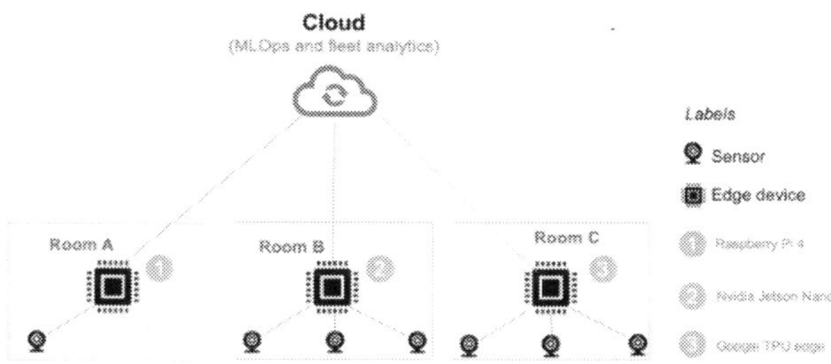

Figure 4. Experimental setup

room's air quality conditions and one edge device to deploy the ML models to and for predicting the changes in the air quality (see Figure 4).

Machine learning models were trained based on three months of historical data from each room, and posteriorly they are deployed on the edge devices in the rooms. The machine learning models used were Multiple Linear Regression (MLR), Support Vector Regressor (SVR), Extreme Learning Machines (ELM), and Random Forest Regressor (RFR). The goal was to predict air quality 15 minutes into the future, inside each room.

A. *Analytics Process*

In this subsection, we discuss in detail the analytics process following our design framework. The experiment included data processing, training of machine learning models, deployment of machine learning models, and the monitoring of models on edge devices.

1) Modeling Approach: In the experiment, we perform multivariate time-series analyses to predict the air quality 15 minutes into the future inside a particular room. With this information, building maintainers could be alerted of possible lousy air quality that needs to be addressed to provide a positive experience for people in the room. For the time being, there is not an integration of the experimental setup with an actuator or the building HVAC system. The collected raw data was sampled every 5 minutes and assembled from 3 months before the experiment. Data column descriptors are listed below. Table III provides some descriptive measures for the data set.

The data descriptors for data collected from IoT devices and their respective data types are shown below:

- *timestamp* - Sampling time (datetime)
- *name* - Name of sensor (str)
- *room* - The room where the sensor is placed or origin of the data (str)
- *room type* - Type of room (str)
- *floor* - Floor where data was generated (str)
- *air quality* - Air quality index altered (float)
- *air quality static* - Air quality index unaltered (float)
- *ambient light* - Light level in the room (float)

TABLE III. DESCRIPTIVE STATISTICS FOR AIR QUALITY INDEX (RANGING FROM 0-500) IN SELECTED ROOMS.

Selected Rooms			
Room name	Room type	Unhealthy air quality frequency	Avg. air quality index (AQI)
Room A10	Office room	2033	61.92
Room A29	Meeting Room	2205	61.40
Room A30	Meeting Room	1085	55.45

- *humidity* - Humidity in the room (float)
- *iaq accuracy* - Indoor Air Quality index altered (float)
- *iaq accuracy static* - Indoor air quality index unaltered (float)
- *pressure* - Pressure in the room (float)
- *temperature* - Temperature in the room (float)

After assessing each room's air quality time-series data, no trend or seasonality was observed in air quality data for any room. However, there is a change over time in the mean, variance, and covariance. To proceed, we extract meaningful features by performing feature analysis and selection.

Feature Extraction: After exploring data and identifying patterns, we found some data parameters or columns that were correlated to the air quality in the rooms. Based on the data analysis, we chose the following parameters or columns for training the machine learning algorithms: *air quality static*, *ambient light*, *humidity iaq accuracy static*, *pressure*, and *temperature*. In order to predict air quality, we added a label column *future air quality* by shifting the column *air quality static* three rows ahead. We also performed a standardization technique for feature scaling, that re-scales the feature value so that it has a distribution with 0 as the mean value and the variance equals 1. With these new features and scaled data, we were ready to start training our machine learning model.

Model Training: We trained four machine learning models on the historical data to predict a future air quality value 15 minutes into the future. To train the models, we perform a 10-fold cross-validation. After assessing each model's performance models were ranked based on performance and is presented here in ascending order:

1) Multiple Linear Regression (MLR)
2) Support Vector Regressor (SVR)
3) Extreme Learning Machines (ELM)
4) Random Forest Regressor (RFR)

Model packaging: To make machine learning inference at the edge and resource-heavy training on dedicated hardware, we have to orchestrate the artifacts by serializing, packaging, and redistributing them to where they are needed. The two primary artifacts considered here are:

- We used a standardization technique for feature scaling to transform our training data. Similarly, we have to scale incoming input data for model inference to predict future air quality. For this purpose, we serialized the feature scaling object to a pickle file (.pkl).

TABLE IV. MODEL TRAINING RESULTS.

Model Training Results			
Room name	Algorithm	Cross Validation RMSE (train)	Test RMSE
Room A10	MLR	5.020	5.875
Room A10	ELM	6.325	6.208
Room A10	RFR	10.710	9.987
Room A10	SVR	6.046	5.977
Room A29	MLR	5.362	4.158
Room A29	ELM	11.202	4.223
Room A29	RFR	11.676	9.208
Room A29	SVR	8.073	4.176
Room A30	MLR	3.648	3.551
Room A30	ELM	7.920	3.895
Room A30	RFR	9.686	7.720
Room A30	SVR	5.177	3.55

- Machine learning models: All trained and retrained ML models are serialized in the Open Neural Network Exchange (ONNX) format. ONNX is an open ecosystem for interoperable AI models. This means serialization of ML and deep learning models into a standard format (.onnx). With this, all trained or retrained models and parameter artifacts are ready to be exported and deployed to test or production environments.

2) Decision making: A properly designed decision making strategy is key to making a system interact with the environment safely. Our strategy was to detect when air quality anomalies occur. The anomalies preceded a situation when a particular room developed uninhabitable conditions. Machine learning models performs regression and a separate layer then detects anomalies.

Evaluation of the strategy was done based on model and system performance. We decide in terms of accuracy of decisions and their usefulness to improve it. From Table IV, we can observe the accuracy of decisions made by the models in terms of the RMSE score. When the detected RMSE value was above 10, a new model was trained on more recent data and deployed to ensure optimal decision making and functioning.

3) Automated accountability: Automated systems enable continuous operations of the system without human or other dependencies. Automation for machine learning based systems is driven by seamless monitoring, continuous integration and continuous delivery as following:

a) Continuous Integration (CI) and Continuous Delivery (CD): Our system is based on multiple edge devices by using continuous integration to ensure model and device freshness. In order to have a seamless continuous integration, two scripts or processes are running inside the docker container deployed in each edge device, as shown in figure 5. These processes orchestrate data pipelines, machine learning, continuous integration, and deployment. The activities of retraining ML models, inference, and monitoring are automated as part of continuous delivery and deployment operations. The two processes are running inside a docker container on each edge device. This way of working is found to provide a reliable system while also being scalable. However, we must note that the implementation is still being revised and improved as this

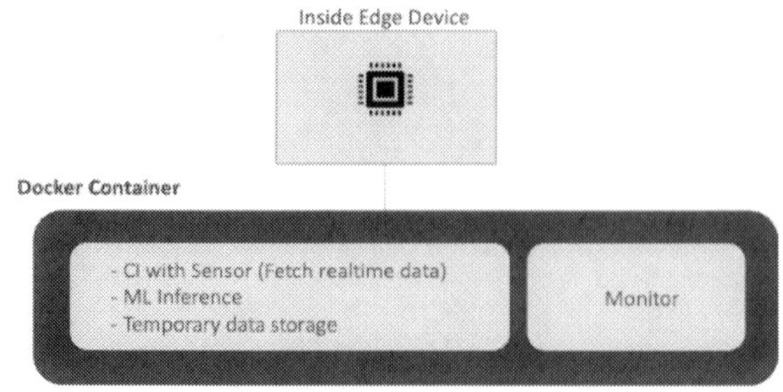

Figure 5. Docker container deployed in each edge device.

is a prototype. In table V, we show the run-time monitoring events that have been detected and handled, as explained in the processes below.

Process 1: This process enables and maintains sensor-to-edge continuous integration by fetching data in real-time. This is done by subscribing to a sensor topic using MQTT protocol. After new data is received from a sensor (which happens every 5 minutes), raw data is pre-processed by discarding or pruning unnecessary data, cleaning, and converting data into features.

A machine learning model previously trained in the cloud is deployed to the edge device inside a docker container. The inference is then made to predict air quality 15 minutes into the future based on variables extracted from sensor data: air quality, ambient light, humidity, iaq accuracy static, pressure, and temperature. After getting a prediction for the real-time data, both sensor data and prediction are concatenated together and appended to a .csv file temporarily stored in the docker container.

Process 2: This process is triggered for monitoring ML model performance at a set time every day (time trigger). When activated, the process evaluates the model drift by evaluating the RMSE for future air quality predictions vs. actual data. If RMSE is greater than or equal to 10, it means that model performance is poor. Hence the process evokes a call to look for and deploy an alternative model from the ML model repository on the cloud.

b) Record keeping: All the models deployed and retrained are end-to-end traceable and reproducible. Auditing and record maintenance enable traceability, validation, explainability (which model is used at a particular time index), reproducibility, and ability to show compliance to data protection regulation.

B. Reliability of fleet analytics

Fleet analytics for the experiment's duration was based on data collected, without any interruptions, from each edge device used in the experiment. Each device's data provided an overview of device performance, based on telemetry data like accelerometer, gyroscope, humidity, magnetometer, pressure, and temperature. Edge device performance was stable overall during the experiment. All decisions were monitored statistically based on defined metrics and thresholds; this enabled the system's comprehensive supervision. The analytics process

TABLE V. ML INFERENCE, CONTINUOUS DELIVERY AND RETRAINING RESULTS.

Realtime machine learning inference at the edge					
S.no	Date of model change	Edge Device	Deployed Model	Model Drift (RMSE)	Model Re-train (RMSE)
1	15-03-2020	Jetson nano 2	ELM	16.39	4.1
2	16-03-2020	Google TPU edge	RFR	14.23	6.3
3	16-03-2020	Raspberry pi 4	MLR	11.91	4.3
4	17-03-2020	Raspberry pi 4	ELM	13.27	8.1
5	22-03-2020	Jetson nano 2	SVR	22.32	6.2
6	24-03-2020	Google TPU edge	RFR	17.11	4.4
7	27-03-2020	Raspberry pi 4	MLR	16.22	4.7
8	29-03-2020	Jetson nano 2	ELM	30.28	8.2
9	30-03-2020	Google TPU edge	SVR	18.12	5.4
10	05-04-2020	Raspberry pi 4	MLR	12.92	3.2
11	10-04-2020	Jetson nano 2	SVR	17.21	5.2
12	11-04-2020	Google TPU edge	MLR	13.42	4.7
13	13-04-2020	Jetson nano 2	ELM	27.29	5.3
14	17-04-2020	Google TPU edge	RFR	17.46	6.9
15	19-04-2020	Raspberry pi 4	SVR	16.32	5.1
16	19-04-2020	Google TPU edge	MLR	11.91	3.4
17	21-04-2020	Jetson nano 2	ELM	23.26	7.3
18	22-04-2020	Google TPU edge	RFR	16.92	7.2
19	24-04-2020	Raspberry pi 4	SVR	17.87	5.2
20	25-04-2020	Google TPU edge	MLR	13.92	5.2
21	25-04-2020	Jetson nano 2	SVR	19.21	7.9
22	26-04-2020	Raspberry pi 4	ELM	23.57	6.4
23	26-04-2020	Google TPU edge	SVR	18.21	5.5

was comprehensively monitored as part of fleet analytics, including model training performance and inference performance in production.

1) Analytics Process: The process of model training, deploying on edge devices, and monitoring the models are covered by Fleet analytics. All models trained and deployed are end to end traceable and auditable in real-time, as seen in the results of the model drift and re-train experiments in Table V. All models trained, deployed, and monitored for fitness were successfully observed without any failures or anomalies. The analytics process implemented for the experiments was based on the strategy devised to make the air quality monitoring system work efficiently with real-time supervision for the analytics process and infrastructure monitoring enabled by fleet analytics.

2) Supervision: System supervision is enabled statistical metrics defined to monitor the business problem. For our experiment, the business problem is forecasting future air quality, looking for signals, and alert using alarms to the building maintenance personnel. In case of future air quality forecasted above 100 aqi the system would alert the users (building maintenance personnel) to regulated air quality in the rooms. For machine learning models, a supervision threshold of 10 RMSE score was set. In case of RMSE crossing 10 RMSE at the end of the day then the model is replaced by another model and retrained on the latest data to improve the model for future use, this process of monitoring the models, deploying for replacing models, and retraining models are automated and enabled by continuous deployment. Fleet analytics (Analytics process) for models performance over time in three edge devices can be observed in Figure 6.

3) Device Analytics: For each device, analytics provided an overview of device performance over some time with telemetry data like accelerometer, gyroscope, humidity, magnetometer, pressure, and temperature. Useful information to monitor edge devices health and longevity, all edge devices' performance was stable overall throughout the experiment without any device failures.

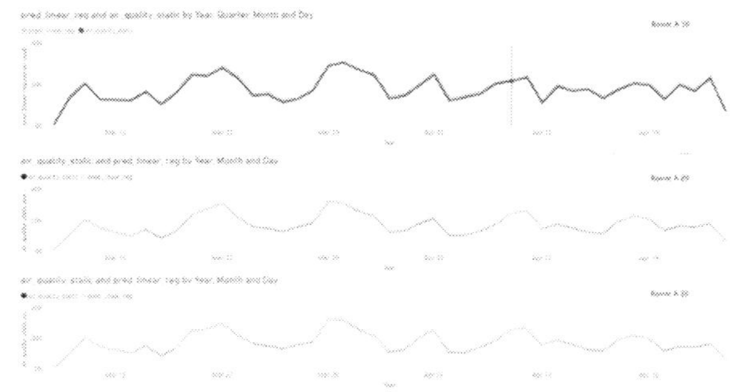

Figure 6. Fleet Analytics - Analytics process

VI. Conclusion

Improving industrial processes using state-of-the-art analytics tools is a challenge despite the plethora of technological advances in IoT. This situation encourages the development of new frameworks with the capacity to bring stability and reliability. This paper presented a novel fleet analytics framework for handling edge IoT devices to improve the decision making process's fleet analytics. Our architecture also allows the user to optimize and scale the process with ease. We tested our framework by four different ML models on three different IoT devices to predict the air quality conditions in different rooms. The obtained results show that our approach is stable and reliable, and the retraining process and deployment was achieved without failure in all edge devices. In the future, we aim to consider scaling targets such as optimization of costs, operational clarity, and resource utilization to facilitate efficient edge-cloud operations at scale. We also plan to explore generalized metrics to evaluate the performance of the proposed framework.

Acknowledgments

E.R. would like to thank TietoEVRY and the 5G-Force project funded by Business Finland. M.W. and L.E.L. thank the support of the Finnish Ministry of Education via the Master ICT for funding.

References

[1] N. Kratzke and P.-C. Quint, "Understanding cloud-native applications after 10 years of cloud computing-a systematic mapping study," Journal of Systems and Software, vol. 126, 2017, pp. 1–16.

[2] S. Singh, Y.-S. Jeong, and J. H. Park, "A survey on cloud computing security: Issues, threats, and solutions," Journal of Network and Computer Applications, vol. 75, 2016, pp. 200–222.

[3] K. Popović and Ž. Hocenski, "Cloud computing security issues and challenges," in The 33rd international convention mipro. IEEE, 2010, pp. 344–349.

[4] W. Shi, J. Cao, Q. Zhang, Y. Li, and L. Xu, "Edge computing: Vision and challenges," IEEE internet of things journal, vol. 3, no. 5, 2016, pp. 637–646.

[5] A. Akusok, K.-M. Björk, L. E. Leal, Y. Miche, R. Hu, and A. Lendasse, "Spiking networks for improved cognitive abilities of edge computing devices," in Proceedings of the 12th ACM International Conference on PErvasive Technologies Related to Assistive Environments, ser. PETRA '19. New York, NY, USA: Association for Computing Machinery, 2019, p. 307–308.

[6] K. Bilal, O. Khalid, A. Erbad, and S. U. Khan, "Potentials, trends, and prospects in edge technologies: Fog, cloudlet, mobile edge, and micro data centers," Computer Networks, vol. 130, 2018, pp. 94–120.

[7] E. Raj, "8 Enablers For Europe's Trustworthy Artificial Intelligence, howpublished = https://www.tietoevry.com/en/blog/2019/07/8-enablers-for-europes-trustworthy-artificial-intelligence/, note = Accessed: 2019-09-30," 2019.

[8] F. K. Shaikh, S. Zeadally, and E. Exposito, "Enabling technologies for green internet of things," IEEE Systems Journal, vol. 11, no. 2, 2015, pp. 983–994.

[9] L. Tan and N. Wang, "Future internet: The internet of things," in 2010 3rd international conference on advanced computer theory and engineering (ICACTE), vol. 5. IEEE, 2010, pp. V5–376.

[10] Y. C. Wu, Y. J. Wu, and S. M. Wu, "An outlook of a future smart city in taiwan from post–internet of things to artificial intelligence internet of things," in Smart Cities: Issues and Challenges. Elsevier, 2019, pp. 263–282.

[11] B. D. Noble, M. Satyanarayanan, D. Narayanan, J. E. Tilton, J. Flinn, and K. R. Walker, "Agile application-aware adaptation for mobility," in Proceedings of the Sixteenth ACM Symposium on Operating Systems Principles, ser. SOSP '97. New York, NY, USA: Association for Computing Machinery, 1997, p. 276–287.

[12] I. Aktaş, "Cloud and edge computing for IoT: a short history, howpublished = https://blog.bosch-si.com/bosch-iot-suite/cloud-and-edge-computing-for-iot-a-short-history/, note = Accessed: 2020-07-26," 2020.

[13] R. D. Statista, "Number of internet of things (IoT) connected devices worldwide in 2018, 2025 and 2030, howpublished = https://www.statista.com/statistics/802690/worldwide-connected-devices-by-access-technology/, note = Accessed: 2020-05-15," 2020.

[14] B. Beyer, N. R. Murphy, D. K. Rensin, K. Kawahara, and S. Thorne, The site reliability workbook: Practical ways to implement SRE. " O'Reilly Media, Inc.", 2018.

[15] H. Adkins, B. Beyer, P. Blankinship, A. Oprea, P. Lewandowski, and A. Stubblefield, Building Secure and Reliable Systems. "O'Reilly Media, Inc.", 2020.

[16] M. Prince, "The Edge Computing Opportunity: It's Not What You Think, howpublished = https://blog.cloudflare.com/cloudflare-workers-serverless-week/, note = Accessed: 2020-07-30," 2020.

[17] L. Bass, I. Weber, and L. Zhu, DevOps: A software architect's perspective. Addison-Wesley Professional, 2015.

[18] A. Raj, D. I. Mattos, J. Bosch, H. H. Olsson, and A. Dakkak, "From ad-hoc data analytics to dataops," in International Conference on Software and Systems Process, 2020.

[19] A. Banerjee, C.-C. Chen, C.-C. Hung, X. Huang, Y. Wang, and R. Chevesaran, "Challenges and experiences with mlops for performance diagnostics in hybrid-cloud enterprise software deployments," in 2020 {USENIX} Conference on Operational Machine Learning (OpML 20), 2020.

Securing the Internet of Things from the Bottom Up Using an Immutable Blockchain-Based Secure Forensic Trail

Bob Duncan
Computing Science
University of Aberdeen, UK
Email: bobduncan@abdn.ac.uk

Abstract—**It has traditionally been the case that the Internet of Things represents the weak link in the corporate information system chain. While research has tried to improve the status quo, this has brought a new challenge to the table. Corporate systems, while generally much stronger than Internet of Things systems, are not, in themselves, totally secure. This is especially true of cloud-based systems. This major flaw arises because of the difficulty in safeguarding the forensic trail of corporate systems. The first thing the attacker does as soon as they have penetrated a corporate system, is to delete all the evidence of their entry from the forensic records of the corporate system, and there is usually very little to prevent this from happening. This is why it is such a challenge for authorities to trace attackers and bring them to account. The forensic trail is often the least protected part of corporate systems, but is arguably the most important from a compliance point of view. We show how it is possible to secure the forensic trail for corporate systems users who adopt these secure IoT approaches, by adopting the straightforward approach we suggest here to protect the forensic trail through the use of Blockchain. This will allow corporates to ensure the overall system can be secured, but more importantly, will provide a means to fight back against the attackers.**

Keywords–Corporate Systems; Internet of Things; Immutable Forensic Trail; Blockchain; Distributed Ledger Technology.

I. INTRODUCTION

The Internet of Things (IoT), a term first coined by Kevin Ashton in 1999 [1] was one of those great inventions that everyone thought would be the next big thing. Until they were implemented, and suddenly, the realisation struck that nobody had really considered how security might be an issue. Since most 'things' were produced with minimal resources, so that they would be cheap to buy, this also meant there was little ability to process the information collected and carried onwards, let alone be able to deal with security. Like all new advances in computing over the decades, it never takes certain people long to figure out a way to abuse the new technology for their own malicious ends.

The applications could be limitless, offering huge potential for operating efficiencies. For example, in some industries, many Supervisory, Control and Data Acquisition (SCADA) systems have been implemented to allow the company to control industrial process over a wide geographical area. Many components are highly specialised, very expensive, and can often only be upgraded once a year when the whole operational facilities are shut down for their annual maintenance program. Many of these SCADA components are decades old, because they are ultra reliable, but very expensive to replace.

However, when some bright spark suggested adding IoT devices all over the area to provide readings, or carry out functions that require people to physically travel to each location, this was seen as a great way to save huge sums on payroll and travel costs. Until those other people figured out there was little to zero security on these cheap IoT devices, and suddenly, they had unprecedented and unlimited access to not only the entire SCADA system, but could often leverage that access into confidential corporate systems because they were entering those systems from a 'trusted' source system. All too often, corporates were lax on the implementation, and review, of anomalous exceptions, meaning intrusions were frequently missed. Oman and Schweitzer [2] expressed concern about how this trend could pose threats to both power substations and SCADA controllers. Creery and Byers [3] were very concerned about how this hybridization of systems could lead to unintended security consequences. Kropp [4] warned of the double increase to risk brought about through the move from regulated industries coupled with the use of networked systems. Ralston, Graham and Hieb [5] carried out a risk assessment for SCADA and Distributed Control Systems (DCSs) networks, and were very concered about the increase in security risks posed.

Thus, those attackers would not only have access to the sensitive corporate system, but they could also cause mayhem by interfering with the SCADA equipment. This allowed for the possibility to shut down gas, water or sewage pipelines, shut off electricity supply, or cause massive damage to the SCADA systems as a whole.

The solution is surely the development of highly secure IoT systems? Sadly, that can only go part of the way to solving the problem. That is because the main corporate systems and the SCADA systems remain weak. In the following decade, Ericsson [6] is concerned about the development of the smart grid, and is concerned that often there is insufficient separation between operational and administrative computer systems, leading to security weaknesses. Wilhoit [7] of Trend Micro, expresses concenns around the importance of these systems, yet their continued lack of security persists. Adding a highly secure IoT system simply means the attacker will go into the main system, then coming from the main source, will have authorisation to get into the new highly secure IoT system, thus allowing them to render the security ineffective.

There can only be one proper solution. We simply need to

protect the one thing all attackers crave — the forensic trail! Will that ensure we finally have a secure system then? Not exactly. Attackers will still be able to get into the system. But now, with the forensic trail preserved, we now have the proof of what the attacker did once they got into the system. This means recovery will be able to become far more focussed than before. With no complete forensic trail to work with, a full search and investigation into all systems becomes necessary to try to work out what has been compromised or exfiltrated. However, with a full forensic record showing who did what, we instantly know what to check.

In 2016, Duncan and Whittington [8] emphasized the vital importance of the need to secure the audit trail. Duncan and Whittington [9] proposed the use of an immutable database to secure the audit trail and system logs. Duncan, Happe and Bratterud [10] proposed a novel method of achieving this using unikernels. Zhao and Duncan [11] considered the possibility of using Blockchain to secure the forensic trail, by considering how secure the Blockchain was in its original use in cryptocurrencies. Zhao and Duncan [12] looked at the possibility of using Blockchain without the cryptocurrecy element as a way forward for securing the forensic trail.

In Section II, we take a look at why companies should care about the implications of legislative and regulatory non-compliance for any company. In Section III, we identify what the Cloud Forensic Problem is, and address why it is such a challenging problem to overcome. In Section IV, we ask whether it is possible to attain compliance without addressing the cloud forensic problem. In Section V, we consider how we might secure corporate systems. In Section VI, we look at the detail of how Distributed Ledger Technology (DLT) might help us achieve a solution. In Section VII, we consider and discuss the limitations of this work, and in Section VIII, we discuss our conclusions.

II. Why Should Companies Care About Legislative and Regulatory Compliance?

Why should companies be concerned about compliance with Legislative and Regulatory compliance requirements? The answer to that is quite simple. Criminals who wreak havoc by attacking online systems are extremely difficult to identify and track down, due to a combination of thier skills in covering their tracks, and also through challenging jurisdictional issues. The primary goal of any attacker is to remove all record of their presence in the system by identifying all elements recording their presence from the system forensic records.

After financial deregulation in the UK during the mid-1980s by the Margaret Thatcher Government, the 'free-for-all' that followed, along with the numerous losses that arose due to unethical behaviour, the Government invited Sir Adrian Cadbury [13] to carry out a review to see what could be done, and this resulted in the introduction of Corporate Governance for public listed companies, together with the introduction of the Combined Corporate Code. This has subsequently been revised and updated, usually every three years, and has accustomed corporates to adhere to the notion of compliance, in this case for corporate governance at the highest levels of these corporates. Of course there has always been the notion that compliance is required with legisalation, as well as many industry regulations.

Large corporates traditionally had a lax attitude to looking after customer data properly, so Legislators and Regulators decided that, since these corporates had a responsibility to look after customer records, which they were clearly failing to do, they would go after these companies. The recent introduction of the EU General Data Protection Regulation (GDPR) [14], took these penalties to new heights, with the power to fine companies who were non-compliant up to 4% of their annual turnover, or up to €20 million, whichever was the greater.

In the US, the US authorities have a raft of legislation to ensure companies do the right thing. Facebook were brought to task last year for privacy breaches, and a settlement was reached of some $3 billion. Of course, Facebook are not yet out of the woods. At they same time as the US intervention, they were also brought to task by the Canadian Authorities, as well as the EU under GDPR. Due to the significant size of the non-compiance, the investigations are being carried out sequentially, rather than concurrently. In the UK, the GDPR, whose regulator is the Information Commissioner's Office (ICO) proposed fines last year of £183.5 millon and £99.5 million respectively to British Airways and the Marriott Hotel Group for privacy breaches. This represents a significant change in approach from both countries.

The US is a particularly litigious country anyway, and when it comes to company wrongdoing, there is no change there. The UK regulator has recently become far more disposed to bring non-compliant corporates to task for their shortcomings. There is no doubt that other jurisdictions have taken notice of this and are also stepping up their approach to mirror these approaches. This means that wherever a large corporate operates in the globe, the regulatory and legislative environment will continue to become far more challenging as time passes. Thus it would make sense to ensure that they achieve compliance with all the relevant legislation and regulation to safeguard their own position.

Since the various legislators and regulators throughout the globe have yet to figure out how to catch cybercriminals with enough consistency to make any meaningful impact, the burden will continue to fall on corporate shoulders. While these shoulders might have been broad in previous years, now that they have had the adverse economic effects of a global pandemic to contend with, even their shoulders will no longer be so broad. This means that the economic shock of larger fines will potentially prove catastrophic over time.

Since the ICO investigation into the British Airways attack started, negotiations have been ongoing between British Airways and the ICO, and due to the huge economic impact of the global pandemic on the airline industry, a much reduced settlement of £20 million has now been reached. While this is significantly less than the proposed fone of £183.5 million, it will still hurt. No doubt the Marriott group will be hoping that their constrained economic circumstances as a result of the global pandemic might now also be taken into account when settling their eventual fine.

When it came into force, the EU GDPR was touted as the world's toughest privacy law, but not all of the 28 EU countries were ready to implement it at that time. During the last two and a half years since then, Countries like the UK, France, Germany and Italy have been starting to flex their regulatory muscles, although many smaller countries are yet to get serious. It is clear that smaller countries like Ireland and Luxembourg, where many tech companies are registered, have yet to bring any successful large action against any US big tech firm. Also, a number of EU countries still do not publish regulatory fines lists. Given the economic dependence of many of the smaller countries, one has to ask whether they are best placed to regulating big tech.

III. The Cloud Forensic Problem (and Why it is Such a Difficult Problem)

All computing systems are constantly under serious attack, and where cloud computing is in use, this can become an even more serious issue. Once an attacker gains a foothold in a cloud system and becomes an intruder, there is little to prevent the intruder from helping themselves to any amount of data covered by legislation and regulation, either by viewing it, modifying it, deleting it or ex-filtrating it from the victim system [15], [16], [17]. Worse, there is nothing to prevent the intruder from gaining sufficient privileges to then completely delete all trace of their incursion, possibly deleting far more records than they need to in the process, leading to further problems for business continuity. Traditional non-cloud systems may also be equally vulnerable, particularly where transaction log monitoriing is not a priority.

This problem is often known as "The elephant in the room" in cloud circles. Pretty much everyone knows about it, yet nobody is prepared to discuss it, let alone try to resolve the problem, due to the difficulty of the challenge it presents. Make no mistake, this is a serious challenge to defend against, let alone overcome. However, not only is it a serious challenge for organisations using cloud, it also presents a major obstacle to compliance with legislation and regulation, thus exposing corporates to much further potential harm.

Once all trace of the intrusion has been deleted, there will be limited forensic trail left for authorities to follow. This means many companies may be totally unaware that the intrusion has even taken place, let alone be able to understand which records have been accessed, modified, deleted or stolen. All too often, companies will believe they have retained a full forensic trail in their systems, but often forget that without special measures being taken to save these records off-site [18], they will no longer be available.

Currently, in any computer system, there must be a complete and intact audit trail in order for the breached organisation to be able to tell which records have been accessed, modified, deleted or stolen. Where the audit trail and all forensic records have been deleted, there remains no physical means for any organisation to be able to tell which records have been accessed, modified, deleted or stolen, putting these organisations immediately in multiple breaches of the legislative and regulatory authorities, leaving them exposed to large potential fines.

IV. Is It Possible to Achieve Compliance with Legislation and Regulation without Addressing the Cloud Forensic Problem?

There can be no guarantee that compliance can be achieved without addressing the cloud forensic problem [19]! It should be noted that this problem also can pertain to conventional systems as well as IoT systems. Looking to the previous section, we can see that there is nothing to prevent an intruder from destroying every scrap of forensic proof of their incursion into any computer system. It is clear that any form of forensic record or audit trail can not therefore be safely stored on any conventional computer system, nor any running cloud instance, nor any standard IoT system.

This means that the only safe method of storage of forensic data will be somewhere off-site from any running computer system. Clearly, separation of the storage from the running computer system would be the preferred solution. the off-site storage must be highly secure, preferably stored in an immutable database, and should especially be held in encrypted format, with all encryption keys held elsewhere.

There are those who say that as long as they are not breached, they will not be in breach of legislation or regulation. While it lasts, that would certainly be true, but consider, how will they be able to tell whether they have been breached, or not? What if they have been breached, and the breach has been very well covered up. They will have no means of knowing whether a breach has arisen, let alone who perpetrated it, how they got in or what they viewed, modified, deleted or ex-filtrated from the victim system. Given the propensity for modern hackers to boast about their attacking prowess, it is not likely that the attack will be missed by regulators for long.

What if a complaint is made that a customer's data has been stolen? The organisation will have no means of proving whether the data has been tampered with, or not. Equally, if, as is most likely, the breach has been extremely well covered up, they will neither have the means of complying with the reporting requirements, nor be able to understand exactly what has been compromised. This begs the obvious question: How do we secure the corporate system properly?

V. How to Address Securing Corporate Systems

Let us first consider what we require. First, we need to ensure the integrity of our systems. This means we need to be able to retain a full forensic trail of all activities within the system. We also need to make it difficult for attackers to access. This means it needs to be separated from the main systems. It should also be difficult for attackers to understand where the records they seek to obliterate are. This would imply that encryption would be a prudent measure to include, along with some form of immutable database.

That does not seem to be a complicated requirements set. Will it be enough? Providing it is kept securely away from the main system, it provides exactly what we need to be able to understand what has happened to our system in the event of a breach. We can see from the complete forensic trail how the attacker got in, what they did from there, and what records they viewed, modified, deleted or ex-filtrated from the system. Investigative agencies can do a great deal with minimal information. How far they could go with a full forensic trail?

To meet these specific requirements, we can turn to the financial system to find a suitable solution, specifically to the area of cryptocurrencies. Anything to do with money is highly attractive to attackers. Cryptocurrencies have to be secure, have to have a bullet-proof audit trail to ensure the provenance of transactions, yet need a high level of privacy, which is possible with the assistance of Blockchain.

Typically, cryptocurrencies use a public blockchain approach, using a great many public "miners" to carry out all the provenance and privacy work using encryption algorithms along with a consensus mechanism to agree the audit trail. This does make the ledger fully public, but also introduces a high element of latency where thousands or hundreds of thousands of miners are involved. The cryptocurrency record becomes effectively immutable after consensus through this DLT. A private blockchain approach could deliver a vastly reduced latency, with the administration being funded by the corporate, whereby they either run their own blockchain system, or they might contract this DLT work in, if such facilities were offered by professional firms. These are the kind of services the big four auditing firms could offer, which could provide high levels of assurance to the corporate users. We shall consider the detail in the next section.

VI. How can Distributed Ledger Technology Help Solve the Problem?

Let us first have a brief look at the detail of how cryptocurrencies work. We will take a brief overview of Bitcoin, since this was the cryptocurrency that was able to get cryptocurrencies off the ground back in 2009. To use Bitcoin, a user must first install a Bitcoin Wallet, which is require in order to pay or to receive money. We will return to this later. The core of the strength of all cryptocurrencies is the Blockchain, which is a Shared Public Ledger (SPL). This ledger is fullly distributed, hence Distributed Ledger Technology. Once a new transaction is made to or from the user's wallet, this transaction is deemed to be 'pending' until it has been verified by a number of 'miners' until consensus is reached, at which point it will become part of the blockchain. This provides the verification of the transaction's integrity in the bitcoin wallet. This process involves entering the transactions into the blockchain in a specific order, enforced by a strict cryptographic process (carried out by the 'miners') to ensure the integrity and chronological order of the Blockchain, in essence, creating an immutable record of all verified transactions. Once entered into the Blockchain, it is not possible to modify or delete these transactions. It is only possible to add a plus or minus transaction at a later date or time, thus ensuring a robust audit trail of all the financial transactions that have been processed. Thus, the blockchain provides the immutable audit trail, and this verifies the user bitcoin wallets.

For our purposes, we do not require a public Blockchain, or SPL, and thus do not need an army of 'miners', all of whom need to be rewarded. This usually happens by awarding them a specific fraction of a bitcoin for their work. Instead, the corporate will need to provide, secure, and pay for, their own private distributed blockchain ledger. Since this is likely to become a target for attack, each of the many versions of the Blockchain the corporate sets up should be stored away from the primary system it is trying to protect. These blockchain systems should be set up with only the absolute minimum software required, with all public facing access removed. All software should be extensively hardened, with no option to delete or amend the Blockchain software.

Then, it is a simple matter for the corporate to decide on precisely what to defend. It is important to be absolutely clear on exactly what needs to be protected, and what will be involved. Clearly, adequate resources will need to be provisioned to collect the considerable volume of data that will be needed. There is no doubt that it will be more expensive to collect, store, and protect this information than under normal operations. However, it is important to realise that instead of being clueless in the face of a successful breach, the corporate will have a considerable amount of verified data to hand, which will clearly help mitigate any potential breach penalties, since very targeted information on the attackers can be passed to both the regulatory authorities as well as to the relevant government agencies, such as police and security services, and so on.

The data collected will also be useful for performing data analytics to discover the footprint used by attackers, which can be used to adapt existing access control systems to become more robust. It would also be ineteresting to have the capability to turn the tables on the attackers.

VII. Limitations and Discussion

Many people point to the significant cryptocurrency breaches we have seen during the past decade:

- Bitcoinica 2012 [20], 46,703 bitcoins stolen followed by another 18,757;
- Mt Gox 2014 [21], $460 million hack, following a previous hack in 2011 of $8.75 million;
- Bitfinex 2016 [22], $72 million hack;
- Decentralized Autonomous Organization (DAO) 2016 [23], $70 million hack;
- Coincheck 2018 [24], $530 million hack.

All very damning evidence for the weakness of Blockchain. Or was it? Zhao and Duncan [25] carried out an investigation on whether these attackes had been able to exploit any weakness in the Blockchain and discovered that:

- Bitcoinica stored large amounts of bitcoin online, rather than in off-line stecure storage;
- Mt Gox attack succedded due to a combination of poor management, neglect and inexperience;
- Bitfinex thought they made their systems more secure, but failed to spot they had created an exploitable weakness, which was duly exploited;
- DAO there was a flaw in their system which could be exploited by a recursion attack. It was duly exploited. Nice return for a couple of hours work.;
- Coincheck did not use secure networks.

Thus it is clear that in every one of these successful attacks, the Blockchain could not be breached. The lesson here is that it is impossible to simply rely on the blockchain alone for good security. Every element of a system must be properly secured in order to ensure the success of the whole.

It is also true that the original aim of Blockchain was to provide a high level of privacy, but Meiklejohn et al., [26], Ober, Katzenbeisser and Hamacher [27], Reid and Harrigan [28], plus Ron and Shamir [29] all observed that Bitcoin delvered much weaker privacy than was first expected. However, since this was based on the use of the public Blockchain, this is not likely to be an issue where a private Blockchain is in use.

Another area of concern arose in observing how some 'miners' exhibited selfish behaviour to try to increase their gains by 'pool hopping'. To try to prevent this, Rosenfeld

[30] drew attention to the mechanism design problem of trying to keep rewards constant over time. Babioff et al., [31], and later Eyal and Sirer[32] expressed their concerns that the mining protocol rules can not be considered to provide true equilibrium strategies if users have the option to withhold information both on a selective and a temporary basis over time. The use of a private Blockchain can remove this issue.

The 2013 introduction of another cryptocurrency, Ethereum [33], opened up the possibility to use smart contracts to extend the capabilities of the Blockchain. It is likely that for forensic trail preservation, this is likely to be something of an overkill.

In 2016, McConaghy et al., [34] presented BigchainDB, a scalable Blockchain database, suitable for big data applications. In this paper, the authors presented a comprehensive description of their proposal, including a full analysis of performance, latency and preliminary experimentation results. They also introduced a new concept of Blockcahin pipelining which provides the mechanism to deliver scalability gains.

In looking at how IoT security could be revolutionised, Liu et al., [35] demonstrated how their proposed solution for a Blockchain based data integrity service framework for IoT data could outperform the use of Third Party Audit (TPA) offerings. Westerlund and Kratzke [36] suggested how the use of Blockchain could help address some of the inherent security issues of using IoT. Qu et al., [37] proposed a Blockchain based credibility verification method for IoT entities. Angin et al., [38] addressed the shortcomings of IoT devices and proposed a solution to improve their security. Dukkipati et al., [39] suggested that a Blockchain backed access control system could offer significant improvements to the security of IoT devices. Li et al., [40] suggested that by uding Blockchain in manufacturing, it could help provide more integrated and secure manufacturing ecosystems. Zhang et al., [41] proposed the use of Blockchain smart contracts for access control to IoT devices.

As we can see, there is a lot of work going on around the possible use of Blockchain as a serious means to improve IoT security. This is most certainly something that is very necessary, but ultimately, if we add a much more secure IoT system to existing corporate systems, then the security of the IoT system could be much better than the existing corporate system. This would result in the weakest link now becoming the strongest link, which will not improve that status quo, rather it will simply turn it on its head.

This is why the simple addition of a Blockchain based forensic trail mechanism to all main corporate systems would even the playing field, security wise, and would offer a means to understand whenever any breach arises. Policing for such an event could be automated into the overall system in order that rapid advance warning can take place, as well as any possible preventive measures that could also be quickly activated. Best of all, the attackers would then leave behind a complete forensic trail of their incursion into the system.

It is important to stress that this is not a 'silver bullet' to solve the security of corporate systems. However, it will clearly provide a welcome solution to the problem of dealing with the protection of the forensic trail that is so often obliterated from corporate systems by attackers in the process of covering their tracks. All too often, the less skilled attackers destroy more data than they need to, resulting in far more difficult challenges for corporate data controllers. This will, however, mean that the addition of a secure IoT system to any existing corporate system can result in a much tighter system, with the bonus of a means to understand exactly what is going on when any attack takes place.

VIII. Conclusion and Future Work

In summary, we can see that the ability for conrporate sysems to have a new tool with which they can more fully understand exactly what is going on as the result of an attack will be a very good thing. This is particlarly the case when the corporate falls under the jurisdiction of many legislative and regulatory bodies, where failure to understand which records have been viewed, modified, deleted or ex-filtrated from the system can lead to punitive levels of fines being levied, as well as the expense and disruption of a lengthy investigation.

It will also be useful to be able to retain the full record of the forensic trail for investigation by the appropriate authorities. These records are not usually left behind, although investigators can do a great deal with fractional forensic snippets that sometimes get left behind in systems after a successful attack. With the full forensic trail now available, this will provide a transformative means for a fightback against these secretive attackers, who have long considered themselves immune to prosecution. While this will not solve the jurisdictional problems, at least the perpetrators can be publicised and added to public watchlists, as well as to various blacklists.

We have proposed how this challenging problem may be approached to ensure that corporate users can be fully compliant with the ever increasing leglative and regulatory requirements that they now have to comply with. Clearly, additional cost will require to be incurred, and there may be a very small impact on latency, but these costs could significantly mitigate the possibility of a huge regulatory fines in the event of a breach. It is also likely that this approach will ensure faster discovery of the occurrence of a breach, thus minimising the potential impact on business continuity.

For our next stage of this development, we propose to set up two small test corporate systems. One system will use existing security approaches, to which we will add a Blockchain secured IoT system, which we will subject to a systematic attack to demonstrate how even the addition of the secured IoT system cannot solve this problem. The second system will be a small test corporate system incorporating the Blockchain secured forensic trail, with added Blockchain secured IoT system to demonstrate how well the whole system can handle an attack. We will then be able to compare both systems and this will allow us to clearly demonstrate the different levels of compliance that could be achieved.

The beauty of this proposal is that it will not involve a major revision of existing corporate systems. Thus no massive expenditure will be required to completely change the system, with all the attendant workload to transfer all the data from the old format to the new. It will simply involve the insertion of a 'software tool' into existing corporate system, with which corporates are already intimately familiar with. Best of all, it is unlikely to involve massive expenditure, which in today's constrained working environment will always be welcome.

References

[1] K. Ashton, "That 'Internet of Things' Thing," RFiD Journal, vol. 22, no. 7, 2009, pp. 97–114.

[2] P. Oman and E. O. Schweitzer, "Concerns About Intrusions Into Remotely Accessible Substation Controllers and Scada Systems," in Power, vol. 20, 2000, pp. 1–16.

[3] A. Creery and E. Byers, "Industrial Cybersecurity for Power System and Scada," in Management. IEEE, 2005, pp. 303–309. [Online]. Available: http://ieeexplore.ieee.org/stamp/stamp.jsp?tp=&arnumber=1524567 Accessed 15 October 2020.

[4] T. Kropp, "System Threats and Vulnerabilities - SCADA EMS," Power and Energy Magazine, IEEE, vol. 4, no. april, 2006, pp. 46–50. [Online]. Available: http://ieeexplore.ieee.org/xpls/abs_all.jsp?arnumber=1597995 Accessed 15 October 2020.

[5] P. A. S. Ralston, J. H. Graham, and J. L. Hieb, "Cyber security risk assessment for SCADA and DCS networks," ISA Transactions, vol. 46, no. 4, oct 2007, pp. 583–594. [Online]. Available: http://linkinghub.elsevier.com/retrieve/pii/S0019057807000754 Accessed 15 October 2020.

[6] G. N. Ericsson, "Cyber security and power system communicationessential parts of a smart grid infrastructure," IEEE Transactions on Power Delivery, vol. 25, no. 3, 2010, pp. 1501–1507.

[7] K. Wilhoit, "Who's Really Attacking Your ICS Equipment?" Tech. Rep., 2013. [Online]. Available: http://www.trendmicro.com.hk/cloud-content/apac/pdfs/security- intelligence/white-papers/wp-whos-really-attacking-your-ics-equipment.pdf Accessed 15 October 2020.

[8] B. Duncan and M. Whittington, "Cloud cyber-security: Empowering the audit trail," International Journal on Advances in Security, vol. 9, no. 3 & 4, 2016, pp. 169–183.

[9] B. Duncan and M. Whittington, "Creating an Immutable Database for Secure Cloud Audit Trail and System Logging," in Cloud Computing 2017: The Eighth International Conference on Cloud Computing, GRIDs, and Virtualization. Athens, Greece: IARIA, ISBN: 978-1-61208-529-6, 2017, pp. 54–59.

[10] B. Duncan, A. Happe, and A. Bratterud, "Using Unikernels to Address the Cloud Forensic Problem and help Achieve EU GDPR Compliance." Cloud Computing 2018: The Ninth International Conference on Cloud Computing, GRIDs, and Virtualization, February, 71–76.

[11] Y. Zhao and B. Duncan, "Could Block Chain Technology Help Resolve the Cloud Forensic Problem?" in Cloud Computing 2018: The Ninth International Conference on Cloud Computing, GRIDs, and Virtualization, no. February. Barcelona, Spain: IARIA, 2018, pp. 39–44.

[12] Y. Zhao and B. Duncan, "Blockchain Challenges for Cloud Users," in Proceedings of the Tenth International Conference on Cloud Computing, GRIDs, and Virtualization, Venice, 2019, p. 6.

[13] A. Cadbury, "The Financial Aspects of Corporate Governance," HMG, London, Tech. Rep., 1992. [Online]. Available: http://www.ecgi.org/codes/documents/cadbury.pdf Accessed 15 October 2020.

[14] EU, "EU General Data Protection Regulation (GDPR)," 2017. [Online]. Available: http://www.eugdpr.org/ Accessed 15 October 2020.

[15] B. Duncan and M. Whittington, "Enhancing Cloud Security and Privacy: The Power and the Weakness of the Audit Trail," in Cloud Computing 2016: The Seventh International Conference on Cloud Computing, GRIDs, and Virtualization, no. April. Rome: IEEE, 2016, pp. 125–130.

[16] G. Weir, A. Aßmuth, M. Whittington, and B. Duncan, "Cloud Accounting Systems, the Audit Trail, Forensics and the EU GDPR: How Hard Can It Be?" in The British Accounting and Finance Association: Scottish Area Group Annual Conference. Aberdeen: BAFA, 2017, p. 6.

[17] P. Tobin, M. McKeever, J. Blackledge, M. Whittington, and B. Duncan, "UK Financial Institutions Stand to Lose Billions in GDPR Fines: How can They Mitigate This?" in The British Accounting and Finance Association: Scottish Area Group Annual Conference, BAFA, Ed., Aberdeen, 2017, p. 6.

[18] R. K. L. Ko et al., "TrustCloud: A framework for accountability and trust in cloud computing," Proceedings - 2011 IEEE World Congress on Services, SERVICES 2011, 2011, pp. 584–588.

[19] B. Duncan, "Will Compliance with the New EU General Data Protection Regulation Lead to Better Cloud Security?" International Journal on Advances in Security, vol. 11, no. 3&4, 2018, pp. 254–263.

[20] L. Constantin, "Hackers break into bitcoin exchange site Bitcoinica, steal $90,000 in bitcoins," 2012. [Online]. Available: https://www.networkworld.com/article/2188554/applications/hackers-break-into-bitcoin-exchange-site-bitcoinica–steal–90-000-in-bitcoins.html Accessed 15 October 2020.

[21] R. McMillan, "Bitcoin's $460 Mliion Disaster," 2014. [Online]. Available: https://www.wired.com/2014/03/bitcoin-exchange/ Accessed 15 October 2020.

[22] C. Baldwin, "Bitcoin worth $72 million stolen from Bitfinex exchange in Hong Kong," 2016. [Online]. Available: https://www.reuters.com/article/us-bitfinex-hacked-hongkong/bitcoin-worth-72-million-stolen-from-bitfinex-exchange-in-hong-kong-idUSKCN10E0KP Accessed 15 October 2020.

[23] D. Siegel, "Understanding The DAO Attack," 2016. [Online]. Available: https://www.coindesk.com/understanding-dao-hack-journalists/ Accessed 15 October 2020.

[24] BBC, "Coincheck: World's biggest ever digital currency 'theft'," 2018. [Online]. Available: http://www.bbc.co.uk/news/world-asia-42845505 Accessed 15 October 2020.

[25] Y. Zhao and B. Duncan, "The Impact of Crypto-Currency Risks on the Use of Blockchain for Cloud Security and Privacy," in The 7th International Workshop on Security, Privacy and Performance in Cloud Computing (SPCLOUD 2018), 2018, p. 8.

[26] S. Meiklejohn et al., "A fistful of Bitcoins: Characterizing payments among men with no names," Proceedings of the Internet Measurement Conference - IMC '13, no. 6, 2013 (pp. 127-140).

[27] M. Ober, S. Katzenbeisser, and K. Hamacher, "Structure and anonymity of the bitcoin transaction graph," Future internet, vol. 5, no. 2, 2013, pp. 237–250.

[28] F. Reid and M. Harrigan, "An analysis of anonymity in the bitcoin system," in Security and privacy in social networks. Springer, 2013, pp. 197–223.

[29] D. Ron and A. Shamir, "Quantitative analysis of the full Bitcoin transaction graph," in Lecture Notes in Computer Science (including subseries Lecture Notes in Artificial Intelligence and Lecture Notes in Bioinformatics), vol. 7859 LNCS, 2013.

[30] M. Rosenfeld, "Analysis of bitcoin pooled mining reward systems," arXiv preprint arXiv:1112.4980, 2011.

[31] M. Babaioff, S. Dobzinski, S. Oren, and A. Zohar, "On bitcoin and red balloons," in Proceedings of the 13th ACM conference on electronic commerce. ACM, 2012, pp. 56–73.

[32] I. Eyal and E. G. Sirer, "Majority is not enough: Bitcoin mining is vulnerable," in International Conference on Financial Cryptography and Data Security. Springer, 2014, pp. 436–454.

[33] V. Buterin and Others, "Ethereum white paper," GitHub repository, vol. 1, 2013, pp. 22–23.

[34] T. Mcconaghy et al., "BigchainDB: A Scalable Blockchain Database (DRAFT)," BigchainDB, 2016, pp. 1–65.

[35] B. Liu, X. L. Yu, S. Chen, X. Xu, and L. Zhu, "Blockchain based data integrity service framework for IoT data," in 2017 IEEE International Conference on Web Services (ICWS). IEEE, 2017, pp. 468–475.

[36] M. Westerlund and N. Kratzke, "Towards distributed clouds: A review about the evolution of centralized cloud computing, distributed ledger technologies, and a foresight on unifying opportunities and security implications," in 2018 International Conference on High Performance Computing & Simulation (HPCS). IEEE, 2018, pp. 655–663.

[37] C. Qu, M. Tao, J. Zhang, X. Hong, and R. Yuan, "Blockchain based credibility verification method for IoT entities," Security and Communication Networks, vol. 2018, n. pag. 2018.

[38] P. Angin, M. B. Mert, O. Mete, A. Ramazanli, K. Sarica, and B. Gungoren, "A blockchain-based decentralized security architecture for IoT," in International Conference on Internet of Things. Springer, 2018, pp. 3–18.

[39] C. Dukkipati, Y. Zhang, and L. C. Cheng, "Decentralized, blockchain based access control framework for the heterogeneous internet of things," in Proceedings of the Third ACM Workshop on Attribute-Based Access Control, 2018, pp. 61–69.

[40] Z. Li, W. M. Wang, G. Liu, L. Liu, J. He, and G. Q. Huang, "Toward open manufacturing," Industrial Management & Data Systems, 2018.

[41] Y. Zhang, S. Kasahara, Y. Shen, X. Jiang, and J. Wan, "Smart contract-based access control for the internet of things," IEEE Internet of Things Journal, vol. 6, no. 2, 2018, pp. 1594–1605.

A Systematic Mapping Study on Edge Computing and Analytics

Andrei-Raoul Morariu, Jerker Björkqvist, Kristian Nybom
Åbo Akademi University
Faculty of Science and Engineering
Vesilinnantie 3, 20500 Turku, Finland
Email: {firstname.lastname@abo.fi}

Jonathan Shabulinzenze, Miikka Jaurola, Petteri Multanen, Kalevi Huhtala
Tampere University
Faculty of Engineering and Natural Sciences
Korkeakoulunkatu 6, 33720 Tampere, Finland
Email: {firstname.lastname@tuni.fi}

Abstract—**The vast amount of data provided by the Internet of Things and sensors, have given rise to edge computing and analytics. In edge computing and analytics, data processing and analysis on sensor input is performed in edge devices prior to sending the results to the cloud. This reduces required processing in the cloud while minimizing communication network utilization and allows cloud resources to be used for other tasks such as decision making. In this paper, we present a comprehensive, unbiased overview of state-of-the-art research on edge computing and analytics. Of the 47 identified papers, several have targeted task scheduling and power optimisation, while data management and engineering, image and facial recognition as well as anomaly detection were not well studied. Simulation remains the most used approach for validation, and research results based on implementations of edge systems in real life environments are still sparse.**
Keywords-edge; analytics; systematic mapping study.

I. INTRODUCTION

An increasing part of new features and added value for machines and technical solutions comes from digitalization and advanced automation. The Internet of Things, collections of Big Data and cloud-based analytics provide potential tools to improve machine reliability, performance and energy efficiency. However, required network bandwidth, data storage and data processing power (as well as the resulting energy consumption) are significant for machines equipped with large sensor systems. Due to these issues, the implementation of analytics systems for condition monitoring, diagnostics and predictive maintenance would be largely unfeasible if not for edge computing and analytics to perform data collection, storage, computation and analysis closer to original locations. Edge analytics can take place on a sensor or other device connected directly to a machine, instead of transmitting the data to the cloud or central data storage, for example. This approach shortens analytics response times and reduces the bandwidth needed for data transmission.

According to analysis by [1], the business drivers supporting edge application use are low latency, cost efficiency, improved operational efficiency and lower bandwidth. However, implementation of edge-based analytics supporting machine diagnostics remains rare. At the same time, a market review [2] has forecast that revenue from condition monitoring applications, which might utilize edge analytics, will almost triple between 2019 and 2023. As such, edge computing and analytics hold significant interest and potential for both companies and research institutes.

This paper presents an overview of state-of-the-art technologies and solutions used for edge computing and analytics. These paradigms are already applied in many areas, such as mobile devices [3], home automation [4], smart cities [5], personal health care [6], automotive and industrial vehicles [7]. The goal of this study was to reveal existing frameworks, infrastructures, methods and algorithms for edge analytics, including their performances and the level of standardization for edge analytic systems. The study was performed using systematic mapping study (SMS) protocol presented in Section II that covered hundreds of scientific publications from several digital libraries.

This study was performed in the context of a Finnish national research project on edge technologies, which has been carried out in co-operation with several industrial companies. The motivation of companies to apply edge computing to their machines relates to condition monitoring and machines diagnostics. The main application areas for the companies are energy production, mobile work machines and related monitoring and AI solutions. Therefore, scientific papers focusing on mobile edge computing were not included and the focus was on industrially applicable solutions.

The contributions of this paper are to provide such an overview and results from applying SMS methodology to this research area. Given that none of the 912 papers found after the initial search provided a similar overview of edge computing and analytics, we deem the results provided in this paper to be relevant.

The paper is structured as follows. Section 2 describes the protocol for the systematic mapping study used to find and evaluate papers in this study. The protocol is described in detail for the purpose of replicability. In Section 3, we present the results of this study, where we also try to answer the research questions presented in Section 2. Potential threats to the validity of this study are discussed in Section 4, and in Section 5, we present our conclusions.

II. THE SYSTEMATIC MAPPING STUDY

This section describes the protocol used for the SMS. The protocol is largely based on the one used in [8], but it has been modified according to the topic of this study.

A. Research Questions

The research questions (RQ) are as follows:

RQ1: Which fields apply edge computing?
RQ2: What methods or algorithms are used in edge computing?
RQ3: What edge framework proposals exist?
RQ4: How do proposed edge framework solutions perform?
RQ5: What is the standardization level for edge computing?
RQ6: How are the edge framework proposals evaluated?

B. Search Strategy for Primary Studies

This section presents our search strategy, which based on the systematic literature review guidelines from [9] and [10].

1) Search Terms: Table I lists the search terms used when searching for original papers for this study. The search terms are derived from the research questions.

TABLE I. SEARCH TERMS WITH ALTERNATE SPELLINGS

Term	Alternate Spelling
edge	
Analy*	Analytic, Analytics, Analytical, Analysis
Algorithm*	Algorithms
IoT	Internet of Things
Complexit*	Complexity, Complexities
Autonomous	
Performance*	Performances
Malfunction	
Defect*	Defects
Anomal*	Anomaly, Anomalies
Machine	
Device	
Comput*	Computing, Compute, Computation
Energy	

2) Search Strings: The search terms listed in Table I were combined into two search strings for use in the digital libraries. These are shown in Table II.

TABLE II. SEARCH STRINGS

#	Search String
1.	edge AND (Comput* OR Algorithm OR Analy* OR Defect OR Malfunction OR Anomal*) AND (Performance* OR Complexit* OR Energy)
2.	edge AND (Comput* OR Algorithm OR Analy*) AND (Defect OR Malfunction OR Anomal*) AND (Performance* OR Complexit* OR Energy)

3) Databases: The search strings shown above were applied to the following digital libraries:

- IEEE Xplore
- ACM Digital library
- ScienceDirect

We decided to start with four libraries, but skipped the SpringerLink database because it did not have the option of extracting papers in a bibtex file format.

The first search string was used for all three databases while the second string was used to search abstracts in the IEEE Xplore database only. This was done to reduce the number of papers found, because the first search string resulted in more than 11,000 papers from the abstract search.

Since the digital libraries have different possibilities for defining search strings, the strings were customized to every digital library. Duplicates were removed from the collected results.

C. Study Inclusion Criteria

The inclusion criteria for primary studies were as follows:

- Written in English *AND*
- Published in a peer-reviewed journal, conference or workshop covering the subjects of computer science, computer engineering, embedded systems, signal processing, or software engineering *AND*
- Describing any one of the following:
  - Methods or approaches for edge computing or analytics
  - Infrastructural or architectural approaches to edge computing and analytics
  - Performance evaluations of existing edge computing and analytics approaches

If several papers presented the same approach, only the most recent was included, unless the contributions of those papers differed.

D. Title and Abstract Level Screening

In this phase, the inclusion criteria were applied to publication titles and abstracts. To minimize researcher bias, two researchers independently analysed the search results. Afterwards, the analyses were compared and any disagreements were resolved through discussion. The screening results were used as a starting point for the full text screening.

E. Full Text Level Screening

In this phase, the remaining papers were analysed based on their full text. To minimize bias, three researchers applied the inclusion criteria on the full text. Here, one researcher screened all of the papers, while the remaining two researchers screened half of the papers each, due to time limitations. The results were compared and disagreements were resolved through discussion. The researchers also documented a reason for each excluded study [11].

F. Study Quality Assessment Checklist and Procedure

The selected papers were assessed based on their quality in terms of contribution to edge analytics. Three researchers assessed the quality of the selected papers with one researcher assessing all of the papers independently, while the two other researchers assessed half of the papers each. After the assessing, the results were compared and disagreements were resolved through discussion between researchers. Any papers not meeting minimum quality requirements, as detailed below, were excluded from the set of primary studies. The output from this phase was the final set of papers.

Table III presents the checklist for study quality assessment. For each question in the checklist, a three-level, numeric scale was used [11]. The levels were: yes (2 points), partial (1 point), and no (0 point). Based on the checklist and the numeric scale, each study could score a maximum of 34 and a minimum of 0 points. If a study scored 8 points or less, it was excluded due to a lack of quality with respect to this study. The reviewing researcher documented the obtained score of each included/excluded study.

TABLE III. STUDY QUALITY ASSESSMENT CHECKLIST, PARTIALLY ADOPTED FROM [8][11]

#	Question
Theoretical contribution	
1	Is at least one of the research questions addressed?
2	Was the study designed to address some of the research questions?
3	Is a problem description for the research explicitly provided?
4	Is the problem description for the research supported by references to other work?
5	Are the contributions of the research clearly described?
6	Are the assumptions, if any, clearly stated?
7	Is there sufficient evidence to support the claims of the research?
Experimental evaluation	
8	Is the research design, or the way the research was organized, clearly described?
9	Is a prototype, simulation, or empirical study presented?
10	Is the experimental setup clearly described?
11	Are results from multiple different experiments included?
12	Are results from multiple runs of each experiment included?
13	Are the experimental results compared with other approaches?
14	Are negative results, if any, presented?
15	Is the statistical significance of the results assessed?
16	Are the limitations clearly stated?
17	Are the links between data, interpretation and conclusions clear?

G. Data Extraction Strategy

We used the form shown in Table IV to extract data from the primary studies. Three researchers extracted the information from the papers with each researcher extracting data from one third of the papers. After the data extraction, the results were double-checked by the reviewing researchers. The extracted data was then used for analysis, applying RQs from Section II-A to obtain answers.

H. Synthesis of the Extracted Data

The extracted data from the papers was analysed to to obtain a high-level view of the different aspects related to edge analytics. The papers were categorised and collective results were extracted. The results from this phase are presented and discussed in Section III.

TABLE IV. DATA EXTRACTION FORM

Data Item	Value	Notes
General		
Data extractor name		
Data extraction date		
Study identifier (S1, S2, S3, ...)		
Bibliographic reference (title, authors, year, journal/conference/workshop name)		
Publication type (journal, conference, or workshop)		
Edge Computing and Analytics Related		
(RQ1) The domain in which the edge analytics are applied (e.g., smart cities, industry, air industry, shipping, heavy/professional vehicles, health sector)		
(RQ2) Edge computing and analytics method or algorithm		
(RQ3) Edge framework (infrastructure or architecture)		
(RQ4) Performance metrics of proposal (e.g., algorithm complexity, computing, data compression, energy requirements, real-time)		
(RQ5) Mentions of standardization level		
(RQ6) Evaluation method (analytical, empirical, simulation)		

III. RESULTS

In this section, we present the main findings of the research. We used search terms such as "edge" and "algorithm*" that are used in several research contexts. Consequently, some findings were not related to edge computing. For example, some papers were related to the analysis of image edges or parsing methods for graph edges, which are not related to the topic of this paper.

As seen in Table V, the initial paper search produced an excessive number of papers. After the initial screening, it turned out that no papers found and published before 2016 were on the topic industrial edge analytics. Therefore, the results of this study include papers published from 2016 onwards. We also discarded papers related to mobile edge computing, as our research relates to the industrial environment. That being said, papers related to fog computing were not discarded, because the technologies used are closely related to edge computing. These are the main reasons to the large number of papers discarded after the title and abstract screening.

TABLE V. NUMBER OF PAPERS IN EACH PHASE OF THE PAPER SEARCH AND SCREENING

Phase	Number of papers
Initial search results without duplicates	912
After title and abstract screening	118
After full text screening	58
After quality assessment	47

After the initial paper search, 912 papers were found after removing all duplicates. After the title and abstract screening, only 118 papers were included in the following phase. After the full text screening, 58 papers were included in the quality assessment.Only a few papers were discarded based on the quality assessment, leaving 47 primary studies for the final analysis. Overall, a significant number of papers were discarded, as their content (e.g., graphs, decision trees) did not relate to the industry domain of edge analytics. Most of the primary studies (38) were published in conference proceedings and the remainder (9) were published in journals.

As shown in Figure 1, the subject of edge computing is trending toward greater interest over time. We note that while there were few papers used from 2019, the initial paper search took place on April 10, 2019. As such, this study most likely does not include all related articles published in 2019.

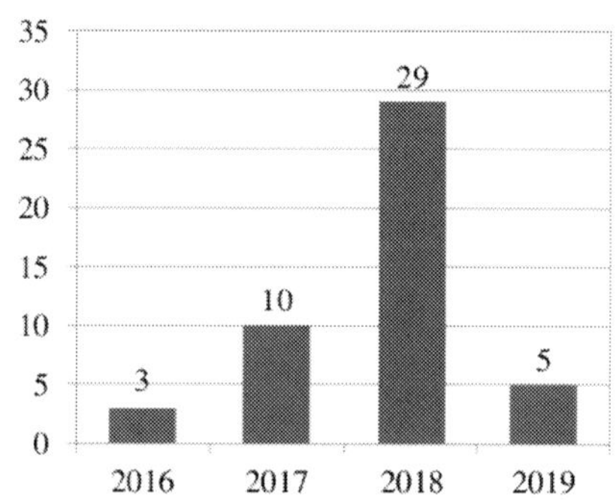

Figure 1. Reviewed papers sorted by publication year

A. Application Domains of Edge Computing (RQ1)

The idea behind RQ1 was to identify domains in which edge computing has been studied, and these domains are illustrated in Figure 2. According to our findings, smart cities and homes were application domain of many primary studies. However, the majority of these studies did not have a specific application domain, providing general contributions that could be applied to several domains.

B. Edge Computing Method or Algorithm (RQ2)

Table VII shows the purpose of algorithms used in the primary studies. Approximately one third of the primary studies relied on algorithms used for task scheduling and operation partitioning, which is expected, since those characteristics are important when implementing edge systems. The second-most addressed use for algorithms was addressing power optimisation, which is also understandable as task scheduling and operation partitioning are closely related to power consumption. A substantial number of papers contained algorithms related to image and video processing as well as data transmission, reduction, and mining. Only a few papers used algorithms related to anomaly detection, audio measurements or time efficiency. In general, Table VII shows that the area of edge computing and analytics is quite new, and more research effort is needed especially in the less addressed categories.

TABLE VI. PRIMARY STUDIES INCLUDED, WITH CORRESPONDING REFERENCES

ID	Reference	ID	Reference
S1	[12]	S25	[13]
S2	[14]	S26	[15]
S3	[16]	S27	[17]
S4	[18]	S28	[19]
S5	[20]	S29	[21]
S6	[22]	S30	[23]
S7	[5]	S31	[24]
S8	[25]	S32	[26]
S9	[27]	S33	[28]
S10	[29]	S34	[30]
S11	[31]	S35	[32]
S12	[7]	S36	[33]
S13	[34]	S37	[35]
S14	[36]	S38	[37]
S15	[38]	S39	[39]
S16	[4]	S40	[40]
S17	[41]	S41	[3]
S18	[42]	S42	[43]
S19	[44]	S43	[45]
S20	[46]	S44	[47]
S21	[48]	S45	[49]
S22	[50]	S46	[6]
S23	[51]	S47	[52]
S24	[53]		

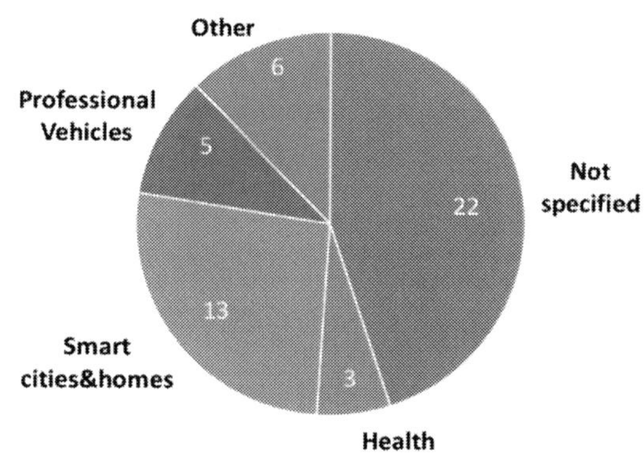

Figure 2. Edge computing application domains from reviewed studies

C. Edge Computing Framework (RQ3)

Figure 3 shows the number of papers that contributed with architectures or infrastructures. However, proposals varied widely and could not be classified further and the distinction between the two terms may be considered vague. This research question was consequently quite difficult to answer. Nonetheless, in our classification, we considered architecture to be device-internal mostly and infrastructure to be an edge-device network.

TABLE VII. TARGETS FOR USING ALGORITHMS IN THE PRIMARY STUDIES

Algorithm Output	Count	Primary Studies	Description
Data Transmission/Reduction/Mining	4	S1, S4, S24, S32	Data management and engineering
Power optimisation	9	S5, S6, S8, S18, S19,S21,S26, S27, S35	Power consumption reduction, anomaly detection
Task Scheduling & Operation Partitioning	16	S7, S11, S13, S16, S20, S23, S26, S27, S31, S34, S40, S41, S42, S44, S45, S47	Decision trees, appliance scheduling, routine handler, offloading algorithm
Anomaly Detection	3	S12, S13, S37	Vehicle anomaly detection, control loops, anomaly detection
Image Classification & Face Recognition & Video Processing & Pattern Recognition	4	S10, S17, S28, S29, S30	Image classification, face recognition, Markov model, image recognition, video processing
Audio Measurements & Time efficiency & Localization	3	S35, S39, S43	Mosquito wing-beats classification, BLE localization, delay reduction

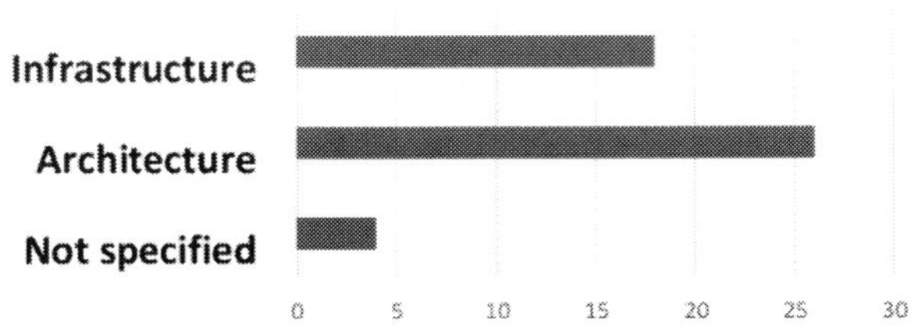

Figure 3. Articles organized by the type of edge framework proposed

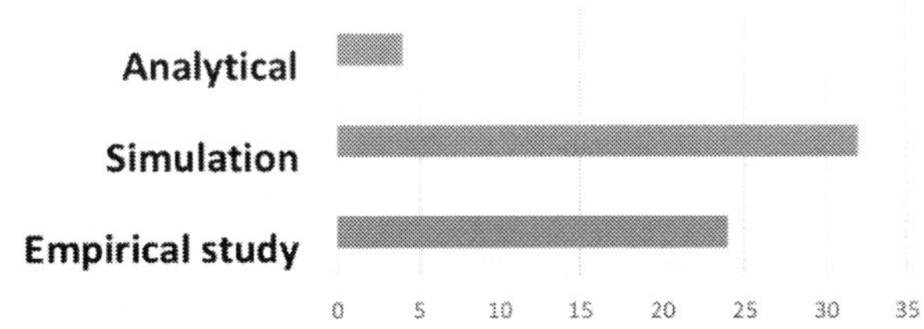

Figure 4. Evaluation methods

D. Proposals Performance

(RQ4)

The purpose of RQ4 was to evaluate the performances of the edge systems presented in the primary studies. As can be seen in Table VIII, 29 primary studies provided energy efficient solutions, mostly by reducing energy requirements for performing tasks. Solutions working in real-time i.e., providing results with minimal but approximately constant delay) were provided by 15 of the primary studies. Five primary studies provided solutions that improved computational efficiency by reducing the time required to complete certain tasks and reducing overall memory usage. Only two primary studies addressed data transmission in edge systems. The remaining nine primary studies measured various phenomena that was not easily categorised.

E. Edge Analytics Standardization Level (RQ5)

In this research, we analysed what level of standardization has been used in edge computing. According to our findings, no primary study mentioned relying on any edge computing-related standard. A few primary studies used standards that are not strictly edge-related (e.g., Controller Area Network, IEEE P1363 and NGSI), but standardization is ongoing for multi-access edge computing within European standards telecommunications institute [3].

F. Proposal Evaluation Methods (RQ6)

Evaluating proposed approaches is an important part of the this study, allowing the effectiveness if each contribution to be acknowledged and compared to other approaches. We analysed the evaluation methods that were used in the primary studies by using analytical, simulation and empirical studies (Figure 4). In the majority of the primary studies, the evaluation was conducted by performing simulations. However, empirical studies were also used in many studies. We point out that in some papers, a combination of these evaluation methods were used. Among the primary studies that were evaluated by empirical studies, case studies were the dominant method chosen. Even though the case studies relied on real implementations for their evaluations, they were mostly applied in lab environments, meaning that the evaluations were controlled by the researchers. Such environments tend to prevent events that occur in real environments.

IV. THREATS TO VALIDITY

A threat to validity of this study is that papers related to mobile edge computing were not included, since this study focused on edge computing and analytics in non-mobile environments. Consequently, some relevant papers may have been missed.

This study also only included papers published from 2016 onward, largely due to the appearance of the term "edge" towards the end of 2015. As such, there may be papers published related to this paper's topic that were published earlier and subsequently missed. There may, however, exist papers published earlier that are related to the topic of this paper, and if that is the case, those papers have been missed.

Another threat to validity is that the screening phases were performed partially by different persons. While one researcher followed the entire protocol from beginning to end, the remaining researchers had varying influence on the screening phases. These researchers may have had different

TABLE VIII. PERFORMANCE METRICS IN THE PRIMARY STUDIES

Performance Metric	Count	Primary Studies	Description
Real-time	15	S1, S12, S13, S24, S28, S29, S30, S34, S35, S36, S39, S40, S43, S45, S46	Computations are performed while the system is running. Results are available with minimal delay.
Computational Efficiency	5	S2, S33, S37, S39, S41	Reduced computation time and memory due to the use of edge system.
Energy Efficiency	29	S3, S4, S5, S6, S8, S9, S10, S11, S14, S15, S16, S18, S19, S20, S21, S22, S23, S26, S27, S29, S31, S32, S34, S35, S38, S43, S44, S45, S47	Reduced energy requirements for performing computations due to the use of edge system.
Data Transmission	2	S25, S45	Reduced response times, improved transmission rates
Other	9	S7, S17, S27, S28, S30, S34, S36, S40, S42	Task scheduling, latency, network performance, flexibility, quality of service, system bandwith, runtime performance

views regarding paper relevancy, causing relevant papers to be excluded.

In all phases where three researchers were involved, except for the data extraction phase, one researcher completed the entire phase independently, while the other two divided the workload evenly between them. Since the workload was divided, some papers may have been excluded because of differing criteria for relevance.

In the data extraction phase, each of the researchers extracted data from one third of the papers. Although each set of extracted data was double-checked by other researches in the group, there is a risk that some data may have been missed.

Finally, we point out that after each phase in the protocol, consensus discussions were held and any disagreements were resolved. Therefore, we feel any threats posed to protocol execution were minimal.

V. CONCLUSIONS

We have presented a systematic mapping study on edge computing and analytics. For the purpose of replicability, the protocol used in the study was also presented. Since the term "edge" is rather new, the papers we identified were all published in 2016 or later.

In our findings, several papers targeting task scheduling and power optimisation while few addressed other targets (such as image and face recognition, anomaly detection, data management and data engineering) to indicate a clear information gap for those fields. Many papers relied on simulating their proposals and few offered real implementations of edge technologies. Many situations, however, are difficult to simulate, because of events that are either unknown, rare or hard to predict.

Almost half of the papers did not specify their application domain, indicating that clear implementation strategies for some proposals did not exist. Among the application domains specified, smart cities and homes were the dominating application hldomains, followed by professional vehicles, the health domain, and various other domains.

ACKNOWLEDGMENTS

This work has been sponsored by the Finnish EDGE Analytics project, funded by Business Finland.

REFERENCES

[1] Frost & Sullivan online publication, "Intelligence at the edge—an outlook on edge computing." [Online] Available: https://store.frost.com/intelligence-at-the-edge-an-outlook-on-edge-computing.html (Accessed Sept. 9, 2019), 2017.

[2] Frost & Sullivan online publication, "Big data analytics in global condition monitoring, forecast to 2023." [Online] Available: https://www.researchandmarkets.com/research/tnfhf2/big_data (Accessed Sept. 9, 2019), 2017.

[3] S. Dey and A. Mukherjee, "Robotic slam: A review from fog computing and mobile edge computing perspective," in *Adjunct Proceedings of the 13th International Conference on Mobile and Ubiquitous Systems: Computing Networking and Services*, MOBIQUITOUS 2016, (New York, NY, USA), pp. 153–158, ACM, 2016.

[4] C. Xia, W. Li, X. Chang, F. Delicato, T. Yang, and A. Zomaya, "Edge-based energy management for smart homes," in *2018 IEEE 16th Intl Conf on Dependable, Autonomic and Secure Computing, 16th Intl Conf on Pervasive Intelligence and Computing, 4th Intl Conf on Big Data Intelligence and Computing and Cyber Science and Technology Congress(DASC/PiCom/DataCom/CyberSciTech)*, pp. 849–856, Aug 2018.

[5] R. Ghosh, S. P. R. Komma, and Y. Simmhan, "Adaptive energy-aware scheduling of dynamic event analytics across edge and cloud resources," in *2018 18th IEEE/ACM International Symposium on Cluster, Cloud and Grid Computing (CCGRID)*, pp. 72–82, May 2018.

[6] S. Nousias, C. Tselios, D. Bitzas, A. S. Lalos, K. Moustakas, and I. Chatzigiannakis, "Uncertainty management for wearable iot wristband sensors using laplacian-based matrix completion," in *2018 IEEE 23rd International Workshop on Computer Aided Modeling and Design of Communication Links and Networks (CAMAD)*, pp. 1–6, Sep. 2018.

[7] Z. Wang, F. Guo, Y. Meng, H. Li, H. Zhu, and Z. Cao, "Detecting vehicle anomaly by sensor consistency: An edge computing based mechanism," in *2018 IEEE Global Communications Conference (GLOBECOM)*, pp. 1–7, Dec 2018.

[8] K. Nybom, A. Ashraf, and I. Porres, "A systematic mapping study on api documentation generation approaches," in *2018 44th Euromicro Conference on Software Engineering and Advanced Applications (SEAA)*, (Prague, Czech Republic), pp. 462–469, Aug 2018.

[9] B. Kitchenham and S. Charters, "Guidelines for performing Systematic Literature Reviews in Software Engineering (version 2.3)," Tech. Rep. EBSE-2007-01, Keele University and University of Durham, 2007.

[10] C. Wohlin, P. Runeson, M. Höst, M. C. Ohlsson, B. Regnell, and A. Wesslén, *Experimentation in Software Engineering*. Springer-Verlag Berlin Heidelberg, 1 ed., 2012.

[11] M. Usman, E. Mendes, F. Weidt, and R. Britto, "Effort estimation in agile software development: A systematic literature review," in *Proceedings of the 10th International Conference on Predictive Models in Software Engineering*, PROMISE '14, (New York, NY, USA), pp. 82–91, ACM, 2014.

[12] M. Saez, S. Lengieza, F. Maturana, K. Barton, and D. Tilbury, "A data transformation adapter for smart manufacturing systems with edge and cloud computing capabilities," in *2018 IEEE International Conference on Electro/Information Technology (EIT)*, pp. 0519–0524, May 2018.

[13] B. Cheng, G. Solmaz, F. Cirillo, E. Kovacs, K. Terasawa, and A. Kitazawa, "Fogflow: Easy programming of iot services over cloud and edges for smart cities," *IEEE Internet of Things Journal*, vol. 5, pp. 696–707, April 2018.

[14] R. Morabito and N. Beijar, "A framework based on sdn and containers for dynamic service chains on iot gateways," in *Proceedings of the Workshop on Hot Topics in Container Networking and Networked Systems*, HotConNet '17, (New York, NY, USA), pp. 42–47, ACM, 2017.

[15] X. Chang, W. Li, C. Xia, J. Ma, J. Cao, S. U. Khan, and A. Y. Zomaya, "From insight to impact: Building a sustainable edge computing platform for smart homes," in *2018 IEEE 24th International Conference on Parallel and Distributed Systems (ICPADS)*, pp. 928–936, Dec 2018.

[16] J. Wang, Y. Hu, H. Li, and G. Shou, "A lightweight edge computing platform integration video services," in *2018 International Conference on Network Infrastructure and Digital Content (IC-NIDC)*, pp. 183–187, Aug 2018.

[17] D. Y. Zhang, T. Rashid, X. Li, N. Vance, and D. Wang, "Heteroedge: Taming the heterogeneity of edge computing system in social sensing," in *Proceedings of the International Conference on Internet of Things Design and Implementation*, IoTDI '19, (New York, NY, USA), pp. 37–48, ACM, 2019.

[18] L. Feng, P. Kortoçi, and Y. Liu, "A multi-tier data reduction mechanism for iot sensors," in *Proceedings of the Seventh International Conference on the Internet of Things*, IoT '17, (New York, NY, USA), pp. 6:1–6:8, ACM, 2017.

[19] B. Tang, Z. Chen, G. Hefferman, S. Pei, T. Wei, H. He, and Q. Yang, "Incorporating intelligence in fog computing for big data analysis in smart cities," *IEEE Transactions on Industrial Informatics*, vol. 13, pp. 2140–2150, Oct 2017.

[20] S. Ci, N. Lin, Y. Zhou, H. Li, and Y. Yang, "A new digital power supply system for fog and edge computing," in *2018 14th International Wireless Communications Mobile Computing Conference (IWCMC)*, pp. 1513–1517, June 2018.

[21] G. Gobieski, B. Lucia, and N. Beckmann, "Intelligence beyond the edge: Inference on intermittent embedded systems," in *Proceedings of the Twenty-Fourth International Conference on Architectural Support for Programming Languages and Operating Systems*, ASPLOS '19, (New York, NY, USA), pp. 199–213, ACM, 2019.

[22] D. Rahbari, M. Nickray, and G. Heydari, "A two-stage technique for quick and low power offloading in iot," in *Proceedings of the International Conference on Smart Cities and Internet of Things*, SCIOT '18, (New York, NY, USA), pp. 4:1–4:8, ACM, 2018.

[23] S. Yi, Z. Hao, Q. Zhang, Q. Zhang, W. Shi, and Q. Li, "Lavea: Latency-aware video analytics on edge computing platform," in *Proceedings of the Second ACM/IEEE Symposium on Edge Computing*, SEC '17, (New York, NY, USA), pp. 15:1–15:13, ACM, 2017.

[24] M. O. Ozmen and A. A. Yavuz, "Low-cost standard public key cryptography services for wireless iot systems," in *Proceedings of the 2017 Workshop on Internet of Things Security and Privacy*, IoTS&P '17, (New York, NY, USA), pp. 65–70, ACM, 2017.

[25] S. K. Bose, B. Kar, M. Roy, P. K. Gopalakrishnan, and A. Basu, "Adepos: Anomaly detection based power saving for predictive maintenance using edge computing," in *Proceedings of the 24th Asia and South Pacific Design Automation Conference*, ASPDAC '19, (New York, NY, USA), pp. 597–602, ACM, 2019.

[26] F. Xiao, L. Yuan, D. Wang, H. Cai, and X. Ma, "Max-fus caching replacement algorithm for edge computing," in *2018 24th Asia-Pacific Conference on Communications (APCC)*, pp. 616–621, Nov 2018.

[27] Z. Zhou, H. Yu, C. Xu, Z. Chang, S. Mumtaz, and J. Rodriguez, "Begin: Big data enabled energy-efficient vehicular edge computing," *IEEE Communications Magazine*, vol. 56, pp. 82–89, December 2018.

[28] Y. Fukushima, D. Miura, T. Hamatani, H. Yamaguchi, and T. Higashino, "Microdeep: In-network deep learning by micro-sensor coordination for pervasive computing," in *2018 IEEE International Conference on Smart Computing (SMARTCOMP)*, pp. 163–170, June 2018.

[29] J. Lim, J. Seo, and Y. Baek, "Camthings: Iot camera with energy-efficient communication by edge computing based on deep learning," in *2018 28th International Telecommunication Networks and Applications Conference (ITNAC)*, pp. 1–6, Nov 2018.

[30] G. S. Aujla, N. Kumar, A. Y. Zomaya, and R. Ranjan, "Optimal decision making for big data processing at edge-cloud environment: An sdn perspective," *IEEE Transactions on Industrial Informatics*, vol. 14, pp. 778–789, Feb 2018.

[31] L. Pu, X. Chen, G. Mao, Q. Xie, and J. Xu, "Chimera: An energy-efficient and deadline-aware hybrid edge computing framework for vehicular crowdsensing applications," *IEEE Internet of Things Journal*, vol. 6, pp. 84–99, Feb 2019.

[32] L. Weijian, J. Yingyan, L. Yiwen, C. Yan, and L. Peng, "Optimization method for delay and energy consumption in edge computing micro-cloud system," in *2018 5th International Conference on Systems and Informatics (ICSAI)*, pp. 839–844, Nov 2018.

[33] B. Confais, A. Lebre, and B. Parrein, "Performance analysis of object store systems in a fog/edge computing infrastructures," in *2016 IEEE International Conference on Cloud Computing Technology and Science (CloudCom)*, pp. 294–301, Dec 2016.

[34] T. Elgamal, A. Sandur, P. Nguyen, K. Nahrstedt, and G. Agha, "Droplet: Distributed operator placement for iot applications spanning edge and cloud resources," in *2018 IEEE 11th International Conference on Cloud Computing (CLOUD)*, pp. 1–8, July 2018.

[35] M. El Chamie, K. G. Lore, D. M. Shila, and A. Surana, "Physics-based features for anomaly detection in power grids with micro-pmus," in *2018 IEEE International Conference on Communications (ICC)*, pp. 1–7, May 2018.

[36] T. Nguyen and E. Huh, "Ecsim++: An inet-based simulation tool for modeling and control in edge cloud computing," in *2018 IEEE International Conference on Edge Computing (EDGE)*, pp. 80–86, July 2018.

[37] T. Rausch, C. Avasalcai, and S. Dustdar, "Portable energy-aware cluster-based edge computers," in *2018 IEEE/ACM Symposium on Edge Computing (SEC)*, pp. 260–272, Oct 2018.

[38] D. Amiri, A. Anzanpour, I. Azimi, M. Levorato, A. M. Rahmani, P. Liljeberg, and N. Dutt, "Edge-assisted sensor control in healthcare iot," in *2018 IEEE Global Communications Conference (GLOBECOM)*, pp. 1–6, Dec 2018.

[39] P. Ravi, U. Syam, and N. Kapre, "Preventive detection of mosquito populations using embedded machine learning on low power iot platforms," in *Proceedings of the 7th Annual Symposium on Computing for Development*, ACM DEV '16, (New York, NY, USA), pp. 3:1–3:10, ACM, 2016.

[40] S. Ning, Q. Ge, and H. Jiang, "Research on distributed computing method for coordinated cooperation of distributed energy and multi-devices," in *2018 33rd Youth Academic Annual Conference of Chinese Association of Automation (YAC)*, pp. 905–910, May 2018.

[41] C. Sonmez, A. Ozgovde, and C. Ersoy, "Edgecloudsim: An environment for performance evaluation of edge computing systems," in *2017 Second International Conference on Fog and Mobile Edge Computing (FMEC)*, pp. 39–44, May 2017.

[42] A. M. Khan, I. Umar, and P. H. Ha, "Efficient compute at the edge: Optimizing energy aware data structures for emerging edge hardware," in *2018 International Conference on High Performance Computing Simulation (HPCS)*, pp. 314–321, July 2018.

[43] K. Kolomvatsos and T. Loukopoulos, "Scheduling the execution of tasks at the edge," in *2018 IEEE Conference on Evolving and Adaptive Intelligent Systems (EAIS)*, pp. 1–8, May 2018.

[44] T. Mekonnen, M. Komu, R. Morabito, T. Kauppinen, E. Harjula, T. Koskela, and M. Ylianttila, "Energy consumption analysis of edge orchestrated virtualized wireless multimedia sensor networks," *IEEE Access*, vol. 6, pp. 5090–5100, 2018.

[45] S. P. Khare, J. Sallai, A. Dubey, and A. Gokhale, "Short paper: Towards low-cost indoor localization using edge computing resources," in *2017 IEEE 20th International Symposium on Real-Time Distributed Computing (ISORC)*, pp. 28–31, May 2017.

[46] S. Li and J. Huang, "Energy efficient resource management and task scheduling for iot services in edge computing paradigm," in *2017 IEEE International Symposium on Parallel and Distributed Processing with Applications and 2017 IEEE International Conference on Ubiquitous Computing and Communications (ISPA/IUCC)*, pp. 846–851, Dec 2017.

[47] C. X. Mavromoustakis, J. M. Batalla, G. Mastorakis, E. Markakis, and E. Pallis, "Socially oriented edge computing for energy awareness in iot architectures," *IEEE Communications Magazine*, vol. 56, pp. 139–145, July 2018.

[48] T. Bahreini, M. Brocanelli, and D. Grosu, "Energy-aware speculative execution in vehicular edge computing systems," in *Proceedings of the 2Nd International Workshop on Edge Systems, Analytics and Networking*, EdgeSys '19, (New York, NY, USA), pp. 18–23, ACM, 2019.

[49] P. K. Sharma, S. Rathore, Y. Jeong, and J. H. Park, "Softedgenet: Sdn based energy-efficient distributed network architecture for edge computing," *IEEE Communications Magazine*, vol. 56, pp. 104–111, December 2018.

[50] I. Petri, A. R. Zamani, D. Balouek-Thomert, O. Rana, Y. Rezgui, and M. Parashar, "Ensemble-based network edge processing," in *2018 IEEE/ACM 11th International Conference on Utility and Cloud Computing (UCC)*, pp. 133–142, Dec 2018.

[51] C. Pan, M. Xie, and J. Hu, "Enzyme: An energy-efficient transient computing paradigm for ultralow self-powered iot edge devices," *IEEE Transactions on Computer-Aided Design of Integrated Circuits and Systems*, vol. 37, pp. 2440–2450, Nov 2018.

[52] X. Li, Y. Dang, and T. Chen, "Vehicular edge cloud computing: Depressurize the intelligent vehicles onboard computational power," in *2018 21st International Conference on Intelligent Transportation Systems (ITSC)*, pp. 3421–3426, Nov 2018.

[53] K. Bhargava, G. McManus, and S. Ivanov, "Fog-centric localization for ambient assisted living," in *2017 International Conference on Engineering, Technology and Innovation (ICE/ITMC)*, pp. 1424–1430, June 2017.

Migration of Data and Applications in the Cloud

Migration of Data and Applications from SharePoint Server in SharePoint Online

Arian Kaçiu
Faculty of Computer Sciences and Engineering
UBT College
Pristina, Kosovo
e-mail:ak30369@ubt-uni.net

Edmond Jajaga
Faculty of Computer Sciences and Engineering
UBT College
Pristina, Kosovo
e-mail:edmond.jajaga@ubt-uni.net

Abstract—**SharePoint Online (SPO) is a Microsoft cloud-based business collaboration platform that is very robust and dynamic. Organizations can deploy and manage SharePoint Server on-Premises or can use SharePoint Online with an Office 365 Enterprise subscription. The platform has been in the market for almost two decades and last year SharePoint hit 100 million active monthly users in the cloud. The platform has become larger in scale, richer in features, and is improving consistently. Thus, SharePoint migration has become even more important, especially migrating into its online version. The SharePoint support cycle changes when a new version is released, which affects also the support for various features. Namely, newly added features and functionalities somehow enforce one to upgrade/migrate to the new SharePoint version. This paper seeks to show the best practices on how to do the migration of the SharePoint platform from one version to another. Five SharePoint migration projects have been described to serve as a case study. Engaging users during the migration process resulted in easier adoption of the new environment by the users and more efficient work from developers' perspective. Moreover, the study identifies 'must have actions' and 'nice to have ones' within each phase in order to do the migration properly. In particular, content owners should be given a date when to finish the clean-up of old/unused data; if they do not do that properly or at all, then at least it should be requested from them to clean-up workflows, solutions, and pages which are not in use, in order to save the time while developing/recreating them.**

Keywords-SharePoint; Data Migration; Cloud; SharePoint Online.

I. INTRODUCTION

SharePoint is a web-based collaborative platform that integrates with Microsoft Office [1]. SharePoint can be deployed and managed on-Premises (SharePoint Server 2019 is the latest version) or can be used Online with an Office 365 Enterprise subscription. It is also available in hybrid scenarios.

On the one hand, both platforms (SharePoint on-Premises and Online) include out of the box a bunch of collaboration, communication, document management and business processes modeling features; and on the other hand, they include the building blocks for many kinds of Modern Workplace solutions through a set of rich application program interfaces (API) and extensibility mechanisms [2]. SharePoint can be used as a secure place to store, organize, share, and access information from any device [3]. Microsoft states that more than 200,000 organizations and 190 million people have SharePoint for intranets, team sites and content management [4].

Like any other application, platform, or framework, SharePoint is evolving continuously over the years. We have a new version of SharePoint on-Premises almost every three years. There can be many reasons, why one should upgrade to the latest versions of SharePoint; few of them are listed below [5]:

1. Support Cycle changes when Microsoft releases a new version – To do proper support we need a deep knowledge & understanding of SharePoint's features & functionalities and help from Microsoft support to keep it running smoothly [5]. At the end of mainstream support, Microsoft no longer issues product updates, only issues security patches. After the expiration of extended support, Microsoft stops issuing patches for that product, which makes that version a security liability to continue using [6]. In Table I, there are shown some version of SharePoint Server together with their Service Pack and the dates when Microsoft will stop supporting them.
2. Features may be deprecated, and additions do occur with new versions - Microsoft stops supporting various features with every new release. A feature can be deprecated in the immediate new version and completely removed in the subsequent versions [5]. The list of features and functionalities that have been discontinued or changed in the SharePoint versions 2013 [7], 2016 [8], and 2019 [9] and the workaround or replacement for them can be found for further reading in the references. There are two options to upgrade in SharePoint on-Premises: upgrade to the new next version, then to the other and so on or use third-party migration tools to upgrade to the desired new SharePoint server version or SharePoint Online.

TABLE I. SHAREPOINT PRODUCT LIFECYCLE SUPPORT [10]

Products Released	Lifecycle Start Date	Mainstream Support End Date	Extended Support End Date
SharePoint 2007 SP3	25/10/2011	09/10/2012	10/10/2017
SharePoint 2010 SP2	23/07/2013	13/10/2015	13/10/2020
SharePoint 2013	09/01/2013	Not Applicable	Not Applicable
SharePoint 2013 SP1	25/02/2014	10/04/2018	11/04/2023
SharePoint 2016	01/05/2016	13/07/2021	14/07/2026
SharePoint 2019	22/10/2018	09/01/2024	14/07/2026

3. One important thing is that when Microsoft releases the new features in any version like SharePoint 2016 or 2019, those features are already tested and are used in Office 365 for several years. SPO/Office 365 includes some distinguishing features [5]. Firstly, SharePoint farms are hosted in Microsoft's cloud infrastructure and Microsoft applies security patches and pushes platform updates. Secondly, Office 365 has committed to 99.9% availability in their Service Level Agreement (SLA) and the cloud version receives more new features [5]. Finally, SPO is licensed on a per-user basis and can be purchased as a standalone service or as part of an Office 365 plan.

   SharePoint on-Premises has some notable features. Firstly, SharePoint farms are hosted within the organization, the organization's IT is responsible for everything like patches, updates, etc. and also maintaining the Active Directory Domain Services on-Premises. Lastly, licensing is done buying Client Access Licenses (CALs) for either each device or person accessing the SharePoint server [5].

   As with other data migration projects, the most important things in SharePoint migrations are planning and analysis. Based on [11], the following steps should be carefully taken into account before and during the migration process:

- Make a detailed inventory of the environment – this helps us to make better decisions and estimates on the effort of the migration. We should have an inventory list of whole structure like site collections, sites, and lists, custom solutions, workflows, pages, users, and groups used retention policies, permissions, large lists or libraries, lists with lookup columns/dependencies to other lists and User Interface (UI) customizations (JavaScript, altered menus, etc.). Nice to have is an inventory list of content types, records, site columns, user alerts, and branding.
- Clean up the old environment - Contact the site/content owners and ask them to do this before the migration starts. They must find and delete unused and duplicated content; break large site collections into multiple site collections; promote large sites into site collections, review and reorganize very large lists. Removing "orphaned users", empty SharePoint groups, unwanted versions and reorganizing lists and libraries with too many columns would be nice too.
- Prepare the destination environment –We must take the time to plan and structure a new home according to the new requirements/needs. It is nice to redesign the landing page if the stakeholders agree with this.
- Communicate with users – Users should be informed about migration before starting it, downtime planned, estimated timeline, the reason for the change and the value for them and possible changes in the environments.
- Start the migration – We must choose the appropriate site template, map SharePoint groups, migrate one by one Site Collection according to the plan, review the migration report/log file and fix the issues, redesign/recreate pages to modern ones and workflows and solutions.
- Post migration – We have to make sure that everything was migrated successfully, test all workflows, check user permissions, set access to read-only/remove in the old SharePoint and redirect users to the new one.

In Section 2 we will explain in details five case studies and the approach used during these migrations. In Section 3 we have a discussion part, where we have discussed lessons learned from these migrations, some critical pitfalls that one must be aware before the migration, comparing the migration methods used here and also what happens when the size is way bigger than the largest size of our case study. In section 4 we have the conclusion, where we have explained the steps for successful migration process, the finding of this paper and also the future works.

II. CASE STUDIES

As a case study, we have used five SharePoint migration projects with which we had experience in the past. The first two are completed in Cacttus Company in Pristina and the others in McKesson Europe AG in Stuttgart for three McKesson Business Units: McKesson UK, Admenta – Italy, and Lloydsapotek – Sweden. In the context of versions, one of them is from SharePoint Server 2007 to SharePoint Server 2010 and the other four from SharePoint Server to SharePoint Online.

A. Upgrade/Migrate SharePoint Server 2007 to SharePoint Server 2010

There are two basic upgrade approaches for the upgrade from SharePoint Server 2007 to SharePoint Server 2010: in-place upgrade and database attach upgrade. An in-place upgrade is used to upgrade all Microsoft SharePoint sites on the same hardware. A database attach upgrade is used to move the content to a new farm or new hardware. One can also combine these two types of the upgrade in hybrid approaches that reduce downtime during an upgrade [12].

There were more than 30 site collections in the old SharePoint 2007 Intranet and the first thing was getting approval from the content owner and delete the unused site collections and move some of the data from different site collections to a new one named Archive. The other 12 frequently-used site collections were prepared for the upgrade. Then database attach upgrade was used with the following steps:

1. Run the Pre-Upgrade Check command in stsadm on the SharePoint 2007 Server to identify and fix the potential upgrade issues before upgrade
2. Set up and configure a new SharePoint Server 2010 farm. Then transfer all customizations to the new farm and tests the environment.
3. Detach the content databases from the old Office SharePoint Server 2007 farm.
4. Attach the content databases to the new farm and upgrade the content.
5. Confirmation that the upgrade has finished successfully and then configures the new farm to start serving requests at the new URL.

B. Migrate of SharePoint Server 2010 to SharePoint Online

The manual migration process, in this case, was performed with the following order:

- First, we created a similar structure of the Intranet including Site Collections
- Then the sites were saved as templates and then moved over to SharePoint Online to the appropriate site collections
- Then the lists/libraries were saved as templates and then moved over to SharePoint Online to the appropriate site collections/sites
- Some of the libraries the documents were moved from the old into the new environment using the explorer view
- Then the forms developed in InfoPath 2010 were moved to SPO by first changing the connection strings in the form
- Workflows have been exported to Visio and then import in the new site and then the config files were modified. Since SharePoint Designer does not provide a direct way to move list workflows and we could not use third-party tools, we used the above way of migrating them by manually changing the config.xoml files between the sites [13].

C. Migrate of SharePoint Server 2013 to SharePoint Online

ShareGate Desktop third party application was used to make the move to SharePoint Online seamless, without impacting the users regardless of how complex the migration project was. It provides a user-friendly interface and it is cost-effective. ShareGate, with its intuitive features, helps to prepare, execute, and validate the data migration whether one is migrating an entire environment or just a few lists [14].

C1. Migration of Swedish Intranet

Swedish Intranet is mainly used to share news and documents with pharmacies. An overview of the Swedish Intranet Inventory is depicted in Figure 1. The Intranet consisted of one site collection with eight sites. The total size was 2.46 GB. There were eight sites with custom master pages, and nine custom features in five of them. The number of checked-out files was nine in six libraries.

Firstly, content owners have been informed to clean up old/unused data from the old environment until a specific date. In order to make it a little bit easier for them, two specific reports in Excel with Unused Documents and Unused Lists for more than 6 months were sent to them. New SharePoint Online Site was created and then the initial content migration was done, from the old one into the new environment. After the initial migration, some issues were found and immediately were fixed. Moreover, all the pages on the new environment were recreated to new modern ones. On the Intranet landing page Newsfeed capability was heavily used to communicate with pharmacies. Since the Newsfeed is not available in the new Office 365 tenants it was decided to use Yammer instead of it. Links in the Top Navigation were also recreated.

After finishing all the above tasks, the end-users were informed that the old Intranet will be set to Read Only for all the users on a specific date and they should update bookmarks in their browsers. After this notification, the site was set to Read Only and a visible banner on the landing page with the PowerShell script and then the final migration has been done. A similar approach can be achieved by setting the site as Read Only in Central Admin and adding a banner on the site landing page with SharePoint Designer, editing page, or a content editor web part.

The visible banner was set on the old Intranet landing page informing the users that the migration is done to the new Intranet. Link to the new Intranet was also present and the information whom to contact if they encounter any error or have any issues using the new version.

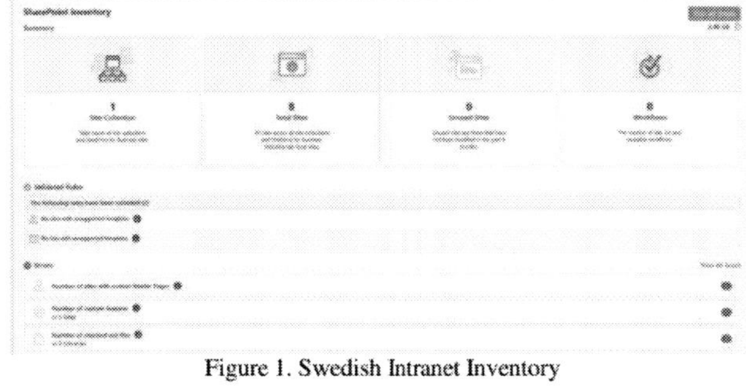

Figure 1. Swedish Intranet Inventory

C2. Migration of Italian Intranet

An overview of the Italian Intranet Inventory is depicted in Figure 2. It consists of one site collection with four sites. The total size was 4.80 GB and there were 21 workflows. There were five custom features in four sites. The number of checked-out files was 84 in 14 libraries.

Since Italian Intranet had similarities with the Swedish one, we followed the same approach during the migration except that Italian Intranet had a huge number of workflows that needed to be migrated/recreated. Also, it was decided that the workflow history list will be migrated only as an 'archive' list and the running instances of workflows will not be migrated. All the items on the lists were workflows were attached were migrated before migrating workflows.

Workflows were migrated from the old to the new environment using ShareGate tool by stopping first the list workflows from starting when the new item is created or modified, and publish them in the old environment. Then the workflows were migrated from the old to the new Intranet and the actions were rebuilt in the new workflows which were not migrated because they were not supported in Nintex Online. Then the conditions to start the workflow were changed to be the same as in the old Intranet and the new workflows were published. Lastly, the content owners were asked to test the workflows.

After finishing all workflows, communication has been done to the end-users, old Intranet was set to Read Only and the final content incremental migration has been done. The banner was set on the old Intranet to inform users about the changes and the new URL of the new environment.

C3. Migration of UK Intranet

UK Intranet is mainly used to share news and documents with all participants and for managing documents within different departments/projects there. As illustrated in Figure 3, the UK Intranet consisted of 30 site collections with 95 sites. The total size was 65.40 GB. There were 14 sites with custom master pages, and 55 custom features in 42 sites. The number of checked-out files was 43 in 19 libraries.

Here we have used a different approach compared with the previous migration of Intranets. It was decided first migrating only the root site collection into the new SPO site

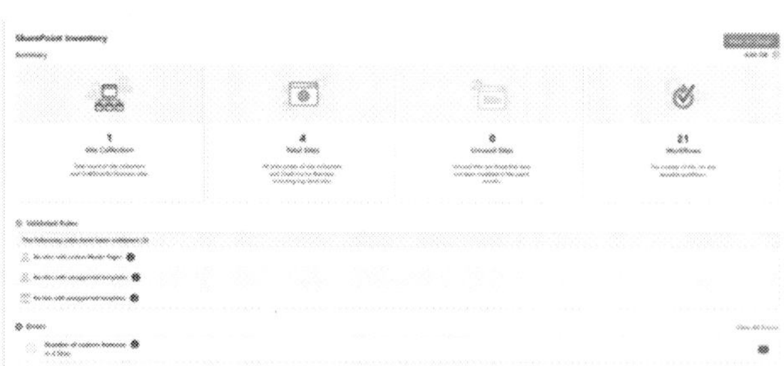

Figure 2. Italian Intranet Inventory

Figure 3. UK Intranet Inventory

and then to go live with this site. All the links to the other site collections in the new site were pointing to the old site collections. Then the other site collections have been migrated one by one and after that, the links in the root site to that specific site collection have been updated. Before going live with this solution, the following things were previously done:

- An initial communication has been sent to all users to inform that migration of their Intranet will start.
- The content owners have been informed to clean up old/unused data from the old environment.
- All the news articles of the actual year were created in new modern pages since previously ones were as the blog posts which is not supported in modern sites
- Training to the communication team was done and a manual was delivered on how to create news articles with modern pages
- The old root site collection was migrated to the new separated site collection
- The new root site collection was used to hold only the news part and some subsites
- IIS redirect was used to redirect users from the old to the new UK Intranet
- The new banner was added to the new root site collection to inform the users about the migration

A new page for the migration plan was created to inform users about timescales and support contact. A report was viewed on the page with the information about when the migration will start and end for each site collections/sites. Also, chart and pie graphics were added with information on how many site collections or sites were migrated and how many others are waiting for. The information on this page was updated frequently when new sites/site collections were migrated and the rows on Excel report were set to green for the migrated ones.

The migration of the site collections was done one by one. Using the script, the site was set to Read Only for 1-3 business days based on the predefined schedule/plan, and banner was added to inform the users that the migration is ongoing in that area. Then the migration started and all the pages on the new site collection were recreated to modern ones. After the migration of the site was finished the banner was changed to the migration is finished and the new URL was there. Since there were lots of pages in each site/site collection we have used a ModernizingPages [15] PowerShell script to do the conversion between the classic pages to the modern ones, and then redo the web parts which were not migrated properly. The description of the code is shown below.

```
$user = "ak30369@ubt-uni.net"
1. $cred = Get-Credential -UserName
   $user
2. Connect-PnPOnline -Url
   https://ubt.sharepoint.com/sites/hr/
   -Credentials $cred
3. $pages = Get-PnPListItem -List
   sitepages
4. foreach ($page in $pages)
5. { Write-Host "Modernizing"
   $page.FieldValues["FileLeafRef"]
   "..."
6. $modernPage = ConvertTo-
   PnPClientSidePage -Identity
   $page.FieldValues["FileLeafRef"] -
   Overwrite Write-Host
   "Done" -ForegroundColor Green}
```

Code from lines 1-3 will prompt for password and creates a context for the other PowerShell commands to use. Code in line 4 will get all the pages in the library named "SitePages". Code in line 5 will iterate over all pages which are saved on variable $pages. Finally, code from lines 6-7 will create a modern version for the classic pages, which will be saved to Site Pages library and named to ex. Migrated_Home.aspx.

After finishing all the site collections based on the migration plan, another final communication was sent to the users to inform them that their Intranet migration is done, and they should ask the Local Support Desk team about any issue.

III. DISCUSSIONS

SharePoint Online is a cloud-based service that helps organizations share and manage content, knowledge, and applications to empower teamwork, quickly find information, and seamlessly collaborate across the organization [16]. Capabilities of SharePoint have expanded greatly from the original 2001 version to SharePoint 2019 and SharePoint Online. SharePoint support cycle changes when Microsoft releases a new version, which affects also the support for various features by Microsoft. Because of this and the coming of new features and functionalities with the new version, there is a must to upgrade/migrate to the new SharePoint version. There are two options to upgrade in SharePoint on-Premises, move through each version as one upgrade or use third-party migration tools to upgrade to the desired version directly and to SharePoint Online. Moving forward, Microsoft will continue its focus on SharePoint Online/Office 365 to make it available and useful for organizations of every shape and size. Office 365 has some distinguishing features. Firstly, SharePoint farms are hosted in Microsoft's cloud infrastructure and Microsoft applies security patches and pushes platform updates. Secondly, Office 365 has committed to 99.9% availability in its service level agreement (SLA) and the cloud version receives more new features. Lastly, some features will never be available on-Premises: Microsoft Graph, Delve, Power Automate, and Power Apps.

After a specified period that the migration has been completed, one should lock the old Intranet to enforce users who still use it in Read-Only mode to switch to the new migrated Intranet. Probably users will complain that they do not have access but they can be informed that they were accessing the old Intranet and they should use the new one in the appropriate URL that is going to be shared with them.

As it is explained in a blog [17], it is always required that the migrations to be of the highest quality and often must balance costs and time while defining their migration roadmap. The lack of resources adds another layer of complexity to the migration process. During our experience with many projects, we found that there is a tendency to take an inexpensive approach, whereby data is directly transferred to the new environment, without much analysis or clean-up. While this may be a relatively inexpensive way to balance the two important parameters of cost and time, it is certainly not the most efficient way. There are some critical pitfalls one must be aware of before upgrading or migrating to a new SharePoint environment [17]:

- *SharePoint Upgrade is the responsibility only of the IT team.* All stakeholders should be consulted, and a consensus emerges regarding the SharePoint roadmap of an organization [17].
- *To migrate, we need only a source and a destination environment.* The new environment must support all the components present in the current environment [17].
- *Consider compatibility requirements of third-party applications' integration.* Before starting with any migration, one must check for the compatibility of all third-party tools with the new environment. Eventually, one should update the tools to a version that is more compatible with the new environment [17].
- *Scatter information.* A SharePoint migration team must map all the information with the relevant metadata. The right set of documents must be identified, along with their versions to be transferred to the destination [17].
- *No documentation of the current legacy system.* Documentation should contain an overview of the architectural and system considerations, with web parts & external data sources. The document should provide also details of all previous migrations or SharePoint upgrade experiences, along with the type of approach used to migrate [17].

External sharing. Users in SharePoint Online can share sites, folders, and individual documents with anyone, who has a Microsoft Account linked to their corporate e-mail address. There is also the possibility to generate Guest Links, which allow Read or Edit permissions to be granted without requiring authentication while allowing the Guest Links to be revoked at any time.

Stay up to date, always. Users of the online version are privileged to get early updates on new releases upgrades than those who use SharePoint On-Premises. Moreover, some features might not be available for the on-Premises at all.

TABLE II. INVENTORY OF INTRANETS

Intranet Projects	Data in Numbers				
	Size in GB	*Site Collections*	*Sites*	*Workflows*	*Custom features*
UK	65.40	30	95	0	55
Italian	4.80	1	4	21	5
Swedish	2.46	1	8	0	9

In Table II, there are shown inventories of the Intranets' contents, from the three last projects before migration took place. Comparing migration method of the Italian and Swedish Intranet with the UK, we have found that the migration pattern we followed in the UK case proved to be the best one. Giving the users direct access to the new Intranet (SPO) at the initial stage of the migration project resulted in more engagement and adoption by the users. Addressing issues appearing in early stages resulted in a smoother migration process, which to the best of our knowledge has not been considered by other related works.

If the total size is way bigger than the largest size of our case studies (65.4GB) or much more workflows or sites are to be migrated, then it will require more time, planning and efforts. Also, we have to keep in mind that the migration performance can be affected by network infrastructure, file size, migration time, and throttling.

IV. CONCLUSION

The migration of data and applications on the cloud outlines one of the most important processes after each application version publishing. A summary of the recommended steps needed for a successful migration process includes the following [11]:

1. Make a detailed inventory of the environment
2. Clean up the old environment
3. Prepare the destination environment
4. Communicate with users
5. Start the migration
6. Post- migration

Content owners should be given a date when to finish the clean-up of old/unused data; if they do not do it properly or at all, then at least we should request from them to clean-up workflows, pages and, solutions which are not used, to save our time while recreating them. The findings in this paper show that in order to have a smoother migration and better users' adoption one should engage users with the new environment as earlier as possible during the migration process.. An insight into user experience with the migration process would be understood by conducting a questionnaire, which is planned as per future works. Other future works include recommendations regarding the custom code solutions and modernization of other customizations and applications to get them ready for migration to SPO.

ACKNOWLEDGMENT

We would like to thank UBT College for supporting this paper.

REFERENCES:

[1] SharePoint, https://en.wikipedia.org/wiki/SharePoint, [retrieved: April 2020]

[2] T. Redmond, Office 365 for IT Professionals (2020 Edition), Tony Redmond, 2019

[3] What is SharePoint?, https://support.office.com/en-us/article/What-is-SharePoint-97b915e6-651b-43b2-827d-fb25777f446f, [retrieved: April 2020]

[4] SharePoint Product Info, https://products.office.com/en-us/sharepoint/collaboration, [retrieved: April 2020]

[5] "4 reasons to migrate to the latest version of SharePoint", https://saketa.com/blog/four-reasons-to-migrate-to-the-latest-version-of-sharepoint/, [retrieved: April 2020]

[6] "SharePoint End of Life", https://sharepoint.fpweb.net/sharepoint/end-of-life, [retrieved: August 2019]

[7] Microsoft, "Discontinued features and modified functionality in Microsoft SharePoint 2013", https://support.office.com/en-us/article/discontinued-features-and-modified-functionality-in-microsoft-sharepoint-2013-bbbb0815-2538-4f1d-b647-1f7f6d508c93, [retrieved: April 2020]

[8] Microsoft, "What's deprecated or removed from SharePoint Server 2016", https://docs.microsoft.com/en-us/sharepoint/what-s-new/what-s-deprecated-or-removed-from-sharepoint-server-2016, [retrieved: April 2020]

[9] Microsoft, "What's deprecated or removed from SharePoint Server 2019", https://docs.microsoft.com/en-us/sharepoint/what-s-new/what-s-deprecated-or-removed-from-sharepoint-server-2019, [retrieved: April 2020]

[10] "SharePoint End of Life", https://sharepoint.fpweb.net/sharepoint/end-of-life, [retrieved: August 2019]

[11] B. Niaulin, "The ultimate SharePoint migration checklist", https://get.sharegate.com/rs/250-JDV-062/images/SharePoint-Migration-Checklist.pdf, [retrieved: April 2020]

[12] "Upgrading to SharePoint Server 2010", https://www.raybiztech.com/solutions/epcm/sharepoint-portal-solutions/knowledge-base/upgrading-to-sharepoint-server-2010, [retrieved: April 2020]

[13] "Migrate SharePoint Designer List Workflows step by step", https://praveensharepointknowledgebase.wordpress.com/2015/03/17/migrate-sharepoint-designer-list-workflows-step-by-step/, [retrieved: April 2020]

[14] "Migrate to SharePoint or Office 365 with confidence", https://sharegate.com/products/sharegate-desktop/migration, [retrieved: April 2020]

[15] N. Nachan, "Transform Classic SharePoint Pages To Modern Look And Feel", https://www.c-sharpcorner.com/article/transform-classic-sharepoint-pages-to-modern-look-and-feel/, [retrieved: April 2020]

[16] Microsoft, "Introduction to SharePoint Online", https://docs.microsoft.com/en-us/sharepoint/introduction, [retrieved: April 2020]

[17] "5 Pitfalls to avoid while you upgrade your SharePoint environment", https://saketa.com/blog/5-pitfalls-to-avoid-while-you-upgrade-migrate-your-sharepoint-environment/, [retrieved: April 2020]

System Operator: A Tool for System Management in Kubernetes Clusters

Jiye Yu
Services Computing Research Dept.
Center for Technology Innovation - Digital Technology
Hitachi, Ltd. R&D Group
Email: jiye.yu.kb@hitachi.com

Yuki Naganuma
Services Computing Research Dept.
Center for Technology Innovation - Digital Technology
Hitachi, Ltd. R&D Group
Email: yuki.naganuma.mk@hitachi.com

Takaya Ide
Services Computing Research Dept.
Center for Technology Innovation - Digital Technology
Hitachi, Ltd. R&D Group
Email: takaya.ide.ap@hitachi.com

***Abstract*—Kubernetes is the most popular container orchestration system for automating application deployment. To adapt thousands of applications' working pattern, Kubernetes Operators are proposed as the default approach for packaging, deploying and managing an application in Kubernetes. Now, different kinds of Operators are developed to support applications in various categories. However, a single Operator only applies to a single application. Users still need to pay effort to deploy, monitor or maintain a system which is formed by a class of applications. Thus, Our System Operator is created to provide a help. It is able to connect applications in Kubernetes by connecting applications' Operator in Graphic User Interface (GUI) canvas. Instead of users, System Operator can help maintain the whole system according to organized pattern. It will be a great help for the flexible utilization of Kubernetes.**

Keywords–Container; Kubernetes; Kubernetes Operator; System Operator

I. INTRODUCTION

Virtual machines used to be one of the best options when companies deploy their services. At that time, OpenStack and Amazon Web Services (AWS)) are famous for its stable virtual server quality. During that period, a large number of software applications are designed in monolithic architecture pattern [1]. Monolithic architecture pattern, trending to integrate all components in one server, tends to cause problems like long building time, poor resilience to failures, incompatibility issues. Then, container [2] is invented to be a new form of operating system virtualization. Kubernetes [3], an open source container platform, is raised by Google to help manage containers and automates many of the manual processes in container's deployment and management. Because of its convenience and powerful advantages, now Kubernetes is becoming the most popular container orchestration tool in IT industry.

Along with the benefits Kubernetes brings to us, it also introduces some new issues. Due to the abundant functionality of Kubernetes, in order to get qualified as a Kubernetes engineer, meticulous training is commonly required. Engineers who are not familiar with infrastructure technology will feel it difficult to try Kubernetes because of its complexity [4].

On the other side, concept Kubernetes Operator [5] raised by CoreOS is designed for packaging, deploying and managing a Kubernetes application automatically. With Kubernetes Operators, people are able to share their knowledge on application management, as well as save effort and time on DevOps. Operators bring convenience to Kubernetes users. However, users still need to deploy Operators by themselves.

With Kubernetes and Operator, more and more companies trend to migrate their legacy systems to modern architecture. However, lack of specialized knowledge becomes a barrier for the migration.

Legacy system requires system management as a entirety, while Kubernetes allows container-specific management of distributed system. Even with Kubernetes Operator's help, engineers need to deploy individual applications and connect them to build an entire system. Engineers who are used to legacy management mode need to try hard to break down barriers.

In the other hand, the Cloud Native Ecosystems like Cloud Native Computing Foundation (CNCF) Cloud Native Interactive Landscape [6] and OperatorHub [7] obtain favorable development. Containers based applications and related Operators are developed and released as Open Source Software (OSS), which are available to anyone. This is a great benefit to develop our proposal, System Operator.

The remaining of this paper is organized as follows. Section 2 gives a brief introduction of System Operator. Section 3 explains how System Operator works and what System Operator can be used to do. Finally, in section 4, we make the conclusion, and list out our future work at the same time.

II. SYSTEM OPERATOR

In order to solve above issues, we designed a new tool, System Operator. System Operator is used to create and maintain systems which are composed by various applications.

System Operator is designed to meet following targets:

1) Easy to use: reduce the requirements on user's knowledge on Kubernetes.
2) High applicability: by choosing proper Application Operators, users are able to create all appropriate systems they want.
3) Expandability: users can apply their own configs to System Operator to achieve their requirements on system maintenance.

The complete workflow of System Operator will be divided into several steps. First, users need to select all necessary Application Operators, connect and configure them to make up a system. Then, System Operator will automatically generate

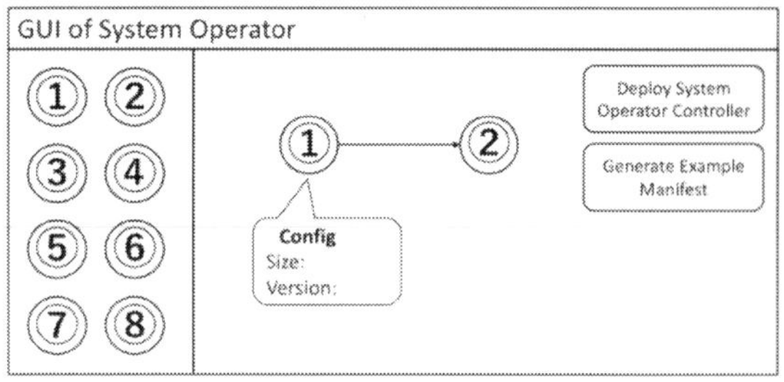

Figure 1. GUI of System Operator

the deployment manifest. Using the generated manifest, users can easily deploy the system to target Kubernetes cluster.

Besides deployment, System Operator can also continuously monitor all resources created by these Application Operators. According to the result of monitoring, adjustment will be executed to keep the system stable. To achieve this aim, there is an issue needs to be solved first. Application Operator is always designed as a black box. Only part of the Application Operators are providing the API for calling corresponding resource's status. Due to this reason, it is not easy for System Operator to get status of resources created by selected Application Operators. Detailed information will be introduced in next section "How System Operator works".

A. *Graphic User Interface (GUI)*

GUI support is important on improving the usability of this tool. Inspired by OpenStack Heat Dashboard [8], GUI of the System Operator is designed as Figure 1. Various kinds of Operator icons are listed on the left side. Users need to select Application Operators with different functions from the left-hand column. Then, drag and drop selected Operator icons to the canvas on the right side. After dragging and dropping Operator icons, users can connect these icons to build the skeleton of their target system. The line used to connect two icons is a directed arrow. An arrow (x, y) is considered to be directed from icon x to icon y, another arrow (y, z) is considered to be directed from icon y to icon z. Thus, icon y is a previous node of icon z, and icon x is also previous node of icon z. These arrows are used to arrange the network traffic in target system.

By connecting the Operators, the skeleton of system will be presented in the canvas. In order to generate the manifest, users are also required to fill the config for each Operator. System Operator controller which is used to manage these selected Operators in Kuberntes cluster will also be deployed by clicking the button on canvas.

III. How System Operator works

System Operator is used to manage the Application Operators instead of human. By monitoring the status of resources, System Operator can make rapid reaction when sudden events happen. In the following subsections, we will introduce how System Operator works from brief architecture to details.

A. *Architecture of System Operator*

Figure 2 shows a brief architecture of System Operator as well as the steps System Operator will do to deploy a system in the Kubernetes cluster.

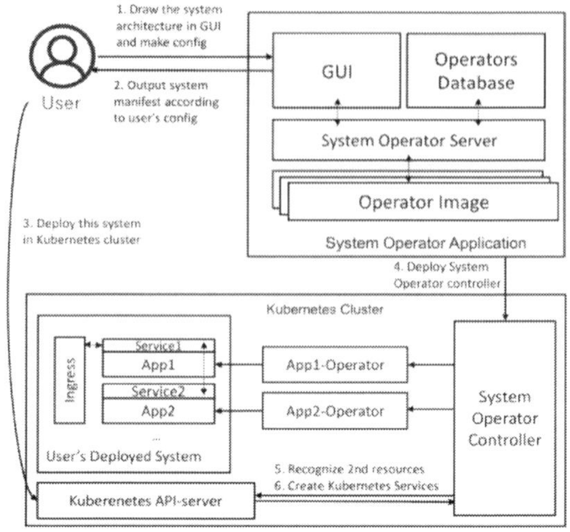

Figure 2. Architecture of System Operator

First, System Operator Application will provide a GUI for accepting user's request, a database and a storage to store the information for Application Operators and Application Operator images. After System Operator accepting user's request (step 1), it will generate a manifest and respond to users (step 2). After deploying of the manifest (step 3), System Operator Application will also deploy corresponding System Operator controller in the same Kubernetes cluster (step 4) to maintain the deployed system. Then, System Operator controller will call Kubernetes API server to recognize all secondary resources of each Application (step 5). At last, System Operator controller in Kubernetes will complete the user's system deployment in Kubernetes cluster by connecting all applications deployed by adding Kubernetes Services among them (step 6). Detailed description will be introduced in following subsections.

B. *Use Kubernetes Service resource to connect applications*

In normal cases, an integrated system is composed by several applications. In legacy system, engineers use IP address or hostname to make the connection for integrated system. In Kubernetes cluster, in order to generate invariable cluster IP, System Operator will use Kubernetes Service resource to bind applications and make the connection. In order to bind Kubernetes Services with application resources, we need to recognize these application resources first. Not only the Custom Resource [9] defined by Custom Resource Definition (CRD), but also the secondary resources of those CRD resources.

C. *Secondary resources*

Secondary resources are defined as resources created by Application Operator and managed by Operator's CRD resources. Taking Nginx Operator as an example, Nginx is the CRD resource and deployment created by Nginx is its secondary resource. For keeping the active status of CRD resources, the status of secondary resources is important. Also, we need to bind Kubernetes Service resources to secondary resources in order to integrate the whole system. That is the reason why we need to recognize all applications' the secondary resources.

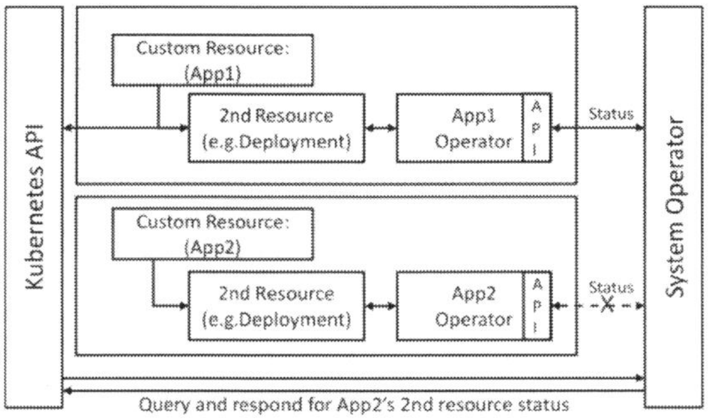

Figure 3. Not all Application Operators provide API for status of secondary resources

D. How to recognize secondary resources

Basically, an Application Operator is designed as black box. Only a few APIs are provided by an Application Operator to communicate with users. In most cases, Application Operator will provide the API to show its secondary resources' status. However, there is no assurance that every Application Operator provides this feature. As Figure 3 shows, without these specific APIs, it is hard for System Operator to recognize secondary resources of Application Operators. System Operator needs to first recognize secondary resources for those Application Operators. Then, System Operator can query secondary resources' status by calling Kubernetes API directly.

As a solution, System Operator can utilize the name and created time of secondary resource to do the reverse inference. In order to accelerate this process, System Operator will maintain a database to record all resource's information collected after manifest applied. Items like resource name, resource type, created time and current status will be recorded in the database. We suppose that there are n Resources in this Kubernetes cluster $(R_1, ..., R_n)$, and in our target system, there are m Custom Resources are deployed $(C_1, ..., C_m)$. What we want to do is to select resources which belong to specified Custom Resource. According to the information recorded in the database, we use following evaluation methods to evaluate the belonging of these secondary resources.

1) Time period evaluation: We define the interval between resource created time and manifest applied time as α. First, we should note that in various Kubernetes clusters, time used to create a resource is not fixed. That means α in various Kubernetes clusters is not a constant. It depends on the transmission delay, computing capability of the hosts and some other factors. In order to keep the accuracy of this evaluation, we need to eliminate this interference caused by the variable α. System Operator will first do dry run several times to create several mock resources. By recording the time difference every time, System Operator can calculate the average value as α in each specific Kubernetes cluster.

Resources whose creating time is close to (manifest applied time + α) tend to be real secondary resources. Either too early or too late will reduce the possibility. To emphasize this characteristic, we can use exponential function to make this evaluation:

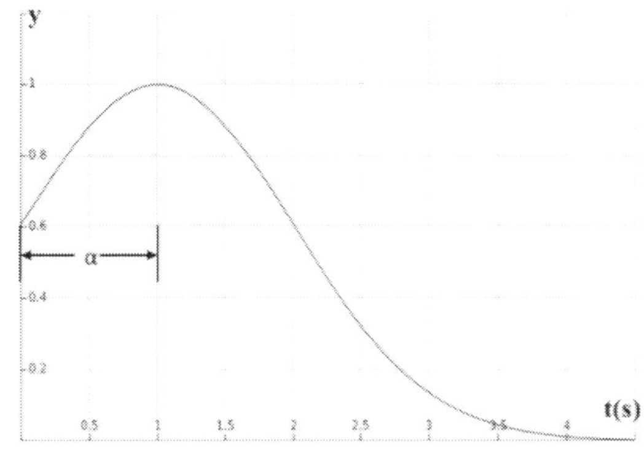

Figure 4. Graph of the time period based evaluation function, suppose $\alpha = 1(s)$

$$y_{ij} = e^{-\frac{(t_{ij}-\alpha)^2}{2}}, \quad (t_{ij} \geq 0) \tag{1}$$

Figure 4 shows the graph of this function. Here, t_{ij} is the difference between Resource R_i's created time and manifest of Custom Resource C_j's applied time. When t_{ij} is equal to α, the evaluation will meet the largest value: 1.

2) Name and label mapping evaluation: According to the convention that the resource name should include the CRD type name as much as possible. We can set the second evaluation equation as follows:

$$x_{i,j} = \frac{(l_{i,j}^1 + l_{i,j}^2)^2}{4L_j^2}, \quad (l_{i,j}^1, l_{i,j}^2 \leq L) \tag{2}$$

Here L_j is the character length of CRD type name of Custom Resource C_j; $l_{i,j}^1$ is the matched character length between Resource R_i's name and Custom Resource C_j's CRD type name; $l_{i,j}^2$ is the matched character length between Resource R_i's label and Custom Resource C_j's CRD type name.

For instance, there are two resources R_1 and R_2, whose names are example-keycloak (R_1) and example-kafka (R_2). R_1's label is $instance = example - keycloak$ while R_2's label is $instance = example - kafka$. Then, comparing with Custom Resource C_1 Keycloak, we can count that $L_1 = 8$, $l_{1,1}^1 = l_{1,1}^2 = 8$, $l_{2,1}^1 = l_{2,1}^2 = 1$. Then, finally calculate the value $x_{1,1} = 1$, $x_{2,1} = \frac{1}{64}$.

3) Joint Evaluation: An much more exact and rational result can be obtained by joint optimization of (1) and (2). We can get the possibility of the belonging of each resource is shown as following:

$$r_{i,j} = x_{i,j} \cdot y_{i,j} \tag{3}$$

For each Resource R_i, we can find the Custom Resource C_j to meet the largest value. Then, we can find out the Custom Resource which Resource R_i belongs to by following equation:

$$\arg \max_{j \in [1,M]} \{r_{i,j}\} \tag{4}$$

We should note that some resources already exist before target system's deployment. That means not every Resource R_i belongs to some Custom Resource C_j. For this reason, we should set an threshold θ_j for each Custom Resource C_j to cut those confusing resources. For a Resource R_i, if its max possibility value $\max_{j\in[1,M]}\{r_{i,j}\} < \theta_j$, we can confirm that this Resource R_i does not belong to any Custom Resource C_j.

Regarding to the estimation of the variable θ_j, there are several algorithms to determine the threshold automatically. Since the possibility $r(i,j) \in [0,1]$, some automatic image thresholding algorithms like Otsu's method [10] can be applied here for threshold determining.

4) Reversing verification: After matching Custom Resources and secondary resources, System Operator needs to do the reversing verification to confirm this resource recognition is correct. Check the network traffic between neighbor secondary resources to verify the secondary resources recognition is a good method. Since System Operator already knows the connection of Custom Resources and traffic according to user's definition, the data stream used for testing should be able to pass through all related secondary resources in turn.

After secondary resources recognition, System Operator can get the status of recognized secondary resources by calling Kubernetes API directly. System Operator will do the regular polling to watch all related resources' status and update them in its internal database.

E. System regulation

Besides system deployment, another function of System Operator is system regulation. In current stage, we have designed two application scenarios for System Operator to handle the whole system. System Operator will do something when:

1) Error happens on secondary resource.
2) Upgrade is executed.

System Operator will watch the status of all secondary resources and make rapid reactions to any changes on the system level. Once unhealthy status happens on any secondary resource, System Operator should send a "stop signal" to all previous Operators of the error one. Here the sequential order of Application Operator can be decided by directed arrows connected in GUI by users.

By default, the Operator received "stop signal" will do nothing, and users can define what should the Operator do properly according to Kubernetes resource ConfigMap. On the other hand, when the unhealthy status recover, System Operator will also send another signal "recover signal" to previous Operators to tell them issue settled. After receiving "recover signal", Operators which have made any changes will revert to the original status.

Similar to the case error happening, when users are making upgrade to some application through Application Operator, System Operator will detect this upgrade action and send stop signal to previous Application Operators. After upgrade, recover signal will be sent as well.

Figure 5 shows an example for application upgrade case. When users applied an updated manifest to upgrade App2, System Operator can easily detect the status change on App2's resource. Then, a stop signal will be sent to the previous node

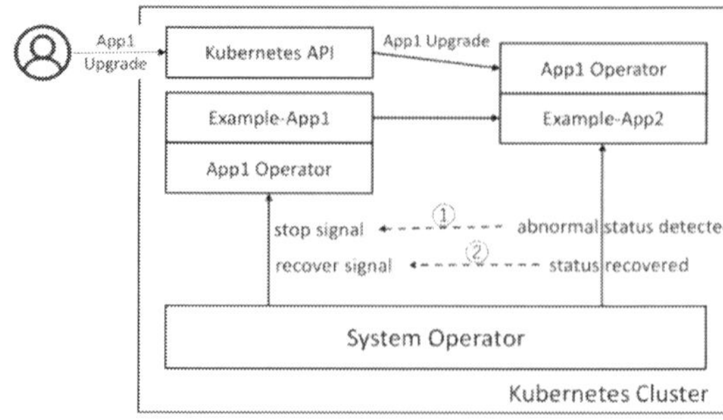

Figure 5. System regulation illustration

(App1). After completing the upgrade, recover signal will be sent to previous node to end this upgrade process.

IV. CONCLUSION

In conclusion, System Operator allows Kubernetes users to design their own integrated system by connecting applications with various functionalities and provide simple approach for deploying this system in Kubernetes cluster, as well as subsequent operations. With System Operator's help, the difficulty of using Kubernetes will be greatly reduced.

We believe that System Operator is a promising project to develop and operate application system in Kubernetes clusters. Currently, we just proposed a basic prototype for it. Details and part of concept are still working in progress. For example, by utilizing Prometheus Operator and Prometheus third-party exporters, we can definitely enhance the monitoring feature for System Operator. Mature and well-tested system "recipe" can be spread among users for efficient system construction. System Operator can be more powerful and useful than it seems.

REFERENCES

[1] M. Mosleh, K. Dalili, and B. Heydari, "Distributed or monolithic? a computational architecture decision framework," IEEE Systems journal, vol. 12, no. 1, 2016, pp. 125–136.

[2] C. Pahl, A. Brogi, J. Soldani, and P. Jamshidi, "Cloud container technologies: A state-of-the-art review," IEEE Transactions on Cloud Computing, vol. 7, no. 3, 2019, pp. 677–692.

[3] D. Bernstein, "Containers and cloud: From lxc to docker to kubernetes," IEEE Cloud Computing, vol. 1, no. 3, 2014, pp. 81–84.

[4] "Kubernetes: Advantages and Disadvantages - The Business Perspective," 2019, URL: https://devspace.cloud/blog/2019/10/31/advantages-and-disadvantages-of-kubernetes [retrieved: July, 2020].

[5] "Introducing Operators: Putting Operational Knowledge into Software," 2016, URL: https://coreos.com/blog/introducing-operators.html [retrieved: July, 2020].

[6] "CNCF Cloud Native Interactive Landscape," URL: https://landscape.cncf.io/ [retrieved: July, 2020].

[7] "Welcome to OperatorHub.io, a new home for the Kubernetes community to share Operators." URL: https://operatorhub.io/ [retrieved: July, 2020].

[8] "OpenStack Documentation: Welcome to Heat Dashboard!" URL: https://docs.openstack.org/heat-dashboard/latest/ [retrieved: July, 2020].

[9] "Kubernetes Documentation, Concepts: Custom Reources," URL: https://kubernetes.io/docs/concepts/extend-kubernetes/api-extension/custom-resources/ [retrieved: July, 2020].

[10] N. Otsu, "A threshold selection method from gray-level histograms," IEEE transactions on systems, man, and cybernetics, vol. 9, no. 1, 1979, pp. 62–66.

International Academy, Research, and Industry Association (IARIA)
412 Derby Way
Wilmington, DE 19810

ISBN 978-1-7138-2165-6

9 781713 821656

CURRAN ASSOCIATES INC.
proceedings
.com